BIBLICAL NARRATIVE LEARNING

BIBLICAL NARRATIVE LEARNING

Teaching Adequate Faith in the Gospel of John

Tung Chiew Ha

PICKWICK Publications · Eugene, Oregon

BIBLICAL NARRATIVE LEARNING
Teaching Adequate Faith in the Gospel of John

Copyright © 2015 Tung Chiew Ha. All rights reserved. Except for brief quotations in critical publications or reviews, no part of this book may be reproduced in any manner without prior written permission from the publisher. Write: Permissions, Wipf and Stock Publishers, 199 W. 8th Ave., Suite 3, Eugene, OR 97401.

Pickwick Publications
An Imprint of Wipf and Stock Publishers
199 W. 8th Ave., Suite 3
Eugene, OR 97401

www.wipfandstock.com

ISBN 13: 978-1-62564-127-4

Cataloging-in-Publication data:

Ha, Tung Chiew

    Biblical narrative learning : teaching adequate faith in the Gospel of John / Tung Chiew Ha.

    xviii + 220 p. ; 23 cm. —Includes bibliographical references and index.

    ISBN 13: 978-1-62564-127-4

    1. Narration (Rhetoric). 2. Storytelling. 3. Learning. 4. Bible. John—Criticism, interpretation, etc. 5. Faith—Biblical teaching. I. Title.

BS2615.2 H1 2015

Manufactured in the U.S.A.   09/23/2015

For
Peck Kiong and Phebe

Contents

List of Charts | viii
Acknowledgments | ix
Introduction | xi

1 **Towards a Biblical Narrative Learning** | 1
2 **The Narrative World That Shaped John's Gospel** | 40
3 **Teaching Faith in John's Gospel** | 78
4 **Learning Faith in John's Gospel** | 109
5 **Practicing Biblical Narrative Learning** | 152

Conclusion | 193
Bibliography | 203
Index | 217

Charts

Chart 1. The Structure of John's Gospel | 82

Chart 2. Literary Set-up of John 6: Showing and Telling | 118

Acknowledgments

This is a revised version of my dissertation accepted at Garrett-Evangelical Theological Seminary in 2012. Praise to the God of grace who called me and placed many people around me to empower me in the completion of this work. This study is made possible through the guidance of Professor Dr. Jack Seymour, Professor Dr. K. K. Yeo, and Professor Dr. Dennis Ngien, who inspired and taught me through the PhD program. They continue to inspire me to imitate their graciousness and fruitfulness in their lives and ministry. Also, my most sincere thanks to the team at Pickwick Publications, you made this book possible.

I am in debt to the many churches I served and worshiped with over the years. My special thanks to William C. H. Ting for his brotherly care and support. Furthermore, I am blessed with caring brothers and sisters. To my brother Dato' Ha Tiung Noon, thank you for the financial support and always there when I need you. Finally, my deepest thanks to my wife Peck Kiong and my daughter Phebe. Your loving supports, understandings, and sacrifices are beyond possible human expression.

Introduction

Narrative is the basic element that informs our being, and narrative learning has been a key way of learning and knowing. The process of narrative learning transcends the limitation of mere propositional teaching where religious concepts (such as faith) are often inadequately presented by teachers and thus eluded the comprehension of many learners. Effective narration is a basic teaching-learning approach that helps learners to transcend different levels of educational and cultural background in appropriating and learning faith. This book seeks to present a teaching method in John's Gospel that benefitted from recent research in narrative learning and a literary analysis of the narrative features in John's Gospel. The end product is a biblical narrative learning that bridges the ancient text and the contemporary reader.

The turn to narrative learning in biblical education is guided by two factors. First of all, narrative learning is a common practice across all culture and learning. It has been a natural learning process from the beginning of human history. Secondly, narrative learning has the capacity to encompass a presentation that brings out the flesh of human experiences. Its importance in human learning has been discounted in the modern world. The turn to narrative learning is in part an attempt to recover the lost created by the Enlightenment. The proponents of narrative learning are unanimous in their critiques of the negative effect of the Enlightenment and the positivists approach to human knowing and learning. McEwan and Egan are particularly representative of the discontent with modernity and its effect on human knowing. They assert:

Introduction

> The storyteller is a victim of an age that values nonnarrative discourse as a measure of sophistication in rationality. . . . Truth, for the tireless promoters of modernity and technical rationality, is measured in terms of standard procedures that demand *an icy, critical stare at the object of study.* In contrast, the story form invites the listener or reader to suspend skepticism and embrace the narrative flow of events as an authentic exploration of experience from a particular perspective. The decline of the storyteller, or narrator, may be read as a symptom of the desire for a certain kind of objectivity, the application of a neutral, unbiased point of view from which to gauge the veracity of knowledge claims . . . we forget the power of narrative to inform and instruct. . . . *especially in education, where a pervasive nonnarrative and behaviorist chill has prevailed.*[1]

In the process of biblical education, the biblical narrative provides a grand narrative that gives the authoritative instruction on living and invites the audience to imitate God's love as the way to experience authentic living. The proposal of this research is to center narrative learning in the biblical stories—specifically, the Gospel of John—and offer the Bible as the anchor for the fluid narrative learning.

Here, I tender a definition that *biblical narrative learning is a process of learning that involves storytelling, specifically telling lived faith experience as Christian testimony, to inform and enable a creation of a new state of understanding and a new level of faith in God. In this process, there are the elements of a narrative, a formulation and presentation of the testimony through a medium, the hearing and interpretation of the story, a reception and imitation of the testimony, and finally, the emergence and retelling of a new testimony.* The media that best make alive the narrative are those that actively engage all senses of human faculty. The oral language and written text with attention to the linguistic feature is in focus here. This engagement of the mind involves use of appropriate linguistic features[2] that create physiognomic expressions.

Biblical narrative learning is a mode of learning and knowing familiar to the church: storytelling, or more specifically, Christian giving witness or testimony of lived faith experiences that is grounded in the biblical

---

1. McEwan and Egan, *Narrative in Teaching*, xii. Author's italics.

2. Stories are basically formed by words arranged into a narration that the audience can comprehend. The representation of the stories can then be further embodied in a script (or screenplay in a movie) and acted out on stage and or captured through media, either audio or visual.

Introduction

narrative. This approach is in line with the church frequent use of testimonies to share their lived faith experiences as a way to teach one another how to live by faith. These testimonial stories can be a simple snippet of their life stories as followers of Jesus. Or on a greater scale, an autobiography of a person's life journey through this world and how the message of Jesus was heard and followed in life. The short testimonies of an event in life are often shared in the church gathering. However, their practices in testimonial storytelling can be informed by current research in narrative learning, both as a form of narrative inquiry and as a process of storytelling to attain deeper reflection and learning. In this, the studies in John's Gospel further adds to the practice of narrative learning, specifically addressing the Christian education goal of learning adequate faith and living a way of life that reflects obedience to God's word through participating in the love of God.

In this study, the Gospel of John is used as the anchor biblical narrative to engage the surrounding narratives. The Gospel of John is chosen for its well-organized and matured biographical form. It has a clear pattern of showing and telling the story of Jesus, the one sent by God to reveal a way of life. The showing is emphasized by the major sign-events aided by the telling sections inserted in between these events. The message of John ultimately asks the audience to remember and imitate a way of authentic living revealed by Jesus; it espouses the wisdom of living in loving relationship with God, self, and others. The characters who encountered Jesus show and tell how to live by adequate (or inadequate) faith in God, his message, and his messengers. Furthermore, the learner who remembers best does so through a process of learning that engages all faculties of human senses.

I propose that the three core tasks of education in the Gospel of John are showing, telling, and living adequate faith. These three tasks together with contemporary understanding in narrative learning help us identify three key components of biblical narrative learning.

1. Components of biblical narrative learning: John's Gospel espouses showing through storytelling that elicits mimesis of the learners. This showing correlates to the components of narrative learning such as events, plot, and characters.

2. The media of narrative presentation: The second key component of biblical narrative learning is informed by the Johannine text. It is a masterpiece in telling and teaching authentic living through skillful use of the dominant language and its literary devices. A good narrative learning depends a lot on the lively re-representation of lived faith

Introduction

testimony that draws the audience's attention and fires imagination. I further identify in the Gospel of John, and propose emphatic use of rhetorical-narrative linguistic devices in the presentation of these lived faith testimonies. The use of deliberative rhetoric in the Gospel of John focuses at a future time, and aims at a better course of action, with the life stories as factual proof.[3] In the contemporary setting the proof will be drawn from the testimonies of both communities of faith past and present, anchored in the Story of Jesus Christ.

3. The anchor faith Story of Jesus and the faith stories of the individuals: faith is learned from biblical narrative and manifested in the one who acquires adequate faith to live in a loving relationship with God, oneself, and others. Here the testimonies of lived faith experiences told by Christians provide the needed data as an information base for learning. Learners draw from this resource and knowledge is gained to form the continual spiral of the faith Story of Jesus on which all faith testimonies are built. The learners will seek and sense (hear, see, smell, taste, touch) the Word, interpret and imagine-inspire (by the Spirit), appropriate what they sense and remember, imitate and claim a way of life. Finally, new experiences of learning to live with adequate faith will be retold. The movement of the Story and stories culminate in wisdom that teaches the learner of faith how to live by faith.[4]

From narrative learning and the Gospel of John, we identify three movements of narrative learning: inquire and invent (creative finding), interpret and imagine-inspire, and imitate and impart. The cycles of telling, imitating, and telling new lived faith testimonies contribute to continuity in the teaching of how to live with adequate faith in the Family of God in changing times and situations. These lived faith testimonies become an integral part of a narrative learning process that grows and contributes to, expands and honors the household of the Family.

OVERVIEW OF THE BOOK

Chapter 1 is an overview of the contemporary understanding and practice of narrative learning. This chapter will provide a foundation for the practice of biblical narrative learning. In most culture, both past and present,

---

3. On the functions of deliberative rhetoric, cf. Aune, *Westminster Dictionary*, 124.
4. I adopt the term "Story" with a capital "S" to denote the Story of Jesus.

Introduction

East and West, narrative learning has been intuitive. I believe this intuitive learning to live a way of life is still common and valid. An effective biblical narrative learning would benefit from careful attention to the contributions of the recent researches on narrative learning. We shall then turn to a comparative biblical model—John's Gospel—for insight into how the faith testimony is told and written.

Chapter 2 will give a comparative cultural, political and religious setting of John's Gospel, highlighting the purpose, and how the author wrote the Gospel. A brief reconstruction of the education during the time of the Johannine community will give us better correlation of the learning problems in the church and show how the Johannine model is informative to the church in addressing her reading and teaching of the biblical faith.

Chapter 3 and 4 present a study on the characters in the six sign-events in John 2–12, and focus on the features of Johannine narrative that excel in re-presenting the Jesus Story. These disciples' decisions to follow Jesus and others who failed to, or postponed their decision to follow Jesus, are narratives that are told with skillful use of literary devices. In the Johannine narrative, Jesus is the anchor to imitate. His testimony of obedience to God is the re-presentation of the call to obey God in love. John taught that by comparison, the characters in the Old Testament narrative failed to adhere to this call to love and obey God. The life story of Jesus in the Gospel of John is the ultimate Faith Story of all faith stories. His teaching and act of obedience till death is a re-presentation of the faith in God worthy of all to imitate.

Finally, chapter 5 shall see an integration of the contemporary narrative learning and the investigation of John's Gospel, and propose a practice of telling lived faith experiences as a process of biblical narrative learning for the church. The testimony telling can be "live," told by the individuals to an audience, or through interview and re-presented in written form to the audience-reader. I will present the three sets of components and the three sets of movements in biblical narrative learning. The concluding chapter will put forth some of the suggestions and possibilities for biblical narrative learning in the church and its contribution to educational leadership.

This book is written with two decisions in mind. First of all, it avoids the debates in biblical studies on how to read and interpret a text. The choice of Bible reading strategy available to the interested learner is immense. The most common approaches are historical-critical, narrative, rhetorical, theological, and cross-cultural hermeneutics that provide a

Introduction

selection of reading strategies that can inform teaching of the Bible in the church. It is sufficient to bring to attention that the contest of interpretations existed and that I have in the best of my judgment adopted the interpretation strategy that best fit the context of this discussion. I will start with where the church is situated and build on this "given." This means that the first choice of interpretive tool is the historical-critical approach in reading the text. However, the narrative learning approach also necessitates the use of narrative criticism in reading the text. Narrative reading is called upon also in view of the genre of the Gospels.[5] Theological interpretation of the Scripture is also necessary as it emphasizes the voice of the reader from her or his social location and theological tradition allows a greater flexibility for the voices of the local churches to be heard.

Secondly, in a sea of information, I acknowledge the limitation of any individual to cover all possibilities on a subject. There is no one learning that can fully incorporate all discussions of the topic. Furthermore, on an abstract subject such as faith, I believe it can only be said that one has adequate faith to move forward in life, never complete faith. At the same time, there is no one learning that is incomplete. We live by the best knowledge and wisdom learned by the available narrative. An eighty-eight-year-old with six years of school education is not necessarily less wise than a twenty-eight-year-old with a PhD under her sleeve. Similarly, the premise of narrative learning entails that each individual possesses the same possibility of learning and teaching something wise about a way of life through her or his lived faith experience. In a biblical narrative learning, no one example of lived faith experiences is supreme except the anchor—Jesus' example. Similarly, none other is inferior to another in teaching faith. Most of all, the beauty of learning faith is that one does not need the whole collection (which is impossible) of faith testimonies; therefore, the futile pursuit of perfection is not a goal in narrative learning. Limited but sufficient, the Gospel of John is a fine example of teaching through selected faith testimonies. Instead of trying to include everything, it is a sufficient work for teaching adequate faith. Similarly, though limited, the church has yet sufficient, supply of lived faith testimonies which she could utilize to teach her

---

5. "Once the genre of a document is recognized, it sets up a sort of compact between author and audience, in which the former attempts to meet certain kinds of expectations associated with that genre of literature, and the audience will be looking for the author to do so." Cf. Witherington, III, *John's Wisdom*, 2. The use of narrative reading to apparently non-narratival text such as the Pauline Epistles has been proposed by Scott, *Paul's Way of Knowing*.

Introduction

members and community. We need to uncover and make them available for teaching.

This book stands on these limitations and of course, there will be areas that will be addressed by future investigation and research in the field among the local churches. I am deeply aware of the limitation and the difficulty of conducting an inter-disciplinary research. I am aware of the warning issued by predecessors in the field using the Gospel and reading it with sociological theories. This approach "runs the risk of incommensurability, anachronism, over-simplification and false deductions."[6] I will draw on the wisdom of the Johannine narrative and the appropriate reading community for guidance as this research is very much a process of uncovering and recovering the reading and teaching of the Bible for the people as it is for me. May this work help the church to grow in strength, and to regain a clear voice over the noise.

---

6. Yieh, *One Teacher*, 4.

I

Towards a Biblical Narrative Learning

Story is the basic element that informs our existence. It is abundantly found in human lives. Every nation, every race, every generation, every community, and every person has at least one story. This basic story can be complex, reflecting the nature of human existence. "We tell them, we live in them, our views of reality, of life itself, are shaped by them in ways beyond our awareness. We make sense of our experience, day by day and across the life span, by putting it into story form. We *are* stories."[1] The use of story in learning has been prevalent in family settings, religious education, and also in many cultural settings. However, the position of narrative learning as an articulated recognized form of education is more recent. It can be said that the Enlightenment and the hegemony of the scientific method had relegated narrative learning to an inferior position. Often, narrative learning became negatively associated with lower world civilization. The postmodern turn opened up a new appreciation on the use of the story and also in the story of individuals *per se*. Re-recognition of narrative learning in the past three decades has spurred much interest in its use in social science.

While stories have been used in many social science studies, in the field of education, this narrative turn is a latecomer, "at least in terms of

---

1. Rossiter and Clark, *Narrative*, 3. Author's Emphasis.

theorizing it."[2] In the recent developments, narrative learning took two routes: narrative learning as within the narrative inquiry into life story research, and narrative learning as storytelling. In general, the former is mainly practiced as researching an individual's human knowing and learning, while the latter has been practiced more often in groups or classroom settings and existed all the while in the history of education. In the field of Christian education, storytelling has been advocated earlier probably because the content of Christian education is very much narrative in nature and is not always bound by the limitation of scientific logic. As a religion that invokes the divine, the concept of Christian education has always remained within the communication of the mystery of God. This communication entails the use of stories to speak the unfathomable of which mere human perception and communication is incapable. However, in a world still very much dictated by the system and method inherited from the modern-scientific the concept of narrative learning remains inferior in the perception of many, including the church, who are always very careful about the continuity of teaching the Truth.

This chapter will begin with the recovery of narrative learning that has taken place in the past three decades or so. It includes the development of a philosophical foundation for narrative knowing in social science research. Then, it shall trace the components, functions, and practices of narrative learning, including in Christian education. It will describe the deficiency in the non-theological perspective on narrative learning, and how these developments can be augmented to provide a more fruitful application of narrative learning. As remedy the theological understanding of personhood is discussed. Human capacity in knowing and learning points to a biblical narrative learning as a way of teaching the Bible in Christian education. Finally, the chapter will culminate with a discussion of the two tracks in narrative learning, one that looks into the search of an individual's life story that is informed by the Bible and able to educate both the self and the others. It is also a narrative learning in the sense of testimony-telling built on researched Christian lived faith experiences.

REVIEW OF NARRATIVE LEARNING

The renewed attention to narrative learning can be understood as evoked by a postmodern reaction to the failed modern agenda to provide answer

2. Ibid., 4.

for every phenomenon and problem encountered in human living. Following the Enlightenment, the rise of scientific knowledge claimed dominance in the quest for knowledge and understanding. Knowledge often came to claim its validity in quantitative measure. The value of life stories that offers answers to life issue such as the unknown element of life after death or the suffering in lives was seen as doubtful data of learning and pejoratively categorized as myths. These stories were dismissed as valid knowledge for education and seen as providing little of useful value, and at times were even considered harmful superstition, to informing a way of life. In a similar way, the ancient biblical narratives are often devoid of its credibility to teach us how to live in the present. While in some parts of the world, narrative learning has remained a key way of learning and knowing, in the West, narrative learning has only been "revived" in recent decades. The recent affirmative research in the West will again help to reaffirm some of the voices through narrative learning by giving them a philosophical base for a practice that is intuitive and indigenous.

Terminologies of "Narrative Learning"

With the various literatures on narrative knowing, narrative learning, life history research, narrative inquiry, biography research, life stories, storytelling, narrative pedagogy, or simply narrative, it seems fit to first of all briefly introduce their usage and then consolidate these terms and gain some coherence in this literature. In general, the terms "narrative knowing"[3] refers to a way of interpreting and understanding human experiences. Jerome Bruner advocated the differentiation and recognition of the narrative way of knowing as compared to a paradigmatic way of knowing.[4] This approach to understanding and explaining human experiences heavily influenced subsequent research on "narrative learning" as a form of knowledge investigation.[5] D. Jean Clandinin focuses on research in the "narrative inquiry"[6] that develops out of a growing interest in the recovery of "life

---

3. Polkinghorne, *Narrative Knowing and the Human Sciences*; Polkinghorne, "Narrative Knowing and Study of Lives."

4. Cf. Bruner, *Actual Minds*, 11. Both Polkinghorne, and Goodson and Gill followed Bruner's argument for narrative learning. Cf. Polkinghorne, "Narrative Knowing and the Study of Lives," 82. Also cf. Goodson and Gill, *Narrative Pedagogy*, 139.

5. Goodson et al., *Narrative Learning*; Goodson and Gill, *Narrative Pedagogy*.

6. Clandinin, *Handbook of Narrative Inquiry*; Clandinin and Connelly, *Narrative*

story."[7] The term "life story" is also used interchangeably with "biography."[8] "Storytelling"[9] as a practice of narrative learning has been applied much earlier in the field of Christian education.[10] Diekelmann and Diekelmann (2009) and eventually Goodson and Gill (2011) use "narrative pedagogy" to describe the process of narrative teaching. With the various nuances of naming the narrative phenomenon, some decided to simply use the term "narrative."[11] In the midst of variances and the number of issues involved, this paper will use "narrative learning" as a general term to encompass references to all of the above. The term "storytelling" will be employed to denote the act of using narrative in teaching and learning. Other terms will be called for where the context, or the original author's usage, requires such specifics.

Charting the Return to Narrative Learning

The first exploration of narrative learning in modern history is attributed to Thomas and Znaniecki's (1918–1920) *The Polish Peasant in Europe and America*. They used life histories to give flesh to the migrant experience and this pioneering work "established life histories as a bona fide research tool."[12] There were a few similar researches in the 1920s and the movement peaked in the 1930s. Then the narrative approach was largely abandoned by social scientists for the next several decades until the 1980s. In the 1980s, with distrust of the previous grand narrative, the emergent postmodern thinking espouses freedom in narratives—the small stories of individuals becoming interesting and put onstage.[13]

Inquiry; Hooley, *Narrative Life*.

7. McAdams, *Stories We Live By*.
8. Birren et al., *Aging and Biography*.
9. Maynes et al., *Telling Stories*.
10. Groome, *Christian Religious Education*; Wimberly, *Soul Stories*.
11. McEwan and Egan, *Narrative in Teaching, Learning, and Research*; Brophy, *Narrative-Based Practice*; Rossiter and Clark. *Narrative and the Practice of Adult Education*; Beattie, *Quest for Meaning*.
12. Goodson and Gill, *Narrative Pedagogy*, 19–20.
13. Cf. Chamberlayne et al., *Turn to Biographical Methods*, 6–7. The authors also give a comprehensive account of the development of narrative learning in the last three decades.

Towards a Biblical Narrative Learning

The turn to narrative learning can be envisaged in four turns, "the attention to relationships among participants, the move to words as data, the focus on the particular, and the recognition of blurred genres of knowing."[14] The relationship between researcher and researched will determine the outcome of the research. The existence of trust on the part of the researched will open up the telling of life story in the "dialogic encounter and collaborative interpretation between the researcher/listener and the teller."[15] The turn to the words as data is a turn from reliance on numbers as accurate pointer to value.[16] This is also in line with the shift from quantitative research to qualitative method. The turn from the general to the particular "signals [the researchers'] understanding of the value of a particular experience, in a particular setting, involving particular people."[17] Finally, the blurring of one way of knowing is replaced by an understanding that there are multiple ways of knowing and understanding human experience. The dominance of a white-Western way of knowing is challenged in many forums, including and especially the post-colonial criticism. This turn to individual voices "allow[s] stories to function as political responses, broadcasting 'voices' that are excluded from or neglected within dominant political structures and processes."[18] These four turns are tied to and built upon the concept of human understanding that has undergone a dramatic shift in the past century.

Jerome Bruner filled the foundation for narrative learning by pointing to a way of knowing that is narrative based. He identified two forms of knowing: the paradigmatic knowing widely adopted from the Enlightenment era, and the narrative knowing which is as old as human existence. Brunner posits that the human mind works in two basic modes: the narrative mode and the paradigmatic mode. In the paradigmatic mode, the ideas are structured by particulars and more often seen in prepositional statements. In the narrative mode, the information is presented in story form.[19] Drawing on the work of Vygotsky, he further argues that the representation

---

14. Pinnegar and Daynes, "Locating Narrative Inquiry," 3, also cf. 7–28.
15. Goodson and Gill, *Narrative Pedagogy*, 35.
16. The numbers are seen as limited representations of what is studied. These numbers do not explain the why and how of the human behaviors. Cf. Pinnegar and Daynes, "Locating Narrative Inquiry," 20.
17. Ibid., 21.
18. Goodson and Gill, *Narrative Pedagogy*, 20.
19. Cf. Bruner, *Actual Minds, Possible Worlds*, 11–14.

of idea always takes these three forms: enactive representation (action based), iconic representation (image based), and symbolic representation (language based). He sees the symbolic-language representation is most mysterious and implies that this is the most efficacious form of representation.[20] However, I would disagree with him on the last point. The linguistic representation is most widely used to convey or present an idea, but the real mystery is in the image it attempts to represent. The ultimate goal of language in a narrative is pointing to an image or more specifically a re-*enfleshment* (re-incarnation) of the event-experience told by the narrator. The image is probably the most mysterious and subject to multiple interpretations. Having said that, it does not mean that language is in any way to be discounted as a carrier of our idea. Language is still our primary tool of representation that animates the storytelling. It is dialogic yet it arrives at an analogous image, and at its best, animatic.[21] Since language remains the primary tool of narrative learning, it is pertinent to understand and appreciate its power and how we can through language *make flesh* a story.

C. S. Song especially points to the role of language as a gift from God that gives us the possibility of communication, by following rules of grammar, syntax, and semantics. Language lives on in the sphere of the individuals and the community, and is both a personal and communal possession. It is the bridge between the personal and community. "Next to kinship, language—and for that matter, dialects—ensures the identity of individuals in the community and maintains the coherence of that community" as it has the power to create affinity and sympathy.[22] Song further poses that religious language is also culturally conditioned and experienced based. "It may be a sublimated form of human experience—human experience inspired, moved, and transformed by a divine power. . . . It may be a an experience caused by a creative power not under our control and not at our disposal. . . . It is by means of language . . . that we seek to express it."[23] In

---

20. Bruner's view on three modes of representation is strikingly similar to the concept proposed by Vygotsky. According to Vygotsky, enactive mode is the mode related to the young age of one. Iconic or imagery representation is associated with age of three and above. Symbolic representation is attained by the time a child who enters school, at the age of seven. Cf. Daniels et al., *Cambridge Companion to Vygotsky*, 254.

21. For more discussions on the representation of ideas or theology through analogical image or dialogic text, cf. Holland, *How Do Stories Save Us*, 71–104. Also cf. Felch, "Dialogism," 73–5.

22. Song, *Believing Heart*, 27.

23. Ibid., 28.

the process of narrative learning, the narration of an event or life is rooted in the acts, formed in the mental image and represented often through the words. In greater details would one see argument that pertains to the issue of "presentation" of faith narrative (chapter 3) where the language or words is specifically expanded to enable an *enfleshment* of the lived-story.[24] This understanding of the role of language in narrative learning precludes some of the problems in life story research.

From the foundation laid by Bruner, many have taken up the task of research in narrative learning. Among them, Ivor Goodson stood out as one who has considerable narrative research under his belt. With a total of 528 interviews with 117 adults over a thirty-six months period, Ivor Goodson and his team concluded that there are two main elements in assessing the life story: the narrative quality, and the efficacy of the narrative.[25] In terms of the narrative quality, a life story narration is assessed by its descriptive or analytical, theorized or vernacular, plot and emplotment (indication of learning taking place).[26] Narrative efficacy is measured by its potential for learning and potential for action.[27] Goodson also concludes from his research interviews that due to the highly unpredictable elements existing in each life, there are various levels of narrative quality and efficacy.

On the other track of narrative learning, using stories as a means of teaching has been validated as efficacious in meaning making. According to de Certeau, one of the (many) defining characteristics of the postmodern condition is succinctly encapsulated by the slogan "Narrative is all, and all is narrative." Our contemporary society "has become a recited society, in three senses: it is defined by *stories* (*recits*, the fables constituted by our advertising and informational media), by *citations* of stories, and by the interminable *recitation* of stories."[28] So modernity's scientific mode of knowledge has finally passed away. Ours is now a *recited* society, a society that is *narrated*.

The postmodern turn to narrative elicits a new way of looking at how humans find meanings in life stories. Dan P. McAdams believes that

---

24. The Word-God incarnated as flesh is key to John. The Word left the world but left with his disciples his words; his words need to be given "flesh" through the use of linguistic devices in narrative learning.

25. Goodson et al., *Narrative Learning*, 12–14.

26. Ibid., 127.

27. Ibid., 13.

28. Hyman, *Predicament of Postmodern Theology*, 21.

"human lives are much too complex for a typological approach, and too socially inflected to support any argument that says the truth resides solely within."[29] He argues, "Truth is constructed in the midst of our loving and hating; our tasting, smelling, and feeling; . . . in the conversations we have with those to whom we are closest; and with the stranger we meet . . . Our sources are wildly varied, and our possibilities, vast."[30] The source of stories is unlimited as "human beings are storytellers by nature. In many guises, as folktale, legend, myth, epic, history, motion picture and television program, the story appears in every known human culture. The story is a natural package for organizing many different kinds of information. Storytelling appears to be a fundamental way of expressing ourselves and our world to others."[31]

Summary

The turn to narrative learning is driven by dissatisfaction with disseminating information merely by propositional statements and disregarding the affective element in a learning process. Brophy pointed out that we may learn a great deal by studying hard facts, procedures and abstract theories which are important to our learning, "but we empathise with one another and we develop a deeper understanding of our world when we listen to stories."[32] We find in storytelling a more positive learning experience, having been released from the confinement of the emotionless-logic-scientific concept of human learning.

The reliance on the scientific and lab-precision knowledge that was born during the Enlightenment is slowly being replaced by a renewed interest in the capacity of lived experiences to form a person. Ritchie rightly concluded from his observation that the new generation is turning away from criticism of personal background in learning. However, there is value in our background for acquiring new knowledge. It is impossible to lay aside one's past at the outset of any serious learning, "if we gain knowledge from the past stories of which we are a part, then our past is a necessary resources in acquiring new knowledge."[33] Narrative learning is a departure

---

29. McAdams, *Stories We Live By*, 12.
30. Ibid., 13.
31. Ibid., 27.
32. Brophy, *Narrative-Based Practice*, 33.
33. Ritchie, *Fullness of Knowing*, 156.

from learning approaches that exclusively focused on either the human behavior, cognitive, or the affective approach. Yet it does not eliminate entirely the contribution of any of the three main learning principles, its fluidity actually enable narrative learner to draw on these principles as they appear in the coming chapters, in which narrative learning is affirmed both affective and reflective.

Many benefits of using storytelling in education were discounted. Storytelling is recognized as an effective way of "depicting reality and of revealing what lies beneath the surface of events. Story-tellers are interested in meaning rather than the recitation of 'facts.' They help us to explore what is significant. They take full account of the human dimension. They are concerned with the interpretation of experience. They invite empathy and participation."[34] This recognition of narrative learning has been actively discussed and gave narrative learning its place in pedagogy.[35] However, there are considerable variations between the practice of narrative as life history inquiry and using the stories as part of teaching material. The next section will analyze the two tracks of narrative learning and how they can complement each other, fill in the shortcoming found in each method, and inform a biblical narrative learning.

THE NATURE OF NARRATIVE LEARNING

A narrative can be a three-hundred-page biography, a simple three-minutes or even a three-line story. It can be an event of a person telling her or his life experiences, or an event where a story is used to teach someone something. Aristotle's analysis of narrative has long ago noted the existence of three basic elements—the beginning, the middle, and the end—set within a plot.[36] Building on the category of Aristotle, Ricoeur further recognizes

---

34. Brophy, *Narrative-Based Practice*, ix.

35. For the documentation of the turn to narrative learning and its philosophical arguments, cf. Chamberlayne, *Turn to Biographical Methods*, 1–52. These authors give a comprehensive account of the development of narrative learning in the last three decades. Polkinghorne's 1996 condensed article is probably the most concise summary of the argument for narrative learning. Many recent researches are built on this foundational work. Polkinghorne, "Narrative Knowing," 77–99. More recently, Pinnegar and Daynes, "Locating Narrative Inquiry," 3–34. Also McDrury and Alterio, *Learning Through Storytelling*.

36. Both Goodson and Polkinghorne recognized the structure of plot in narrative. However, the contribution of Aristotle has been left out in their discussions. Conversely,

what he called "concordance" and also "discordance" in the plot of the story that gives the twist in the story, makes it interesting and grabs the attention of the listeners.[37] Cortazzi and Lin added, "Stories have a trajectory or *plot structure* with a clear beginning, some crises or turning-points and their resolutions which constitute the body or middle, and a final resolution or ending, in which there is generally strong human interest in the events and *motivations* of story characters and how they solve problems, overcome difficulties or create coherence in their life."[38]

On this foundational and time-tested understanding of the basic three elements in a narrative, current understanding of narrative has become more refined. While the basic pattern of a story consists of three elements, the characteristic of the story told varies as the story takes on various fashions and in a variety of possibilities, as many as there are individuals. Not all storytelling would have the same flow or pattern. Some are more organized while others loosely organized. Focusing the task of narrative learning as taking place in an individual telling one's own life experiences, Goodson and Gill see the key elements in a life story research with a simple category—in terms of the descriptive and analytical quality of the narrative while forgoing other fine characteristics that may not be employed in an individual's narration. The more descriptive and analytical (or evaluative) narrative can be a result of a more reflective mind that examined the life experience in greater depth. The continual internal reflection or self-conversation can be more sensitive and contributing to the meaning making of the narrator.[39] The narration of the individual is one of the most pristine and available sources of story.

The identification of the sources of stories helps us better differentiate the type, its aim, and the plot in these stories. Rossiter and Clark named four sources of narratives in terms of individuals, family, cultural, and organizational origins.[40] In a slightly different classification, alongside Schank, Brophy named five types of narrative. The official stories are usually

---

Paul Ricoeur, on whom they both relied heavily for their research philosophy, devoted a hefty chapter on Aristotle's *Poetic*. Cf. Ricoeur, *Time and Narrative*, 1:31–51. Cf. Goodson, *Narrative Learning*, 13. Also cf. Goodson and Gill, *Narrative Pedagogy*, 7, 104–6. Also cf. Polkinghorne, *Narrative Knowing*, 18–20. Polkinghorne, "Narrative Knowing," 86–88.

37. Cf. Brophy, *Narrative-Based Practice*, 43.
38. Cortazzi and Lin, "Narrative Learning," 651. Author's emphasis.
39. Cf. Goodson and Gill, *Narrative Pedagogy*, 58–61.
40. Cf. Rossiter and Clark, *Narrative*, 21–28.

Towards a Biblical Narrative Learning

broadcast to a large audience, often with an exhortation and often originating with government, business, or voluntary organizations. Secondly, the invented or adapted stories, made up to describe experiences or to relay what we have imagined, often with embellishments and perhaps reordering events to make a more coherent tale, often created for entertainment rather than to persuade. Third is the first-hand or experiential story of personal experiences. These stories are often altered in order to appeal to particular listeners. Bausch further breaks down the religious personal story into four types: stories that signify self-discovery, stories that signify an impact experience relating to mystery and its demand, the story that signifies mystical experience, and stories that signify conversion experience.[41]

A fourth type of story is the second-hand story that we relay, having heard them from someone else and remembered them. Finally, culturally common stories are those which we have imbibed from our social and cultural environment and which we use both to make a point about our experiences and to demonstrate our membership of a particular group. This type of story can be encapsulated in a short phrase or "ossified stories" as they become culturally embedded over time.[42] These pithy and short stories are important as they assist memorization and enhance the ability to retrieve relevant stories from memory being an important skill in many fields.[43] These sources of stories may be named differently, but they are readily found in all regional and cultural settings.

These stories are often told to different audiences at different times, places, and with some purposes. As a process of storytelling, Brophy identified these key elements in narrative learning.

1. *Setting:* Every narrative has a setting. It can be a place—real or imagined—where the action happens. It has to be a dramatic but believable setting, one which the listener can picture and imagine, and enable the listener to make assumptions and presuppositions out of the story.[44]

2. *Causality:* Narratives capture and express cause and effect. "Causality is at the heart of nearly all modern understandings of the world. . . . In narrative, these elements of the plot, coupled with actions of the

---

41. Cf. Bausch, *Storytelling*, 173–94.
42. Cf. Brophy, *Narrative-Based Practice*, 40–41.
43. Ibid., 41.
44. Ibid., 42, 44.

characters, enable the listener to identify the starting point (cause) and what occurs, perhaps much later, as a result (effect)."[45]

3. *Plot:* A narrative plot is "the container within which we find both events and causality. . . . Plot is at the heart of narrative, because it not only relates events to one another but crucially also the transformations that occur between them . . . the plot enables the listener to establish the causality. . . . The plot is never explicit; rather it is inferred by the listener from the discourse. At the same time, different discourses may have the same plot, . . . But because certain plots are frequently encountered, they achieve familiarity and enable the listener to explore meaning in the particular context of the story and the storyteller."[46] A narrative needs a plot that keeps the interest flowing because new events keep occurring, which catch the attention, often by being unexpected yet maintaining the temporal linkages throughout.[47]

4. *Style* and *Point of View:* Narrative style refers to the way in which the narrative is presented. It includes point of view of the narrators, or the narrative's "focus" or "angle." The point of view is usually revealed by the voice which is used.[48]

5. *Character:* Character is a critical element of narrative, as "the listener's understanding is formed in relation to the characters who 'act' in the narrative. Listeners relate to characters emotionally, which greatly affects what they hear and the meaning they ascribe to it."[49] Narrative presents "characters we can empathise with—or hate—so that we relate our own lives to theirs; character development which assists in making the narrative believable because it reinforces the sense of time

---

45. Ibid., 44.

46. Ibid., 45.

47. Ibid., 42.

48. "The first-person singular tells us that the point of view is that of a participant in the story (known as *autodiegesis* if a person is telling their own story or *homodiegesis* if telling someone else's). The third person, single or plural (*heterodiegesis*), tells us that we are hearing the story as observed by someone external to it, but a person who has knowledge of what has happened and often claims understanding of the thoughts and feelings of the protagonists. The third person can also be used to create what is called an 'objective' point of view, where no attempt is made to penetrate the thoughts and feelings of the actors, but the story is narrated simply as a series of events which happened." Ibid., 45–46.

49. Ibid., 46.

passing as well as confirming our knowledge that people change as they experience more."[50]

6. *Narrative Presence:* Narrative presence refers to the listener's relationship to the story, which in the extreme can involve feelings of being transported into the action, of being part of the narrative.[51]

7. *Hermeneutic and Proairetic Codes:* These two sets of code work to create suspense in a narrative and lead the audience to ask anticipatory questions such as "who did it?" or "What happened next?"[52]

The working of these intertwined elements of a narrative is useful to pedagogy, "all those aspects which the listener brings to the experience, including shared knowledge, emotions . . . leads to 'realisation,' . . . connections are made with prior knowledge and beliefs leading to reconstruction of the mental world of the listener."[53]

The Functions of Narrative Learning

There are various suggestions on the functions of narrative learning to consider. As a process of self-narration, it is a site for learning as one constructs her or his identity through an "ongoing internal conversation and external accounts that are undertaken as a genuinely lifelong process."[54] It enables one to dialogue with oneself and others, both in private and in a public place.[55] McEwan and Egan asserted, "Narratives form a framework

---

50. Ibid., 42. Goodson and Gill further identified seven basic plots in narrative: comedy, tragedy, rags-to-riches, the quest, overcoming the monster, voyage and return, and rebirth. Goodson and Gill, *Narrative Pedagogy*, 103.

51. Brophy, *Narrative-Based Practice*, 46. For more discussion on the emotion factor in narrative, also cf. Goodson and Gill, *Narrative Pedagogy*, 81–85.

52. "Roland Barthes introduced these terms to describe the two different ways in which suspense can be created in a narrative. The hermeneutic code refers to elements of the plot that raise unanswered questions, . . . so we keep our attention on the unfolding story until all these loose ends have been tied up satisfactorily (or left for us to ponder). . . focused on answering the question, 'who did it?' The proairetic code is simply the actions which occur and which will have consequences—we wait to find out what these will be so our attention is caught by anticipation of the outcome. What happens next?" Brophy, *Narrative-Based Practice*, 47.

53. Ibid., 47.

54. Goodson et al., *Narrative Learning*, 131. Also cf. Goodson and Gill, *Narrative Pedagogy*, 43–46. Similarly, cf. Polkinghorne, *Narrative Knowing*, 146–55.

55. Cf. Beattie, *Quest for Meaning*, 46–71.

within which our discourses about human thought and possibility evolve, . . . the function of narrative is to make our actions intelligible to ourselves as well as to others."[56] It can also be, as with feminists, "*designed pointedly to introduce marginalized voices into the record.*"[57]

In the act of storytelling, the "function of stories is chiefly to equip students with knowledge that will later prove to be useful . . . has to do with *what we want students to be like as human beings*, . . . include the values we want them to hold, the characteristic traits we want them to exhibit, the views of the world and of themselves we want them to cultivate, and so forth."[58] Bausch elaborated on the multiple functions of stories: to provoke curiosity and compel repetition; as a bridge to our existence in the culture and to others; to help us remember; to restore the original power of the word; to provide escape; to evoke in us right-brain imagination, tenderness and therefore wholeness; to promote healing; and to provide a basis for hope and morality.[59] On a different note, objections to narrative learning generally fall under the "questions of reliability, subjectivity and representativeness."[60] How do we know the veracity of a story? T. Patrick Burke claims, "The story itself cannot tell us that. It always pretends it happened. That is where philosophy comes in, and science and history." Our philosophy and science may tell us that it simply did not happen, "and history is a form of science; but science always carries a question mark. In the end the decision whether the story is true or not hangs on our philosophy."[61] Burke's argument remains within the thought of modernity and a good representation of the challenge narrative learning might encounter in application. Polkinghorne counters that the "use of stories to convey the reasons and purposes of people's actions reaches back to humankind's prehistory. . . . Changes in the philosophy of science have removed the barriers to the use of narrative data. . . . The recovery of stories for the study of lives provides researchers the opportunity to study lives from the point of view of

---

56. McEwan and Egan, *Narrative*, xiii.

57. Maynes et al., *Telling Stories*, 6. Author's italics. On the role of feminist on narrative, also cf. Bausch, *Storytelling*, 26–27. For the use of narrative learning as a critique of ideology, also cf. Hooley, *Narrative Life*, 177–212.

58. McEwan and Egan, *Narrative*, 4.

59. Bausch named thirteen characteristics of story. Some of them are summarized here. Cf. Bausch, *Storytelling*, 29–63.

60. Chamberlayne et al., *Turn to Biographical Methods*, 3.

61. Burke, "Theologian as Storyteller," 212.

Towards a Biblical Narrative Learning

those who live them."[62] These issues will be further regulated when the Bible is placed and recognized as the anchor in a biblical narrative learning.

While there are various ideas on the functions of the stories, the basic understanding on the function of narrative has been widely accepted and identified with Ricoeur's analysis of Aristotle's *Poetics*. Ricoeur suggested that stories are constructed by the use of *mimesis* and *emplotment*. Mimesis denotes the way in which, in constructing a story, one imitates events from life. Brophy succinctly summarized Ricoeur's three stages of interpretation based on mimesis and emplotment:

> *Mimesis* 1 refers to our basic competencies in the use of conceptual terms, our practical understanding of actions, goals, motives and agents. The storyteller and the listener have preconceptions which give meaning to the situation before any attempt is made to build and share the narrative.
>
> *Mimesis* 2 relates to the field of action, the context which invests meaning. It is here that we use emplotment, giving the narrative structure.
>
> *Mimesis* 3 is concerned with temporal structures, the "now" and "then" of lived time which are related to the narrative itself and thus provides the intersection where the time of the listener and the time of the narrative intersect. In this way, listeners are exposed to new understandings of their worlds, and thus to new possibilities for action.[63]

Ricoeur's theorizing of the learning that takes place within a mimetic act can be further understood in the mimesis theory of Rene Girard.

Girard argued that mimesis is a key to human learning and improvement. While in a world that highly values innovation, it seems that imitation is incompatible to innovation. He points to mimesis as a way to innovation. He challenges a false conception of mutual exclusivity of imitation and innovation. He asks, "To begin with, is there such a thing as 'absolute innovation'?"[64] He adds, "The Latin word *in-novare* implies limited change rather than total revolution—a combination of continuity and discontinuity."[65] He analyzed the process of imitation in this way:

---

62. Polkinghorne, "Narrative Knowing," 99.

63. Brophy, *Narrative-Based Practice*, 43. For a similar iteration of Ricoeur on mimesis, cf. Goodson and Gill, *Narrative Pedagogy*, 103–5.

64. Girard, *Mimesis and Theory*, 238.

65. Ibid., 244.

> In a first phase, no doubt, imitation will be rigid and myopic. It will have the ritual quality of external mediation. After a while, however, the element of novelty in the competitor's practice will be mastered, and imitation will become bolder. At that moment, it may—or may not—generate some additional improvement, which will seem insignificant at first, because it is not suggested by the model, but which really is the genuine innovation that will turn things around . . . concretely, in a true innovative process, it is often so continuous with imitation that its presence can be discovered only after the fact, through a process of abstraction that isolates aspects which are inseparable from one another.[66]

With reference to observations in business and industry, Girard pointed to the transition of nations in Europe, the United States, Japan, and Korea and so forth, where, from being imitators, each subsequently became innovators. He stated, "The metamorphosis of imitators into innovators occurs repeatedly, but we always react to it with amazement . . . the only shortcut to innovation is imitation."[67] In the process of mimesis,

> All imitators select models whom they regard as superior . . . the superior achievement of the one, which motivates the imitation of the others. . . . When we imitate successful rivals, we explicitly acknowledge what we would prefer to deny—their superiority. . . . The mimetic urge can never be repressed entirely, but it can turn into counter-imitation. The losers try to demonstrate their independence by systematically taking the course opposite to that of the winners. Thus, they act in a way detrimental to their own self-interest. Their pride turns self-destructive.[68]

The possibility of real change is possible in a mimesis process when the tradition is respected: "The main prerequisite for real innovation is a minimal respect for the past and a mastery of its achievements, that is, *mimesis*. To expect novelty to cleanse itself of imitation is to expect a plant to grow with its roots up in the air."[69] Mimesis is a necessary interaction of the narrator and the audience in order to achieve a new or innovative understanding of the human self. For human development, it is contributing to imitate. On the goodness of mimetic desire, Girard points out, "what Jesus advocated is mimetic desire. Imitate me, and imitate the father

66. Ibid., 238.
67. Ibid., 239.
68. Ibid., 240.
69. Ibid., 244.

through me, he says, so it's twice mimetic. Jesus seems to say the only way to avoid violence is to imitate me, and imitate the Father. So the idea that mimetic desire is bad makes no sense," except when the mimetic generates mimetic rivalry.[70] Mimesis is the core vehicle in the storytelling and learning, meaning-making process. It is tacit and allows room for divine action in this intuitive mental activity. It is capable of enriching our imagination when we respect and open ourselves to our inherited tradition and stories.

Life story in all its richness, Dan P. McAdams said, functions adequately as "an act of imagination that is a patterned integration of our remembered past, perceived present, and anticipated future" where both author and reader come to appreciate "its beauty and its psychosocial truth."[71] Our lives are surrounded by stories in various forms and guises found in various cultures and settings. "The story is a natural package for organizing many different kinds of information. Storytelling appears to be a fundamental way of expressing ourselves and our world to others."[72] It is a means for the preservation of a people, a tradition, and inspiration for the next generation. On a similar note, Rossiter and Clark recognizes the effectiveness of using narrative but hesitated to draw a close to any narrative, because "stories don't really have endings, or at least not fixed or solid ones."[73] However, they failed to acknowledge that each and every story could be a completed unit as it is told, and serves its function as is.

McAdams names this ongoing presence of narrative as "generativity" of a personhood in a process of "(1) identifying, (2) living, and (3) changing the personal myths that shape and give meaning to our lives."[74] However, he also warned that the story is "not to provide . . . simple recipes for human happiness and understanding, in the manner of the proverbial self-help book in popular psychology."[75] Ivor Goodson and his team of researchers even conclude that narrative learning is neither a necessary nor sufficient condition for leading a happy and rewarding life.[76] It shall be argued that the lacking in Goodson's view is in fact the problem of postmodernity. When an anchor for a meaning scheme is denied, all reflection and

---

70. Girard, "Goodness of Mimetic Desire," 63.
71. McAdams, *Stories*, 12.
72. Ibid., 27.
73. Rossiter and Clark, *Narrative*, 170.
74. McAdams, *Stories*, 253.
75. Ibid.
76. Goodson et al., *Narrative Learning*, 133.

meaning making is adrift and without this reference, there is no measure of what is good, true, and beautiful.

The generativity of adulthood is a key goal among adults as each tried to leave behind a legacy of some sort for their descendants. We highly value life achievement as a way of living aiming at passing on of a good honorable name in the family and the community.

Goodson made a similar observation as Dan P. McAdams who observes that telling one's life story is a process that most people find rewarding.[77] Goodson and Gill further claimed that Mezirow's transformative learning theory is too dependent on crisis events to occur to initiate the transformation.[78] They argue that narrative learning "does not rely on an experience of disorientation in order to question the premises of one's values or beliefs, nor is it necessary for a person to feel critical and discontented about his/her own assumptions."[79] Instead, they posed: "Transformation through narrative learning is enhanced understanding about oneself and the other, one's lived experience as a person over time, one's position in the world, and how histories, cultures and socio-political forces have shaped who we, as human being were, who we are now, and the journey we have traveled so far and the journey we are to travel together."[80]

It is true that life does not always contain disorientation dilemma and transitions, but when these events took place they always initiate a process of critical reflection. Furthermore, the events are necessarily disorienting to create the maximum impact. In fact, they were self-contradictory when they acknowledge that we are "shaped"—implying the presence of external forces—by "histories, cultures and political forces" both in the past and now. Furthermore, as also Girard contended, how can we be "enhanced" if there is no substance (either traditions, rituals, or stories) of comparison? Given these weaknesses identified, it shall be argued that the conclusion of Goodson and Gill is weak and mostly due to their unwillingness to acknowledge the role of "meta-narrative," a crucial reference point for comparison or mimesis. The false state of ideal fluidity they embrace is not tenable if there is going to be a more consistent and meaningful narrative learning. A grand narrative is necessary to which the respondents can readily refer as they reflect on their past, see their present, and peep into the

---

77. McAdams, *Stories*, 253.
78. Cf. Goodson and Gill, *Narrative Pedagogy*, 116–17.
79. Ibid., 117.
80. Ibid.

future. It is this writer's proposal that the presence of a referential narrative that is adequate for mimesis, such as a religious narrative, (in this case, Christian faith narrative contained in the Bible), makes a huge difference to the process of narrative learning. The necessity of the Bible is the ground and anchor in a spiral of narrative learning, both in the process of life story reflection-inquiry and storytelling itself.

Narrative Learning and Human Development

As life is examined and the story told, narrative learning is able to contribute to our understanding of faith development in a way our current theories of human becoming fail to. While most theories on human development focus on the description of the process of human growth, narrative learning is capable of giving meaning to human life in a completed state. This capacity of narrative to give completeness of humankind is more so when it is told in relation to a greater narrative such as the religious narrative—the Bible of Christian faith. I will use the faith development theory put forth by James W. Fowler as a starting point to show that story has the power to complete a person's life development.

Fairly speaking, from the life stories and interviews Fowler conducted in understanding human development, his faith development theory may be understood in terms of the stories that are present in each stage of life. At the first stage, the intuitive-projective stage, the example, mood, action, and stories of the people nearest to the child is formative for a child's development. In the second stage, the mythic-literal stage, the stories (myths) expanded and the child tends to understand these stories literally. In the third stage, synthetic-conventional, there is the emergence of narrative and myth in the young person. However, at this stage, the personal myth is in a nascent stage of development. The person has some idea but not "owning" that myth. In the fourth stage, the individuative-reflective stage, the young adult in reference to the other myth/stories is shaping his or her own myth, and in turn, their vocation in life. In the fifth stage, conjunctive faith, as a person enters his adulthood (30–60), his or her personal myth comes to almost a full circle.[81] Donald Capps notes that most of the autobiographies are written at this age group as one "would stop for a moment and engage in self-reflection. . . . If any literary genre is fundamentally about the identity

---

81. Cf. Fowler, *Stages of Faith*, 119–98.

vs. identity confusion conflict, the personal autobiography is surely the genre."[82]

The final stage, the universalizing stage, the person has become a myth—a legend like Ghandi, Mother Teresa—that Fowler finds is so rare.[83] Fowler also finds it difficult to clearly delineate the stages once a person enters adulthood. The usefulness of Fowler's final stage is often questioned as to its usability if so few people are able to attain this level of faith development. Furthermore, Fowler did not deliberate on the people who are disabled, or do not live to a good old age to "qualify" under the later stages of life development. Are these people excluded from achieving a full life?

Fowler sees faith development as life related to self, others, and God, as a way of finding meaning, or more of a foundational form of meaning that sustains a person's belief and action in life. From this intricate relationship, every person has a life story, regardless of length in time. The same applies to the life development of a disabled person to live as "normal" people do. In these exceptional lives, their life stories, at times, need to be told by and in relation to others. In cases where a child died young, or a child born disabled, the community (family or church who recognizes the precious presence of these lives) will seek to give meaning to these lives. The community can relate to their experiences of the lives of these children or underprivileged and bring them to fullness. The bravery of the child who faced the fear and pain of illness and death can be told, documented, and shared. The narrative functioning in these life stories can be as powerful and, at times, even more effective to elicit transformation in the hearers and/or learners than those who lived much longer. The process will be examined in greater detail in chapter 5 as the various factors that give rise to a biblical narrative learning will be examined.

Stories as Content of Narrative Learning

Storytelling has been the age-old practice of passing knowledge and wisdom from generation to generation. Stories "appeal to experience. The narrative is much richer than the analysis in its real-life application."[84] They help societies to conserve and reuse knowledge generated from past experiences.

---

82. For Capps, the identity vs. identity confusion stage is peg at the fifth decades of life, contrary to Erikson's adolescence. Capps, *Decades of Life*, 89.

83. Cf. Fowler, *Stages of Faith*, 199–213.

84. Brophy, *Narrative-Based Practice*, x.

Towards a Biblical Narrative Learning

Stories possess "subtle, half-hidden rhythms of what it is like to be human, to live."[85] Furthermore, stories may "address an individual situation, but still open up a new world of experience and understanding. As such, they provide insights which the bare 'facts' can never reveal."[86] Stories can also "circumvent the subconscious defence mechanisms of their listeners . . . An arresting introduction, . . . together with an unexpected conclusion may be used as mechanisms both to catch the listeners' attention and to hook the story, and its point, into the memory—to make it stand out from . . . the sleep-inducing factual presentation."[87] Because behind the story is a real person that has lived that experience, in turns, that experience can captivate the audience or reader. Furthermore, by introducing a new element into the knowledge experience of the audience, the story created the learning appetite. Or in another word, the new element creates a familiar yet strangeness to the audience.

Similarly, Rossiter and Clark argued that storytelling can "make information more memorable and more believable than if presented in another format such as a report or handbook or lecture."[88] It shall be argued that if other forms of presentation are forgettable, as older research has indicated, the experience of narrative learning, especially one that engages our full senses, is most powerful to implant memory in the audience and learner. This effect is brought about by the capacity of storytelling to engage both of our left and right brain. Furthermore, stories of lived experiences are perceived as more believable in terms of their reality factor.[89] Stories are powerful as they "engage learners at a deeply human level. Stories draw us into an experience at more than a cognitive level; they engage our spirit, our imagination, our heart, and this engagement is complex and holistic."[90] In the process of teaching the Bible, this thesis seeks to demonstrate that storytelling will act as a concrete and real example that empowers, serves as a guide for coping with life issues, crosses major and minor milestones, nurtures growth in faith—faith as representative of abstract lesson object. Living in the postmodern multi-tasking culture, we need time and space

---

85. Ibid., 33.

86. Ibid., 36.

87. Ibid., 37. Brophy is also careful to point out, "It is not the argument of this book that stories are, of themselves, sufficient as a basis for professional action." Ibid., 37–38.

88. Rossiter and Clark, *Narrative*, 27.

89. Ibid., 27.

90. Clark and Rossiter, "Narrative Learning," 65.

for reflection—guided by the stories of faith. Stories are the central source of knowledge base that informs our meaning scheme. In reflecting on the stories of our past experiences, our cultural tradition, and our faith stories, one learns the concept of what it means and how to live as an authentic person.

Summary

Narrative learning is a rather fluid process of learning. It can be a process of learning that occurs when one reflects and tells a past event in life. It can also be a process where the storytelling is teaching to elicit meaning making. In both incidents, there is a complex process of interaction between the teller and the others. Reflection, telling, interpretation, reception, and transformation are all possible overlapping parts of this process. Within this process, narrative learning helps the storyteller make sense of the past of the self through the others. A person's life, be it the storyteller's own or the character in the story, can be completed by the storyteller's interpretation and presentation of the life lived. Narrative learning also has the capacity to teach perspective on the future as one contemplates what the past has taught them in this process of inquiry. As a storytelling process, when a storyteller or teacher tells a story in a well-crafted (animated by the wise use of words) presentation, the storytelling is efficacious in creating a long lasting memory in the audience or learner that will, at the moment of engagement, produce guidance and wisdom to the most appropriate decision and action.

THE PRACTICE OF NARRATIVE LEARNING

The practicing of narrative learning has received wider acceptance in the recent decades in medicine, law, social work, and more recently, education.[91] Narrative learning has been variously and loosely linked to many forms of inquiry into life history and presenting the life story. This section will specifically focus on the convergence of these two processes of narrative

---

91. Cf. Brophy, *Narrative-Based Practice*, 33. Also cf. Merriam et al., *Learning in Adulthood*, 209.

inquiry and using the narrative as storytelling in the field of professional education and Christian education.[92]

When narrative learning is seen as a process of learning through the telling of life experiences or life stories, Goodson argues from the theory of Ricoeur, "narrative is not a product nor is it a set of tales about individuals and their communities. It is a process, a journey that leads to learning, agency and better understanding of oneself, others and one's purpose in the world. . . . Life stories are not end products but the beginning of the social process of narrative encounter."[93] Goodson and Gill are right to recognize narrative learning, in their view, as an unending process but they ignore the possibility of a narrative becoming an end product at a certain moment. The moment a narration is given, even when the "final outcome" has not been reached or revealed, the narrative has the potential of being an end product—a story, even when in suspense—that can invoke thoughtful contemplation. A narrative, regardless of its length, as seen in a story that seems to leave an open ending, is an end product in itself. However, a so-called end product can also be viewed as "not ended." A sequel or numerous sequels can be added to a completed story, in written form or in performance. Therefore, in the practice of narrative, a learning moment can take place at any point. This makes it hard to distinguish between an "inquiry" that informs and that which educates the *self* and/or the others. The learning moment can occur within Goodson's five-stage spiral process: narration, collaboration, location, theorization/meaning making, and direction.[94] It can also occur when a story is told. This process will be dealt with in chapter 5 where the three movements of a biblical narrative learning process that incorporates both narrative inquiry and storytelling will form the main substances of the discussion.

---

92. In this research, I will be using the terminology "testimony" as a category that includes all life stories short and long, from a five-minutes sharing of a life event to a full biography of a Christian life. For the possibilities of labeling the various types of narrative and life history research, see Goodson and Gill, *Narrative Pedagogy*, 21–22.

93. Ibid., 102.

94. Ibid., 102, 118–21, 125–30.

Narrative Learning in Adult Education and Career Training

For Clark and Rossiter, the three basic steps in learning though stories: hearing, telling, and recognizing the stories.[95] In this process, the learners give meaning to experience, but it is more than pulling an example from a collection of personal experience. The learner makes a connection with a cognitive understanding of a concept and links that to his or her own experience. In making this connection, new learning occurs.[96] Storytelling can take the forms of fiction, case study, example from practice, role-playing, or critical incidents. Brophy added that narratives could take a number of forms in practice: "storying" the curriculum, storytelling, and autobiography.[97] The learning process of a course in studies itself can be examined and interpreted to become a story about the subject studied.[98] The autobiography has been a long tradition that included diaries and journaling, blogs, and educational biography in which human experiences in various situations are recorded. These stories of past experiences become guides pointing to possible future action.[99]

In the field of medical practice, Diekelmann and Diekelmann identify the practice of narrative learning in three key settings: schooling in terms of attending, learning in terms of listening, and teaching in terms of co-responding and co-responsibility.[100] By schooling, Diekelmann and Diekelmann refer to a state of engaged attendance, an attentiveness that enable the human being of openness to be alert to the possibilities of understanding. This amplified understanding moves schooling beyond mere transfer of information and ability to give an identical output where the individual is made into a predetermined whole.[101] In schooling, the participant with whatever is given, by his/her presence, is offered the world as a dialogical experience.[102] Thus, the act of listening is not rote repetition nor a mere exercise of the ear, it is "presupposed by the experience of listening and understanding, not as a causal chain of events, but as a practical and

---

95. Clark and Rossiter, "Narrative Learning," 65.
96. Ibid., 64–65.
97. On storying the curriculum, also cf. Rossiter and Clark, *Narrative*, 74–75.
98. Cf. Merriam et al., *Learning in Adulthood*, 209–10.
99. Ibid., 210.
100. Cf. Diekelmann and Diekelmann, *Schooling, Learning, Teaching*, 191–250.
101. Ibid., 193–97.
102. Ibid., 216.

prudent historically situated belonging-together."[103] Instant reaction and response or creation of a new idea, meaning, and action plan is possible in the process of hearing, identification and resolution.

Listening allows knowledge to occur through "narrative telling of something, the effective self-finding of disposedness, . . . a participatory and historically particular experiencing."[104] In this fluid engagement, the "human being of openness as a listening attendant in the open clearing is always already ahead of itself as possibility. It is not a fixed entity, soul, psyche, ego, substance, subject, or person."[105] With insight gained, the listener may take the matter to heart or lacking one, hold back attending to the subject matter.[106] It seems that a considerable amount of uncertainty remained in the listening-learning process.

Finally, Diekelmann and Diekelmann cited the phenomenological view of Heidegger and Gadamer that the human being is never restricted or reduced to "some biological or theoretically determined static phenomenon."[107] In the didactic process, teaching "turns on the richer notion of belonging-to wherein co-responding is the primary groundless ground . . . teaching teacher is not an ultimate agency or the activity of a subject."[108] Teaching as co-responding shifts the traditional fixation and transfer of knowing onto a path that begets path. In this shift, the expert is no more than a replaceable part of a technical mechanism.[109] In a sense, it is teaching without teachers, yet the teacher and students are both present. It is the interplay of schooling as attending, learning as listening, and teaching as co-responding. The three elements constitute "a melodic line wherein these phenomena are never without each other and are always already moving alone as difference."[110] Diekelmann's three-stage narrative learning can be informative to a class setting in teaching the Bible. This

103. Ibid., 219.
104. Ibid., 220.
105. Ibid., 227.
106. Ibid., 238–42.
107. Ibid., 265.

108. Ibid., 272–73. The role of the teacher is open to different views. The role of the teacher is not limited to the presenter of the knowledge, but their personal integrity in part determines the learning. A person of worthy standing is granted better hearing. Aristotle also recognized the ethos of a narrative as one of the three key features. This may be developed further in rhetorical studies of pedagogy.

109. Ibid., 283, also cf. 278–79.
110. Ibid., 292.

reminds us of the importance of physical presence, and the full engagement of the individuals in the narrative learning process. This form of narrative practice will be most relevant in a classroom setting such as adult Sunday school. It is also a useful reference for biblical narrative learning since the attending aspect of narrative learning requires the presence of the learner and by their presence, makes possible full engagement of our five senses in narrative learning.

Narrative Learning in Christian Education

In 1980, Thomas H. Groome advocated a form of narrative learning in Christian religious education. He rightly reminded us that education is as old as human consciousness.[111] Groome advocated for the use of the story in Christian religious education. He built his *praxis* way of knowing on Aristotle's notion of three-tier human understanding: *theoria*, *praxis*, and *poiesis*.[112] In the process of human knowing and learning, Groome sees the becoming of *self* as a four-fold socialization:

a. externalization

b. objectification

c. internalization, and

d. the self/social dialectic.[113]

He contends, "Formal education only plays a small part in our participation in and formation by the social consciousness of the race. *Far more formative is the influence which arises simply from living within our social context.* . . . We are formed to be who we are through interaction with our social and cultural context. In other words, self-identity is socially mediated and maintained."[114] Though Groome does not employ the term narrative learning in his shared praxis approach, his understanding and using of the little stories in relationship to the Story corresponds to the socially-situatedness of narrative learning. His usage of storytelling also corresponds to the process of engagement with the self and the others. I will very briefly introduce here Groome's core concept of narrative learning. I shall return

---

111. Groome, *Christian Religious Education*, 5.
112. Ibid., 153.
113. Ibid., 109–15.
114. Ibid., 107.

to these components when I propose a biblical narrative learning based upon the discovery of Johannine pedagogy. The components of Groome's shared praxis approach call for:

a. present action,

b. critical reflection,

c. dialogue,

d. the Story (of Christian Bible and traditions),

e. the Vision (of Christian Bible and traditions), and

f. present dialectical hermeneutics.[115]

The interplays of these six components give rise to Groome's five movements of shared *praxis*:

a. Naming present action

b. Participants' stories and visions

c. Christian community Story and Vision

d. Dialectical hermeneutics between the Story and participants' stories

e. Dialectical hermeneutics between the Vision and participants' visions.[116]

In practice, he encourages freedom in

a. variations and sequence of movements,

b. timing and shared praxis,

c. the environment of shared praxis,

d. relationship of theology to Christian religious education, and

e. liturgy and a shared praxis approach.[117]

Anne E. Streaty Wimberly also recognizes the power of storytelling and applies the story-linking process in the African American congregation. In some way, her approach is similar to Groome's. She proposed four phases in story-linking:

Phase one: Engage the everyday story

Phase two: Engage the Christian faith story in the Bible

---

115. Ibid., 184–97.
116. Ibid., 205–23.
117. Ibid., 223–31.

Phase three: Engage Christian faith stories from the African American heritage

Phase four: Engage in Christian ethical decision making.[118]

Wimberly did not break new ground in her story-linking method. She did point out an important aim of using narrative in teaching the congregation: it is a process that is liberating and ushers in wisdom.[119] The achievement of wisdom is from relating our stories to the Story from God.[120]

Both Groome and Wimberly focused on the storytelling aspect and did not elaborate on the process of gathering the participants' or the teacher's stories used in teaching the Bible. Karen Massey also subscribes to the importance of narrative in teaching the Bible. Similar to Groome and Wimberly, Massey sees the interplay and dialogue between God's story and the community's story. Different in Massey is that she placed a clear emphasis on the person's individual story which is implied in Groome and less so in Wimberly. Massey stressed the importance of the self in narrative teaching of the Bible, "the biblical story, the community's story, and the person's life story, meet in individual Christians . . . they integrate themselves in one person, clash in another, or get reinterpreted in another."[121] She also added an important observation in the use of narrative learning: "it invites learners to remember."[122] It shall be analyzed that remembrance is one of the key purposes in the Johannine narrative strategy.

Summary

While narrative learning has always been practiced in all cultural settings from old to present, the use of narrative in learning is fairly recent in the professional practices. The philosophical turn to narrative filled the foundation and validated the use of fluidic narratives as a meaningful engagement in learning. In the present field of both secular and Christian education, narrative learning refers to two levels of engaging the learners. On one level, narrative learning is both the content and the process of learning through one's narration of their own lived live-experience(s). On the other level, the

---

118. Cf. Wimberly, *Soul Stories*, 39–57.
119. Ibid., 12–13.
120. Ibid., 3–12.
121. Massey, "Narrative Model," 202.
122. Ibid., 202.

education process uses storytelling as content reference to meaning making. This form of narrative learning has also been recognized, explored and proposed in Christian education. Thomas Groome pioneered the use of story in Christian religious education while Wimberly spoke of a story-linking process as a way of learning and making meanings. However, neither had he ventured deeper into researching a life story and its necessity in narrative learning. Biblical narrative learning will draw on these practices and proposes a need to combine the two levels in narrative learning.

THEOLOGICAL HUMAN UNDERSTANDING AND NARRATIVE LEARNING

From the various advocates for narrative learning, it becomes clear that there are different approaches to describe narrative learning both in theory and practice. This is precisely because of the complexity and variety of narrative learning. However, these researches mostly took place outside the scope of the religious setting and are overly dependence on the human faculty of learning and media. As a result, consideration for the divine intervention in human learning, and the *remythologizing* (in Vanhoozer's term) possibility in narrative learning are left out and greatly diminished the voice of narrative learning in Christian education.[123] The next section will try to argue for a theological perspective to human understanding and how this is relevant to the process of human learning and meaning making. One crucial element in understanding the Christian pursuit of human knowing and learning is how we can possibly learn *from* and *through* the divine presence. Sensitivity to the tradition of the Church reminds us to reconsider the theological underpinning for narrative learning that is fluid and seems to go against the Christian idea of the existence of a God-given Truth.

Conservatives among the Church would be wary of narrative learning since this approach is linked to postmodernism and its train of identifications. A link of narrative learning to postmodernism invokes the claim of the death of Truth and a close connection to liberal thinking. However, C S Song rightly informs us that God uses story in both the Old and New Testaments to convey His act in history. He further reminds us that "God has endowed human beings with the imagination of the soul and the facility of words to tell over and over God's story of creation as part of our stories and

---

123. Vanhoozer, *Drama of Doctrine,* and *Remythologizing Theology.*

to integrate our stories into God's story."[124] We have a wealth of stories that numbered, "as many as the inhabitants, who account for more than half of humanity.... This world of stories is the world of real people of flesh and blood,"[125] We are an undeletable part of these stories, "stories to which we are not outsiders but insiders, not strangers but participants, stories that tell us as much about ourselves as Christians as about our fellow Asians, we begin to realize how much the story of Jesus... is reflected in them. What we need most is a theological mind... to cultivate the theological imagination that can help us image God and perceive God's activity in the stories."[126]

The ministry of Bible teaching calls us to be faithful in engendering the faith of the community in order that people might live an authentic Christian life, to love and obey our life-giving Creator-God. In the process of knowing and learning, different suggestions on how best to approach the task at hand emerge. The suggestions vary as each comes from a different perspective. Some of these suggestions would negate the role of divine intervention and view personhood entirely as a social construct. We find the inconclusiveness of non-theological understanding of human beings as they excluded the divine intervention in forming a people. One does not reject nor diminish the contribution of various suggestions, especially those of social scientific enquiries, to our knowing and learning. However, for humankind created in the likeness of the image of God, to attain an authentic personhood requires us to be anchored in the divinely gifted personhood, modeled in the incarnated Jesus Christ, given by grace to us through the Word, written by the various witnesses and storytellers.

The Postmodern Self and Meaning-Making

The recent turn to narrative learning has been variously discussed in terms of how we know and how this knowledge is usable in our learning process. The rise of modernity understood knowledge as it begins and makes possible within the *self*. Kant promoted the self as "the locus of autonomy and free decision."[127] This sense of optimism in the human capacity continued till probably the early 1970s when the postmodern understanding of *self* took shape and the *self* became de-centered. Thiselton notes that

124. Song, *Believing Heart*, 65.
125. Ibid., 67.
126. Ibid.
127. Thiselton, "Postmodern Self and Society," 555.

with the postmodern, the *self* "no longer regards itself as active agent carving out any possibility with the aid of natural and social sciences, but as an opaque product of variable roles and performances which have been imposed upon it by the constraints of society and by its own inner drives or conflicts."[128] The postmodern self is a constructed identity that floats in uncertainty. They experience a loss of hope that Thiselton identified as "sprang at least in part from the collapse of any norm or truth that might otherwise be independence of someone else's power-interest, into sexism, racism, or socio-economic competition."[129] He further pointed out that if "*the self of modernity had been the right to hope, but wrong with the basis and on which it built its hope. Perhaps the postmodern itself had been right to despair* if will-to-power exhausted the content of all reality, *but wrong in its assumption that this exhausted all that might be called 'real.'*"[130] If indeed the popular rhetoric that there is no truth with the "T" stems from this erroneous base, then we should look at the possibility of a theological self-understanding found on the Word of God as an anchor for hope. Thiselton speaks of the necessity of this anchored hope, "without this promise, the transition from the selfhood of optimistic modernity to the postmodern self has deeply destructive social consequences. First a loss of stability, loss of stable identity and loss of confidence in global norms or goals breeds deep uncertainty, insecurity and anxiety."[131] Mark R. Talbot points out that if we are to function in anything like a distinctly human way, we must rise above "the sum of our physiological drives."[132] This calls for a Christian education that is anchored in the unchanging Word with an intentional task of teaching the Bible and reconstruct, within the fluidity of our current context, an authentic living revealed through the Word incarnated.

Human Being as Responsible Learner

How much can one know and how does one learn to live an authentic life according to the way proposed in the Bible? Dennis Ngien reminds us, the "Triune God who does not reserve goodness for himself, but *resolves*

---

128. Ibid., 555–56.
129. Ibid., 578.
130. Ibid., 579. Author's italics.
131. Ibid., 562.
132. Talbot, "Learning from the Ruined Image," 172.

to communicate."¹³³ God initiated the revealing throughout the history of humankind. The revealing climaxed in the incarnation of the Word in Jesus. The showing and telling in Jesus is efficacious to deliver humankind caught in the struggle for freedom from bondage of ontological, ethical, and epistemological anxieties as they seek to live life in truthfulness, seeking goodness and beauty.

Building on the work of Barth and Buber, Anderson pointed to the uniqueness of the human being in a state of co-existence.[134] In this state of co-existence, the singularity of humanity is determined in relation to the others, and one can only be an authentic individual in relation with another.[135] Barth articulated in a fuller sense the relationality of humans with God and others and explains, "Adam as the solitary male could never bear the divine image and likeness."[136] Our pursuit to be in the likeness of God is made possible in our relationship to God and to one another informed by, taught by, and through the stories and writings of the community of faith. "Christ's apostles were not scribes, but messengers. . . . The Word of God spoken . . . through human agency."[137]

We are able to rise above our other-determined being because each individual is also a responsible being. Anderson argues this difference with an existential approach in that "subjectivity is a conclusion rather than the starting point of theological anthropology."[138] We are "subjectively free as well as subjectively responsible to discriminate our own being *as it occurs* within the order of God's creation."[139] In sum, learning to live an authentic personhood lies within the range and reach of everyone. It is a movement toward a relationship with God. This is a reversal of what Donald K. McKim described, "Humanity as a whole is infected with what Augustine called

---

133. Ngien, *Gifted Response*, 59. Emphasis mine. Though Ngien's research relates mainly on the worship aspect of the human encounter with God, it also directly correlates to the human knowing and learning as worship is also a form of coming to know God with a further emphasis on the response of human to God. The task of learning about a Christian way of life inevitably affects the way one approaches and worships God. As Ngien points out, "The moment of understanding is precisely the moment of doxology." Ibid., xvi.

134. He terms this condition as co-humanity. Cf. Anderson, *On Being Human*, 44.

135. Ibid., 45–46.

136. Ibid., 77.

137. Ngien, *Gifted Response*, 116.

138. Anderson, *On Being Human*, 56.

139. Ibid., 60, author's emphasis.

'concupiscence,' or self-centered desire, which directs one toward the self as the center of attraction instead of toward God." It is determined by the circumstances (the others), depending on its hostility or friendliness, and opens up or narrows down the range of possibility for determining one's own being. "But each one is to seize the opportunity as best as possible. Failure to achieve will constitute a loss of authentic self."[140] This authentic self is a reflection of the relationship existing in the triune God in whose likeness humans are created.

Robert Louis Wilken named six areas that make personhood in the likeness of God. First of all, he calls to attention human participation in a spiritual world through the unique quality, be it called soul, or spirit, or mind that gave rise to language, produces works of art, establishes communities with memory, and sets human life off from all other forms of life.[141] Secondly, he claims the mystery of the human being that is made in the image of mysterious God. Thirdly, he named freedom of human orientation toward excellence as we seek to transcend ourselves. His fourth point recognizes the sinful nature of the human being but the reality of sin does not eradicate the image that is hidden beneath. Thus, we are to recognize and recover the fifth features of the human being through Christ, the perfect revealer of God. Christ redeemed us that we may have fellowship with God. Sixth, this fellowship occurs within the physical and spiritual aspects of human life.[142] This image is recovered through the stories God given us by the Word.

Authentic Living as Anchored in the Word of God

The history, and at the same time, the direction of human becoming is presented through the stories in the OT and NT. The stories have been told among the communities in the ancient past and continued to the present church. Those who have ears, the Lord proclaimed, should *hear* the Word and be transformed by this knowing. However, the stories of the Bible show more often a people who had not sufficient fear of God, resulting in not hearing God well enough. The warning from these stories of failure to hear and fear God set the mood when John the Baptist introduced Jesus to the

---

140. Ibid., 61–62.
141. Wilken, "Biblical Humanism," 17–18.
142. Ibid., 18–27.

teaching ministry. Jesus came to us as human and revealed God.[143] Jesus is the Word incarnated and gave us the fullest presentation of what it means and how to be human beings. He has taught his students to continue telling the story of salvation and the way to live as household of God. Jesus casts light on the uniqueness of human beings through the Word of God expressed in the personhood (life story) and teaching of Jesus. Jesus' story and teaching provides a way to restore the sinful human nature that distorted authentic way of life and impaired our response-ability to God.[144]

The community of God has been charged with the responsibility to safeguard and manifest this redeemed life as we imitate Christ.[145] Lints points out the importance of recognizing and embracing the sociality of the Christian community and leave behind the "solitary minds" of modernity. He reminds us of the necessity of being "covenantly bound to the people of God as a reflection of the triune God."[146] We are now able to achieve this through the indwelling of the Holy Spirit in the community of God. Our communication with God in enabled through the Spirit. "The double-movement of the Trinity constitutes the condition of the possibility of true worship: God descends to our flesh in the Son, revealing his gracious will in the Spirit; conversely the Spirit draws us through the Son to . . . the Father."[147] This relational personhood, living and practicing faith in a community of faith, is what Grenz describes as the "ecclesial self,"[148] as the Holy Spirit gathers them into the dynamic of the divine life. Through the Holy Spirit, Christians come to share the relationship that the Son enjoys with the Father. It is important to acknowledge that, on our own, we are unable to comprehend God.

With the presence of the Word and the Spirit, the Father bestows on the believers, by virtue of their being "in Christ," what he gives to the Son,

---

143. The role of Jesus as revealer of God is one of the key themes in the Gospel of John (see John 1:14–18). The interpretation and teaching of this interpretation is a process that could benefit from a closer look at the Wesleyan quadrilateral and other biblical hermeneutics.

144. Cf. Anderson, *On Being Human*, 93–103.

145. Paul imitated Christ and urged the Corinthians to follow his example (1 Cor 11:1).

146. Lints, "Imaging and Idolatry," 224.

147. Ngien, *Gifted Response*, xvi.

148. Grenz highlighted the shape of the faith community. "The image of God does not lie in the individual per se, but in the relationality of persons in community." Grenz, "Social God," 89.

making all believers members of his household. Thiselton points out the outcome of a relationship in Christ:

> The renewed self does not remain entirely victim to the social, moral, or cause-and-effect forces that determined its historical situatedness.... Although forces from the past still operate, the Holy Spirit also bring about a process of transformation "from ahead," which loosens and eventually breaks the ties which bind the self to its pre-given situatedness.... transformation from a failed or distorted "image" of humanness into the "image" of Jesus Christ.[149]

Thiselton further explains that the process of creative transformation through the Holy Spirit "begins in the present, even if as partial 'first fruits' only.... because the Spirit transposes self-interest, conflict and bids-for-power into *love for others* (for individuals and groups) *and for the Other* (for God and for whatsoever is not self)."[150] By the Spirit, they participate in "the Son's act of eternal response to the Father."[151] Grenz concludes:

> Personhood, then, is bound up with relationality, and the fullness of relationality lies ultimately in relationship with the triune God. Creating this relational fullness is the work of the Spirit, who places humans "in Christ" and thereby effects human participation in the dynamic of the divine life. Moreover, being "in Christ" entails participation in the narrative of Jesus, with its focus on the cross and the resurrection ... an identity-constituting narrative, ... and thereby are the ecclesial new humanity.[152]

The Christian community has learned to live a way of life through the Story and sustained by the theological recognition of who we are.

Summary

The relational living points to the task of Christian education as a knowing and learning process anchored in the community of faith. In this process, the stories of the people of God are presented in relation to the Story. In this Story, we are the participants and imitators of Jesus whose incarnation

---

149. Thiselton, *Thiselton on Hermeneutics*, 561.
150. Ibid., 576. Author's italics.
151. Cf. Grenz, "Social God," 91–92.
152. Ibid., 92.

becomes the referential character whom we imitate for authentic personhood embodied in living out love in God and one another. Jesus presents a personhood centered on love and obedience to bring justice to the livelihood of authentic human living. In this participation, we imitate the master story and become the continuing stories showing and telling for others possibilities of authentic living. Thus, the task of Christian education entails a learning experience utilizing the unique social and cultural context of each people group. In it, the attractiveness of our stories relates to, offers, and invites fellow pilgrims in attaining authentic living.

In the way the learning through dialogue of the Story and story, Vision and vision advocated by Groome, the imitation of Jesus is active in a narrative learning process. In the biblical narrative learning, imitation involves more than the story, it includes the presentation, and the creation of new narratives, based on the lived Christian faith experiences. The experiences can vary and encompass faith experiences lived in different life challenging issues or moments of jubilation in diverse settings. This imitation of living life by faith will be further explored in chapter 3 and 4 where a literary reading of John's Gospel informs our narrative learning.

NARRATIVE LEARNING AND ADULT LEARNERS

In practice, we have witnessed the use of stories as a rich resource in many churches. The use of stories at times transcended areas untouched by the many theological ideas. Stories or testimonies have a huge impact in the formation of the Church. The huge success of the charismatic movement has been largely fueled by testimonies. These mega churches use testimonies of healing to their best benefit. However, in these settings, the power and function of testimony have not been fully articulated and interpreted in relation to the biblical tradition. This lacking in biblical support in understanding the lived faith experiences has caused differences in the churches, and weakened the power of these narratives.

Towards a Biblical Narrative Learning

Recognizing that in this global setting, we recognize the necessity to affirm narrative learning for the church. This affirmation is significant for Christians living in a different social setting, unfamiliar and, at times, uncomfortable with theology or philosophy that promoted individualism.[153] The recent recognition of the non-Western way of knowing and learning further opens a way for the global Christian to dialogue with the dominant western way of knowing and learning.[154] Recent researches done on non-Western perspectives in learning have expanded the space for exploring the differences of the non-Western learners.[155] In fact, the non-Western perspective has always existed but was less studied and even less published in the world outside their context. Similarly, there are many stories of a Christian way of life among the local church that are hidden in the memory of those who lived these experiences. Only a small fraction of these life stories are shared in the church.

The practice of sharing personal testimony in the small group or fellowship gathering is a significant source and practice of biblical narrative learning in teaching a Christian way of living. The testimonies of the church members have been an active agent in presenting the life stories of the believers. These testimonies can be a snippet of their experiences living as followers of Jesus. Sometimes, these testimonies are shared in writing. Less frequently, an autobiography is written to tell a Christian's life journey through this world and how the message of Jesus was heard and followed in life. Recently, there are also Christian bloggers who posted their live experiences and reflections. Others have also used social networks or blogs as means to connect and share. The venue for narrative sharing is vast and varied.

How would the church best adopt narrative learning in teaching the Bible among the congregation? The strangeness of narrative learning as a personal investigation into one's life may be constrained by the church's

---

153. Tyron Inbody points out that the relationship between the belief and practice in the last quarter century has shifted from pure speculative philosophy. Now, "The language of the social science has tended to replace the stranglehold philosophy had on theology throughout most of Western Christian history. It has become the language of theologians who are willing to use the wisdom of secular culture to help Christians understand their faith." Cf. Inbody, *Faith of Christian Church*, 25.

154. Cf. Merriam et al., *Non-Western Perspectives*.

155. Merriam, Caffarella, and Baumgartner recognize the dominating and colonizing of the Western tradition in the non-Western world through Western science. They advocate the alternative perspectives to our understanding of learning a knowing from non-Western perspectives. Cf. Merriam, *Learning in Adulthood*, 219–25.

culture of self-enclosure. The older generation is, in general, not comfortable to have their personal life brought into the open, at the risk of being scrutinized. Yet they have a wealth of life stories that are teachable stories to the younger generation. Their stories are essential to ensure the continuity of the Christian way of life, and consolidation of their faith. Their stories need to be researched, documented, and told—though not necessarily in that order. To foster both tracks of narrative learning among the local church, we will need to 1) introduce life story research, 2) affirm and encourage their current practice of sharing testimony and develop that into a mature form of storytelling, 3) use these stories in educating the church. The practice introduced by Groome and Wimberly are worthy references to the task of biblical narrative learning. This idea of narrative learning as storytelling is not alien to the Church, but theorizing it may take time to introduce, to learn, to familiarize and become comfortable with.

CONCLUSION

Not many new ideas have surfaced in recent years since narrative learning was revived in the nineties. The Aristotelian root reinterpreted by Ricoeur provided the foundation to narrative learning and has been used to argue for the present trend in narrative learning. Most of the recent writings are recycling the few ideas on the narrative way of knowing, the method of narrative inquiry, the relationship of the researcher and subject, the nature and functions of narrative, and the use of narrative in practice. The non-theological understanding of human knowing leads to a postmodern instability, and at times, a free redefinition of what is human, and how and what we can know. Theological understanding of the human way of knowing and the source of knowing prepares a way to reexamine our learning process through the stories of the Bible and points to a way of narrative learning and teaching the Bible.

The Gospel writers remembered what they had experienced in Jesus. Beyond what they had heard about Jesus, they interpreted them in line with the tradition and responding to the needs of their unique audiences. They drew on the Jewish Scripture available to them in Greek to explain what they had witnessed and experienced. Their interpretations and presentations in writing tell the story of Jesus' life, ministry, teaching, death, and resurrection. They further recorded the story of Jesus in relation to the disciples and the people of the time. How does the author of John's Gospel stand out in his writing and how does he intend to teach his audience? And how does his work inform us in a biblical narrative learning? The next chapter will bring us into the world that shaped John as a learner-teacher, and his teaching in John's Gospel as a well-honed storyteller.

2

The Narrative World That Shaped John's Gospel

The first-century Palestine world under the Greco-Roman rules and influences sets the backdrop of the Johannine writing. The lives of the people were challenged under the tension of contesting groups fighting for control over religious, political, and social (especially educational) matters. The group having ability to control any or all of these realms of lives held its grip on the way of life of the community. In many ways similar to the Church, the Johannine community at large may have been consciously facing the pressure of living under such adverse conditions, while their way of life, and their practice of faith in real life was threatened and shaped by the surrounding narratives that encompassed the three major aspects of their lives. John, as a leader in the nascent church, saw the challenges that threatened this young faith tradition. He wrote an account of the faith and taught his faith community to believe in Jesus Christ the Lord, and no matter what the adverse conditions were, to remain in this faith. This chapter aims to highlight the challenges of Johannine community that are strikingly similar to the situation in the Church and flesh out the implications of how the churches educate their members in living their faith.

The first section presents the world of the Johannine audiences and how John sought to educate them in the face of these challenges through

John's Gospel. The second section shall look at the educational details of the Johannine context and show how the Johannine community successfully "survived" the cultural changes by their syncretism of the Hellenistic challenges. Finally, the chapter will address the purpose of John in writing a life story of Jesus, and how John presented Jesus in a new light: John wrote a testimony of Jesus as a *bios*.

THE WORLD OF JOHANNINE COMMUNITY AND THEIR CHALLENGES

The background of John's Gospel, according to J. Ramsey Michaels is not significantly different from that of the other three Gospels. He argues that the main issues are similar and the Synoptic Gospels shared the Jewish Bible with John's Gospel, Second Temple Judaism, and primitive Christianity.[1] Within a broad setting of first-century Palestine under the Roman rule, the general cultural climate is probably static and we should not anticipate drastic and rapid changes in a short span of less than five decades. While John's Gospel shares with the Synoptic Gospels the influences of Greco-Roman socio-politics and culture, as a product of a later period, it does command some special attention in relationship to its composition and purpose of writing. Traditionally, most Johannine scholars recognize that the Gospel was written specific to its audience and situation.[2]

Though it is difficult to speak of "Jewish Christian" in the first century Palestine, the basic group within the Johannine faith community was probably Jewish Christian.[3] Todd Klutz points out, "neither in public perception

---

1. Cf. Michaels, *Gospel of John*, xi, 4. For a similar opinion, also cf. Smith, *Theology of John*, 56.

2. The earliest comment on this sectarian origin of John's Gospel is by Irenaeus (c. AD 180). In *Against Heresies*, he attributed the authorship of the Gospel of John to an authoritative figure, Apostle John, one of the twelve disciples of Jesus, who wrote the Fourth Gospel to his faith community in Ephesus around the late first century CE, addressing the various issues challenging the faith belief and practice they were facing. Recent scholarly works have several suggestions for the place of writing, but there is a lack of consensus. Brown stood by Ephesus as the locale. Cf. Brown, *Introduction to the Gospel of John*, 204. As for the date of writing, the general consensus is late first century CE.

3. Esler points out, "The term 'Christian' and 'Christianity' are anachronistic for at least the early part of this period, until the end of the first century CE and even for some time beyond. Not only was the word *Christianos* (which appears only three times in the New Testament: Acts 11:26 and 26:28; 1 Pet 4:16) not used by those who followed Christ as a term of self-designation until later, but 'Christian' conveys such particular

41

nor in religious practices were 'Christianity' and 'Judaism' universally distinguished from one another at the beginning of the second century CE."[4] The diverse elements in the practices among the Jewish Christians of the first century made it difficult to use these terms in general. Consequently, cautious scholars abandon the words "Jew/Jewish" and "Christian/Christianity." Instead they use *Ioudaioi* in referring to "Israelites and non-Israelites alike—people who lived in or (although residing in the Diaspora) were oriented to *Ioudaia* (Judaea) and its holy city, Jerusalem, and the temple within it."[5] In most churches outside Jerusalem, the composition of their members was probably Hellenistic.

The Hellenistic period was a time of syncretism.[6] Tessa Rajak points out that to distinguish between Jews and Greeks was common in Second Temple Palestine. However, to set up the two cultures as incompatible, fixed systems, standing center stage, in opposition to one another, is to be avoided as the two cultures were deeply intertwined. By the first century CE, "Greekness" had been an intrinsic part of Judaism for some centuries.[7] A broad definition for the term "Hellenistic" would refer to

> the general diffusion of Greek culture among those peoples conquered by Alexander as a consequence of his Hellenizing policies, a cultural programme actively pursued by his successors. It included the establishment of Greek as the international language of politics and commerce, the introduction of Greek cultural and civic institutions into those cities among the peoples Alexander had incorporated into his empire.[8]

The Hellenistic dimension of the Jews owes its strong presence to a few factors. Most immediate and pertinent are the extensive Hellenization during the Hasmonean rule, Herod's active promotion of it, and the

---

associations from the later course of the movement as to obscure an important aspect of its rather fluid and developing identity at this early time." Esler, *The Early Christian World*, 22.

4. Klutz, "Paul and the Development of Gentile Christianity," 169.

5. Horrell cites Rohrbaugh and Malina in their arguments for this change in terminology. Reasons for the change include the tendencies to relate the term "Jew" with the past and subsequent history of this people. Cf. Horrell, "Early Jewish Christianity," 137.

6. Koester, *History, Culture, and Religion*, 164.

7. Cf. Rajak, "Location of Cultures in Second Temple Palestine," 3–4.

8. Martin, "Graeco-Roman Philosophy and Religion," 55.

"dramatically-expanding Jewish Diaspora."[9] There were adoptions of Greek names in addition to their Hebrew names.

The impact of these cultural contacts brought significant changes to Jewish living; "In measuring the urban dimensions of this interplay between Judaism and Hellenism—from the material culture, to the institutions, languages, and diverse social and religious practices—the impact of the latter on Jerusalem must be judged to be most significant."[10] As a development of cultural history, Hellenization affected all Jews, not only those of the Diaspora, but also the Jews of Palestine. "But in the diaspora especially in the Greek cities, the results of Hellenization were much more profound."[11]

Koester points out "only a small portion of the Jewish people offered resistance to the further spread of Hellenism, . . . the majority of the Jewish people became thoroughly Hellenized."[12] During the syncretistic process was the mutual permeation of various elements of the different cultures and religions.[13] As with other religions of the Hellenistic and Roman period, "Christianity became deeply enmeshed in the syncretistic process, and this may very well have been its particular strength. Christianity began as a Jewish sect with missionary ambitions, but it did not simply arise out of Judaism, . . . more than the other religions of its time, was able to adapt itself to a variety of cultural and religious currents and to appropriate numerous foreign elements until it was ready to succeed as a world religion—thoroughly syncretistic in every way."[14] Christianity was rapidly Hellenized and appeared in the Roman world as a Hellenistic religion.[15] In Jerusalem, the guardians of the Temple and its cult and the interpreters of the law were the priests. "Outside of Jerusalem, especially in the *diaspora* outside of Palestine, Jews had long since learned to adjust their religion to the new

---

9. Cf. Levine, "Second Temple Jerusalem," 56–66.

10. Ibid., 65. Rajak sees the most obvious influence on the Palestinian land is the buildings and institutions rather than the people. He points out the Second Temple constructed under Herod was so influenced by the architecture of the day it "could scarcely have been mistaken for a Greek shrine." Cf. Rajak, "Location of Cultures in Second Temple Palestine," 5.

11. Koester, *History, Culture, and Religion*, 224.

12. Ibid., 97.

13. Ibid., 166–67.

14. Ibid., 167.

15. Ibid., 40.

situation . . . Thus, a new tradition of interpretation was developed in the synagogues which was no longer controlled by the priests."[16]

The Johannine community consisted mainly of poor people living in the Diaspora.[17] The size of the Diaspora was significant and their influences probably grew in the presence of the Temple authority and gained greater autonomy. The establishment of the church among them further propelled them into redefining their own faith practice. A medium figure puts the population of the Jews in the Diaspora at five million while the Jewish population in the land of Israel in the first century numbers at two and a half million.[18]

In terms of economic activities and the related political position, the significance of the Diaspora Jews in shaping the new Christian community is indelible. Irina Levinskaya's study on the first-century Jewish Diaspora gives evidence from epigraphs and literatures of the time that the Diaspora Jews were in Antioch, and in Ephesus where the Johannine community was situated.[19] Some of the Jews in the Diaspora had become quite prosperous.[20] There are evidences of educated Jews, even physicians, among them.[21] While for some cities the records of Jews are few, Levinskaya's study shows "concrete"[22] (inscriptions) external evidences of the influential positions of the first century Jewish Diaspora communities. The Jews in the Diaspora were able to hold the coveted *civitas Romana* and even municipal

---

16. Ibid., 405.

17. For the economic situation of the first-century Greco-Romans Jewish population and their economic activities, the following authors provide significant insight. Meeks, *First Urban Christians*. Skarsaune, *In the Shadow of the Temple*. Goodman, *Judaism*, 52–59. Fiensy, "Composition of the Jerusalem Church," 214–15. Friesen, "Justice or God's Will," 18–21.

18. Cf. Skarsaune, *In the Shadow of the Temple*, 91. The total number of Jews in the Diaspora ran into many millions in by the first century CE Philo of Alexander records the total number of Egyptian Jews alone at one million. Adolf Harnack (1908) calculated the four to four and a half million Jews in the Roman Empire. Salo W. Baron (1972) calculated eight million.

19. They were also in several cities in Asia Minor including Miletus, Pisidian Antioch, Iconium. Records of Jewish communities also indicate the presence of Christian groups in the cities of Macedonia and Achaia, namely Thessalonica, Berea, Athens and Corinth. There were significant activities of the Jewish communities in Rome with records of no less than fifteen synagogues retained. Cf. Levinskaya, *Diaspora Setting*, 127–52, 153–93.

20. Ibid., 128–32.

21. Levinskaya, *Diaspora Setting*, 138, 147.

22. Pun intended.

office in the cities of western Asia Minor.[23] The Diaspora Jews were active in acquiring wealth, attaining status in the upper strata of their community and creating a powerful association with the authorities. These urban elites were dependent upon maintaining close relationships with both Jewish religious authorities and Roman political entities in order to protect their various possessions.[24] The mundane life of the Johannine community living in the Diaspora is reminiscent of the lives of the post-immigrant Christians living in foreign countries. The successful syncretism of the Jews living in Diaspora has its implication for the migrant Christians living in a complex cultural setting. They tend to seek harmony rather than oppose conflicting forces and hence avoided any creative conflict. The church has been mostly silent on critical social issues. On the issue of biblical and theological differences, most of the times the migrant Christians also tended to avoid direct confrontation. Lack of clear response and a strong message of Christian integrity will put the testimony of the Christians in dire situation in the midst of competitive voices.

Contestation of Christ's Testimony

While the early Christians managed the Hellenization in a fruitful manner, the Pharisees with their long arm of influence through the presence of the synagogues was a major concern for both Diaspora and Palestinian Jews. James Newsome describes the Pharisees community as follows.

> They bound themselves together by a common commitment to the strictest possible observance of the Torah, an observance that was, of course, understood in terms of their own body of Torah interpretation. Anyone who did not live up to the discipline of their teaching could not participate in their fellowship. It appears, in

---

23. Meek, *First Urban Christians*, 14.

24. In the extremely hierarchical Greco-Roman society, maintaining one's status is a necessity to survival and well-being of the rich and powerful. For example the citizenship of Paul brought its benefits such as lighter penalties in court cases. "One of the effects of this stratification within the empire was the desire for wealthy individuals in the provinces to have a place within the higher circles of Rome." Gill and Gempf, *Acts in Its Graeco-Roman Setting*, 108. Bruce Malina describes the defensive strategy of the honorable individuals and how they formed alliances in order to maintain, safe guard and preserve their entitlements in the competitive world. Cf. Malina, *New Testament World*, 89–106.

fact, that the term by which they originally referred to one another was not Pharisee, but *hever*, meaning *companion*.[25]

Vincent Martin describes the Pharisees as "a self-conscious group forming a network of strict observant people, and intent on the study of the Law and the traditions of the past sages."[26] The Pharisees developed a strong sense of community among the members of the group.

According to Josephus, although the Pharisees were themselves quite a small group, they were influential with the masses.[27] He reckons the number of Pharisees who refused to take an oath of loyalty to the emperor in the time of Herod as 'above six thousand' throughout the kingdom.[28] Despite their relatively small number to the Jewish population, they were prominent in the Jewish religious system in the first century. They were able to sway decisions in the Sanhedrin by their authority in the interpretation of the Law. Stemberger points out,

> The fact that the Pharisees increase in importance in the later Gospels . . . and that the Pharisees increasingly dominated the scene after 70 CE, and evolved into the rabbinate. . . . the fact that the early Christian communities were especially involved in disputes with the Pharisees could mean that the traditions of the Pharisees also played a role in their own circles.[29]

Wenell observes the influence that the Pharisees had gained "through their oral interpretation of its regulations," resulting in their partial control of Second Temple society.[30] Their claim to have the authoritative interpretation of Torah also stacks their control over salvation. As in their social setting, the two main media of redemption and salvation were the temple and the Torah.[31] They "were convinced that *they* were the way for Israel, the assured way to regenerate the people and make them ready for welcoming the Messiah."[32]

---

25. Newsome, *Greeks, Romans, Jews*, 115.
26. Martin, *A House Divided*, 58.
27. Josephus, *Antiquities*, 13.298
28. Ibid., 17.42. Cf. Goodman, *Judaism*, 41.
29. The influences and development of the Pharisees into the Rabbinic Judaism tradition are discussed more fully in Stemberger, *Jewish Contemporaries of Jesus*, 140–41.
30. Wenell, *Jesus and the Land*, 79.
31. Moxnes, *Economy of the Kingdom*, 106.
32. Martin, *House Divided*, 59.

The Narrative World That Shaped John's Gospel

The implication of the considerable presence of the Pharisees on the faith practice of the Johannine community is the control on who has the authority to interpret the Scripture. This became a ground of contest after the destruction of the Second Temple. Without the presence of a ruling Temple, while other groups such as the Essenes and Sadducees disappeared, the Pharisees are believed to be the core group that developed into the Rabbinic Judaism and represented the sole controlling power of the Jewish faith.[33] They probably became the main challenger to the Johannine community on the matter of faith in God and the appropriate way of living faithfully in relation to God and his commands. They claimed new leadership in interpreting and teaching the Scripture for the Jewish community. This group is also among the audience of John's writing.

John was writing to his Family and, at the same time, all his contemporaries whose lives are inexplicably related to the lives of the Johannine community. Jerome H. Neyrey helpfully distinguishes two contesting voices within the all-encompassing Johannine audiences: the insiders and the outsiders. The insiders gave maximum honor to Jesus while the outsiders vilified him.[34] He cites the role and status of the significant characters in John's Gospel, and their identification and relationship to locations or territory are some of the key criteria that separated the vituperative outsiders and the encomiastic insiders in the audience.[35] Those significant insider-characters received high status, and are those who exhibit a high level of understanding of who Jesus is. These insiders with the highest status are the man born blind (John 9) who boldly proclaims his alliance with Jesus, and the Beloved Disciple, who had physical contact with Jesus and alone recognizes the Risen Jesus.[36] Neyrey elaborates on how the places, sacred or profane, and where one stands to proclaim or worship, set one apart as insider or outsider. Neyrey identifies many places in John's Gospel. While the Temple and synagogue become off-limits to Jesus and his disciples, the houses (such as where the wedding was held in Cana and houses where

---

33. Pharisees is occasionally used in the Gospel of John, but Sadducees completely dropped out of the picture. The disappearance of Sadducees and collapsing of the Jewish religious group into one group is probably reflected in the singular use of "the Jews" in John's Gospel.

34. Neyrey's reading would presume reading the final form of the Gospel of John. Cf. Neyrey, *John in Cultural and Rhetorical Perspective*, 13.

35. Ibid., 3–84.

36. Ibid., 45–56. Also see Neyrey, *Gospel of John*, 7–9.

many others event unfolded) become a "*fluid* sacred place" for them.[37] Neyrey's studies disclose that the Johannine community, after the destruction of the Temple—the sacred place of worship and center of instruction—initiated their separation from Jewish heritage and religious way of life.

Summary

In sum, the Christians living in the first century Greco-Roman world are mainly people of low income. Many either moved to or remained in the foreign land. Some of them have shown significant success living in the major cities. Though they were surrounded by foreign cultures, they were not swallowed into them. Their way of living was strongly Hellenized and they had taken full advantage of this Hellenization syncretism. The Jewish Christians in the Diaspora were successful in negotiating their way through these challenges. Removed from their homeland, the Diaspora Christian Jews depended on the synagogues as the center of their religious activities. In the next section, it will become obvious that the synagogues were also their centers for educating the young, exerting the most significant influence on their way of learning, knowing, and the way of life.

THE EDUCATION AND SOCIAL LIFE IN JOHANNINE COMMUNITY

Language and education, the imperialistic Roman Empire, and the social convention of honor-shame are three key factors that impacted the Johannine community. These elements also correspond closely to the religion-influenced political problems, and social convention of family honor.

Language and Education

In the first-century Greco-Roman world Greek language and Greek methods of education dominated culturally.[38] The dominance of Greek language in the eastern part of the Empire that included Asia Minor and Palestine also dictated the literature and content of studies for students.

---

37. Cf. Neyrey, *John in Cultural and Rhetorical Perspective*, 83. Author's italics.
38. Koester, *History*, 41.

Within the Hellenistic cultural milieu, they established a three-tier education system. There were the primary school, gymnasia (secondary), and school of rhetoric (advanced).[39] The primary schools were normally run by the administration of the Hellenistic cities, while the "gymnasia, even if they were in fact sponsored by private associations, were viewed as a public and communal responsibility."[40] The school of rhetoric was limited and only found in some of the major cities. More often, instruction in rhetoric was private and had to be paid for by the student or his parents, making it available to the rich only.[41]

In the primary schools, children from the age of seven to fourteen learned reading, writing, music, arithmetic, and athletics. The classroom would be in a shop near the town center.[42] The methods of instruction were simple rote learning where one started by learning the alphabet and then reading and writing of words and sentences. Memorization and copying were the main learning methods with greater emphasis on memorization. Ferguson poses that the emphasis on memory was probably due to "a survival of earlier times when this was the only or principal means of preserving and transmitting information."[43] "In their fifteenth (or seventeenth) year the young men went to the gymnasium for a one- or two-year period (the so-called *ephebia*, where athletics and preliminary military training predominated)" for the secondary education.[44] There, they received instruction from a *grammaticus* (grammarian) paid by the parents. In addition to learning the grammar, they also began to learn the poets, reading primarily Homer and Euripides.[45] "The method of instruction was for the teacher to read aloud a passage and then explain it in detail. . . . The student then read the passage aloud and were questioned on it."[46]

For the Jews, their learning followed the same stages as did Greco-Roman education. However, the aim of Jewish education in the first-century

---

39. Also cf. Ferguson, *Backgrounds of Early Christianity*, 109.

40. Koester, *History*, 93.

41. Ibid., 93.

42. Cf. Ferguson, *Backgrounds of Early Christianity*, 109.

43. Ibid., 110. Also cf. Koester, *History*, 93.

44. Koester, *History*, 93.

45. Ibid.

46. The teacher taught in detail "textual criticism, meaning of words and idioms, references to mythology and history, points of grammar, figures of speech, and moral lessons to be learned." Ferguson, *Backgrounds of Early Christianity*, 110.

differed from the culture surrounding them. While the Hellenistic education had the formation of the human person as its goal, the aim of Jewish education was a religious one. They learned the Scripture and the oral traditions of the scribes.[47] Besides the home education system, there was probably a primary school run in the Synagogue, but that was not widely available outside of Jerusalem until the second century AD. Secondary schools existed earlier (second century BC) and were known as *beth midrash* (house of instruction) or *beth talmud* (house of learning [oral law]) available in both the homeland and in the Diaspora.[48] Here, mostly beginning at the age of thirteen, students studied the law. The learning center was in an adjoining building of the synagogue and supported by the synagogue.

After the destruction of the Second Temple, the development of Jewish education grew and this increase in Jewish teaching centers would augment their education activity and influence. In his studies on the existence of Torah centers and rabbinic activity in ancient Palestine, Ben Zion Rosenfeld identified both the location and personnel in teaching activities of the sages. There were numerous synagogues built in Palestine and beyond at the end of first century. During the period after the destruction of the Second Temple (70–132 CE), within the near vicinity of Judea, there was "an increase in the number of rabbinic centers relative to the two preceding generations, but it is their geographical dispersion that is informative. The rabbinic centers were ... distributed throughout other areas of Judea."[49] He explains the impact of this moving away from the major center into minor centers. "This dispersion of spiritual centers represented a significant expansion of rabbinic activity and influence across Judea. The sages resided in the small towns and villages of Judea, ... They lived among the people and were involved in society ... enable them to gradually develop into a religious leadership with widespread influence."[50] He found similar increase in Caesarea "a well-established rabbinic center ... the third and fourth generations of the talmudic period ... it was the scene of activity of twelve to fourteen sages in each generation, respectively."[51] Though Rosenfeld didn't

---

47. Ibid., 109, 112.
48. Ibid., 112.
49. Rosenfeld, *Torah Centers and Rabbinic Activity*, 87.
50. Ibid., 87–88.
51. Ibid., 223. Also see 85–89, 220–22, 255–56 for the summaries of the distribution in each region. Rosenfeld gives a detailed count of the number of Torah centers and sages in various time periods in different regions in Judea, Galilee, and the regions to the East. The maps on the distributions of these centers are particularly informative and

explore further geographical locations, he suggested a high possibility of widespread Jewish teaching centers in the Diaspora where the synagogue as teaching centers originated and probably a later introduction to the Palestine region after the destruction of the Second Temple necessitated the adoption of this form of religious learning centers.

In addition to schooling, the establishment of public libraries also serves as a site of education for the literate. Koester points out that with "the production and sale of books in larger quantities, literary works were increasingly available to the general public."[52] The literate public was accessible to the city libraries financed through public or private funds, and smaller libraries found in the gymnasia and schools. The libraries usually held the same works, "with the smaller libraries having only a limited selection: the classical Greek authors, with the poets (especially Homer and Euripides) being more fully represented than prose writers and philosophers; and handbooks, textbooks, and compendia."[53] Besides, those who cannot afford the cost of education were accessible to other means of learning. "The classical poets were available for reading everywhere, but they could also be heard: in the theaters poetry became accessible to the illiterate public as well as to the educated reader."[54] Other sites of learning included theater that was found in every city, and in many cities in addition to the theaters, there were odium, *stoa* (covered colonnade), and auditoriums where people gathered for public lectures, discussions, and competitions of poets, orators, and singing.[55]

For the privileged few who pursued Greek education, there was advanced learning focused on rhetoric that could include some philosophy, astronomy, history, depending on the profession aspiration of the students. The teaching was usually done by either wandering popular scholars, by private teachers established in the cities, or in institutions of learning in educational centers in major cities.[56] For the Jews, advanced study was in the form of learning from a great scholar. After the destruction of the

---

summarize his finding. Ibid., 297–300.

52. Koester, *History*, 94.
53. Ibid., 95.
54. Ibid.
55. Ibid.
56. Cf. Ferguson, *Backgrounds of Early Christianity*, 111.

Temple, and later Jerusalem, the advanced learner would probably go to one of the academies, such as the one at Jamnia.[57]

While the majority of the population lived in poverty does not mean that the poor were illiterate. There are indications, based on the evidence of the papyri, that the literacy rate of Hellenistic time was high, possibly higher than at any period prior to modern times.[58] This would be true for the Jews who received their education at home. The education of early Christians was influenced by the Hellenistic milieu and at the same time they sought to focus on different content of learning. Learning could take place both at home and or at an established institution. The main language of learning was Greek while the people most probably spoke in Aramaic. In this multi-lingual society, the early Christians successfully used what was available to them and spread the Story of Jesus. John's Gospel is a product of such a complex environment.

First Century Roman Empire and Her Demand on the Early Church

In general, the Roman Empire was lenient to the existence of established religious groups. Expansion of a temple or religious center for the established religion was often left to the jurisdiction of local authorities. But Christianity, which was spreading quickly in many areas, did not fit the Roman concept of a legitimate religion. Their existence relied much on their "acquiesce in the existence of Jewish religious communities which were established in numerous cities, . . . the Jews had ancient privileges in most areas, even if these were not always uncontested, and they were a nation which could claim possession of a long tradition."[59] However, the Jewish religion could only be exercised in the absence of disturbance and interference, and "only so long as the responsible authorities were willing to grant certain privileges."[60]

Under the banner of Jewish religion, "Christian itinerant missionaries were free to preach anywhere, just like other wandering preachers and philosophers of the streets and marketplace, and their followers would

---

57. Ibid., 112.
58. Ibid., 111–12.
59. Koester, *History*, 365.
60. Ibid., 226.

normally be left unmolested."⁶¹ However, problems arose if local authorities thought that the Christians had caused unrest, or if competitors or ill-meaning outsiders petitioned them to the local authorities. Such was the situation numerously reported in the Book of Acts, making the ministry of the early Christians perilous. Probably on a greater scale, the members of the Jewish diaspora communities experienced insecurity of living as few had the rights of full citizenship. Furthermore, Koester points out that anti-Judaism had its origin in the Diaspora and was closely connected to the contrast of different cultural and religious traditions existing side by side.

The Jewish Diaspora was repeatedly subjected to "anti-Jewish" actions and persecutions that found their literary expression as early as the Hellenistic period.⁶² The weight of living under the imperialistic Roman Empire increased in the later development of the early church. Together with the disapproval of the Roman's way of life, the anti-Roman Empire rhetoric became the root of an antisocietal structure in John's Gospel. Malina and Rohrbaugh identified the antilanguage in John's Gospel and stressed that the Johannine community was not a liminal group, but clearly they were against the way of life in the world. They were antisociety.⁶³

While the elements of contesting the imperial Roman Empire are identified in the writings of Paul and the Gospel of Mark, John's Gospel was less often seen in a similar context.⁶⁴ Warren Carter proposes that the Johannine text speaks to the real-life daily presence of the imperialistic Roman Empire.⁶⁵ Carter argues that the presence of the Roman Empire has been neglected in Johannine studies.⁶⁶ He proves his point by examining the "rhetoric of distance" in John's Gospel. His argument is built on a few observations on the Johannine audience. Firstly, he placed the audience at the end of the first century, and its "possible interaction between John's text

---

61. Ibid., 365.

62. Ibid., 226–27.

63. They also give a comparison table for the differences between liminality, society, and antisociety. Cf. Malina and Rohrbaugh, *John*, 59–61.

64. Horsley particularly argues for the Gospel of Mark to be read as a struggle against the repressive Roman rule. Cf. Hosley, *Hearing the Whole Story*, 121–48.

65. Cf. Carter, *John: Storyteller*, 170–72.

66. He argues that the presence of the Roman Empire should receive similar attention as in the studies of other NT documents such as in the Pauline Epistles. He also argues that the individualistic and sectarian-synagogue approaches are insufficient to understand the issues that challenge the way of living in the Johannine community. Cf. Carter, *John and Empire*, 3–11.

and Jesus-believers in the last decade or so of the first century."[67] Secondly, he accepts the earliest view of John's Gospel as having been written at the Roman Asian capital of Ephesus, a city where the people are accommodating to, and comfortable with, the Roman imperial ideals. In this context, John's Gospel

> addresses Jesus-believers whose lives are, . . . too accommodating, too comfortable, too 'at home' with the Roman world. With its rhetoric of distance and differentiation, the Gospel seeks to disturb cozy interactions and ready participation in Roman's world by emphasizing Jesus' challenge to and conflict with the Roman world, by delineating an either/or dualistic worldview, and by emphasizing the alternative world created by God's life-giving purposes manifested in Jesus.[68]

Carter concludes that the Johannine text "participates in the complex, diverse, and societal political management of reality," the Gospel "work[s] hard" to non-violently contest a Roman vision of way of life and a challenge against this order.[69]

A violent contest of the Roman Empire would endanger both the Jewish communities at large and the Johannine community in particular. The community had seen the Christian evangelistic efforts among the Jews grew so much so that they were threatening the stability of the synagogue.[70] With the expansion of the Christian community and the Jewish effort to reposition themselves after the destruction of the Second Temple, both communities were defending themselves. Both groups tried to find ways to survive in the empire, including efforts to maintain status and honor as well as access to power. Kysar aptly describes the position of the Johannine community, namely they "felt caught between their allegiance to their Jewish roots and their new conviction that Jesus was the long awaited Messiah . . . . John may be the record of a group of subordinates trying to live with the dominant imperial power, while claiming that their Lord was greater than the emperor."[71] This is the backdrop of John 11:48, claiming that "the Romans will come" if Jesus as they perceived was rocking the stability of their precarious existence under the Roman watchful eyes. The existential

---

67. Ibid., ix.
68. Ibid., 14.
69. Cf. Carter, *John: Storyteller*, 171. Also, cf. Carter, *John and Empire*, 14, 15, 335.
70. Cf. Kysar, *John the Maverick Gospel*, 28.
71. Ibid., 27, 29.

reality was a crucial factor when the members of the Johannine community considered their choices in life.

The contest among the various people groups extended beyond the material goods to include the social convention on honor. The honor-shame and patron-client social relationship in the Second Temple Palestine is one of the social conventions that may hold the key to reading the relationships and conflicts in the early church. Both Greeks and Jews shared the honor-shame and patron-client relationship. The social relationship of patron-client and friendship within the honor-shame culture is a strong convention of public opinion, a social force that has its hold on the people, one possibly even stronger than the religious moral regulatory power.[72]

Moxnes points out that a break to take place in the patron-client relationship was rare. The only way to break from the system was by rebellion against the system in the first century.[73] The existing Pharisees might be led by the social convention to expect the new sect of Christianity to maintain a proper relationship (in the sense that they were patrons, the Christians as client). Any other form of relationship might have led the Christians to be viewed as a rebel group broken away from the established religious system. Furthermore, honor is pertinent in reading the Scripture for the important reason that having honor determined who talked and who listened. If the members of the Johannine community wished to retain the benefit of being considered part of the larger Jewish community, then they would be responsible to share the carrying of the duty of upholding the honor of the group, since then "kin members are embedded in each other and shared a common honor status."[74]

The break away for the Christian group would necessitate someone who was acknowledged as honorable and commands the obedience of the people. In John's Gospel: the honorable Jesus.[75] Neyrey points out that John's Gospel contains elements of an encomium to defend the honor of Jesus. Neyrey especially cites John 7 where "the conflict was all about, namely the worth, reputation, and status of Jesus—his honor rating."[76]

---

72. Ferguson, *Backgrounds of Early Christianity*, 66–71.

73. Moxnes, *Economy of the Kingdom*, 45–6.

74. Malina and Rohrbaugh, *John*, 116.

75. This defense is seen in the Johannine description of Jesus, who is promoted as one that is from God (John 1:1–18), more than the vision of their ancestor Jacob who saw the ladder (John 1:51), more honorable than even Moses (John 3:14; 5:46).

76. Neyrey, *John in Cultural and Rhetorical Perspective*, 226.

As an honorable man, Jesus' claim about his status as Christ, Son of God, should lead us to have faith in him, to listen and obey him. Malina and Rohrbaugh also emphasize the importance of maintaining the honor of the household name. The believers are brothers and sisters of Jesus, the eldest Son of God. It is every Christian's calling to do what is necessary to keeping up the honor of the Family.[77]

The notion of family honor is deeply rooted in our moral code. We make decisions in consideration of the honor of the group we identify with. At exceptional times, the privilege of honor overrides theological considerations. We expect a way of living that honors God when this honor is challenged by other contesting religions surrounding them. Some of the obvious challenges are how Christians handle wealth (acts of grace to the needy), eradicate sins (teaching people to live as holy people), and address social justice (corrective actions or contributions toward building a fair, prosperous, and peaceful society). The believers' way of life could negatively or positively contribute to the integrity of a Christian namesake.

Summary

Looking at the social setting of the Johannine community through their education experiences indicates a community accessible to at least basic learning. Where economic conditions disallowed this luxury of higher education, there were other means of learning such as the theater and, for the Jews, their home and synagogues were available. These basic needs of their lives would be threatened if the Johannine community would no longer be considered part of the larger Jewish community. Furthermore, the political situation also pressured them to stay under the umbrella of Judaism in order to avoid unwanted persecution from the local authority. The contest of maintaining the group's honor added the necessity for the members of the Johannine community to defend their beliefs and a relevant way of life. They were also challenged to choose whom they would give honor to and submit to. These were the common issues surrounding their livelihood. What John sought to address would be relevant to the church. It was the aggregation of meager things in daily life experiences into life-sized challenges that John tried to address.

Often, the congregational are not dealing with the tsunami, but the little waves that beat up the shore and unnoticeably erode the shoreline,

77. Cf. Malina and Rohrbaugh, *John*, 116.

THE NARRATIVE WORLD THAT SHAPED JOHN'S GOSPEL

leaving the people weaker and weaker in their defense against the greater threat when it appears. In the late first century, there wasn't any immediate sudden increase in persecution in Ephesus. John's Gospel was really preparing the believers to delve deeper in their faith.

PURPOSE OF WRITING JOHN'S GOSPEL

The strategies available to read a text help to argue for multiple reasons in the purpose of John's Gospel. However, with its well-constructed content, John points to some specific aim in its writing. There are three main teaching purposes in John's Gospel. First and foremost, it is written to foster the faith of the believers in a shifting life setting where the believers were undergoing challenges to their way of living. To achieve this aim, the writer sought to foster remembrance of Jesus in them. Finally, he crafted his writing to re-present Jesus, the Son and revealer of God, in a refreshing text that enhances and prolongs the audience's perception.[78] While three key purposes are identified, they support one another to visualize adequate faith, leading to wisdom, and enable sound judgment for a way of living that glorifies the honorable Family name of God's household. This household includes a small group in a village or city, a sectarian, or the universal church.

Writing Purpose as per John 20:30–31

The teaching purpose of John has centered on whether it is to bring nonbelievers to faith or to deepen the faith of existing believers. D. A. Carson revisited the debate on the purpose of John based on the tense of the word *pisteusēte* used in 20:31. Carson agrees with Fee's argument that the tense there is present subjunctive. He also shares Fee's caution on placing too much weight on the tense alone. Fee argues that the present tense in this verse presupposes a document intended for those who are already members

---

78. It is possible that the author of John deliberately wrote in a manner that created an entirely different hearing or reading experience, namely to create understanding and remembrance. The composition of John's Gospel may not have been in direct reference to the Synoptic but certainly he has knowledge of them. For a good assessment of the relationship of the Synoptic and John's Gospel, cf. Schnackenburg, *John*, 26–43. Also cf. Brown, *Introduction to the Gospel of John*, 90–104.

of the believing community.[79] Fee also sees the confirmation in the fact that "those who 'confess' Jesus in this Gospel in the language of this sentence (that Jesus is the Christ, the Son of God) are not coming to faith, but represent those from within a context of faith, who must be encouraged to a deeper measure of that faith, in the sense of deepened understanding (e.g., Nathanael, Peter, Martha, Thomas)."[80] Although Carson disagrees with Fee on the implication of the present tense, he acknowledges the majority of scholars lean on the argument put forward by Fee.[81] Charles H. Talbert is among those who see the Fourth Gospel as confirming Christians in their faith.[82] Raymond E. Brown in his late work reiterated his stand on the purpose of the Fourth Gospel as stated in John 20:31, "These things have been recorded so that you may have faith that Jesus is the Messiah, the Son of God, and that through this faith you may have life in His name." He emphasized the Gospel was written more to "intensify people's faith and make it more profound" instead of to evangelize.[83] Moloney sees the Johannine community inclusive of both Jews who did not believe in Jesus and Jews who did believe but deficiently.[84] With this view, Moloney avers that the writer of the Gospel is not addressing either "the Jews" or Christians of inadequate faith, but rather writing "to encourage the faith of his community and like-minded Christians."[85] In its finished form, John's Gospel is teaching the community of faith how to continue living as the Family of God.

Argument for social memory in the Gospel tradition further reinforces the view that the Fourth Gospel was written as a document to build and sustain the faith of the believers, though seen more as selective in memory and purpose. Tom Thatcher also works on the memory aspect and asks: Why did John—living as he did in a culture where most people couldn't read, fewer could write, and no one regretted that fact at all—*write down* his

---

79. Cf. Carson, "Syntactical and Text-Critical Observations," 701.

80. Fee quoted in ibid.

81. Though Carson was reluctant to make a conclusion here but pointed to more studies. Ibid., 714. Elsewhere Carson has indicated his stance, "I confess, I remain part of the small but unrepentant bands of those who think that the primary purpose of the Fourth Gospel was the evangelization of Jews, proselytes, and God-fearers in the Diaspora." Carson, "Challenge of the Balkanization of Johannine Studies," 145.

82. Talbert, *Reading John*, 64.

83. Brown, *Introduction to the Gospel of John*, 152. Also see, Brown, *John*, 1:lxxvii–lxxviii.

84. Brown, *Introduction to the Gospel of John*, 76.

85. Ibid., 79.

ideas about Jesus?[86] Thatcher proposes the work of John was both an archive and rhetoric to preserve the memory of the Jesus tradition and to address both the external social and the internal conflict with the Antichrists.[87]

The primary purpose of John was not evangelical or missionary. It was addressed to the Christian community by one of their esteemed leaders and was designed to educate them in their struggle in that local situation. "It was an intrachurch document, a Gospel intended for the family."[88] It teaches the audience how to remain in God. As this work will present, John the learner turned teacher utilizes his own learning experiences through the years he learned from Jesus, added his own lived faith experiences, and bears witness to Jesus that draws others to imitate this faithful living.

Composition of John's Gospel

Recently, more scholars have favorable opinions on the composition of John's Gospel in stages over a period of time, caused by a series of events within its specific audience group. Mark Alan Powell suggests that what we have is possibly even a fourth or fifth edition.[89] Urban C. von Wahlde gives the most comprehensive argument that the Gospel is a composite of three editions.[90] Von Wahlde has forcefully demonstrated through his textual studies on John's Gospel, that the changes of social setting in John's Gospel led to the three editing process. He employs seven criteria to identify the editions: the *aporias* (gap in the text) as markers of editing, changes in terminology, doublets, *wiederaufnahme* (repetitive resumptive), style, Synoptic comparison, and differences in theological.[91] His proposal of the three editions began as early as AD 55 and stretched till the end of the century.

Von Wahlde identifies the first edition (AD 55–65?) that includes a complete narrative of Jesus ministry (including his Passion, Death, and

---

86. Thatcher's focus is on the evangelist's act of writing of the Fourth Gospel. Thatcher, *Why John Wrote a Gospel*, xv.

87. Ibid., 23–49. Thatcher also mentioned other reason for John's writing, such as having a written text elevated the status of the Jesus tradition in the Graeco-Roman context (37–8).

88. Kysar, *Maverick*, 29.

89. Cf. Powell, *Introducing the New Testament*, 173.

90. Cf. von Wahlde, *Gospel and Letters of John*, 6, 10–12.

91. Ibid., 12–16.

Resurrection) and including all the miracles of the present Gospel.[92] The second edition (AD 60–65?) sees the development of Johannine theology out of their conflict with the synagogue that become critical.[93] The third edition (AD 90–95?) is written soon after the death of John the Elder. In between the second and third edition are the Johannine Letters (65–70?) that addressed an internal crisis. The final and third edition was written to solidify previous teaching and "addresses new issues and makes explicit other beliefs of the community."[94] The issues identified as pertinent to the third edition include belief in bodily resurrection of the dead; the importance of rituals such as baptism, the Eucharist, and forgiveness of sins; clarification on the relationship with the Synoptic tradition, and "the authority and insight of the Johannine community enshrined in the witness of the BD and the leadership of the Great Church symbolized by the person of Peter."[95] Von Wahlde recognizes that with three editions in John's Gospel, the makeup of the community is not so clear, but is confident that the evidence still points to a community located in Ephesus.[96] While von Wahlde's three-edition argument proposes that each edition attended to a specific issue in its time, he does not elaborate on these specific issues that led to editing or addition.

Olsson offers an explanation for the change in the Johannine community living among the Diaspora Jewish community.[97] He points out that in the post-Second Temple Jewish community, "the Pharisees/rabbis began to urge greater unity among the Jews. At the same time, Jewish Christians became more conscious of their faith in Jesus as the Messiah and also more open to Gentiles."[98] Olsson further poses that due to different forms of

---

92. Ibid., 50.

93. Ibid., 51–52.

94. Ibid., 52–54.

95. Ibid., 54. On the addition of John 21, especially the narrative of Peter and BD, the pericope is most probably a late addition to address the leadership issue. The passage is seen as reconciling, even subsuming the Johannine community to the Great Church. If there were indeed a competition of authority (both in terms of text and leadership), Johannine authority would actually have seemed more authoritative before his death and his community could have felt higher in the organization for almost thirty years from the time of Peter's death till BD's death.

96. Ibid., 54.

97. For a history of the development in the research of the relationship between the Johannine community and the Synagogues, cf. Olsson, "All My Teaching," 209–10.

98. Ibid., 217.

The Narrative World That Shaped John's Gospel

Birkat ha-minim toward the end of the first century there were some Jesus believing Jews who "drew back to traditional Judaism by not confessing Jesus as Messiah, others confessed him and had to leave the synagogues."[99] This separate group was isolated from other Jews. "They were Greek-speaking . . . and influenced by Hellenistic thought and language."[100] The situation of the Johannine community contributed to a final edition of John's Gospel which includes an accumulation of the challenges and the community leader's concern.[101]

Summary

John is clear and specific in his teaching purpose. He began with a well-crafted prologue (John 1:1–18) that highlights the direction of the message and again explicitly told his audience that he writes to teach (John 20:30–31.) The audience was the immediate community within his reach and the writing intended to address the various issues that accumulated within the community. With the passing of the first generation apostolic authority, living in the midst of different interpretations of religious living, a new interpretation of Jesus' story is needed. Within the presence of the Synoptic, the writer decided to present Jesus within his community's understanding of who Jesus is and how they should remember Jesus. Furthermore, this memory should guide the community in their way of life amidst the conflicting voices. John wrote the story of Jesus and his disciples in a manner that seeks to maximize the effect of learning and remembrance.[102] To achieve this, he presented his interpretation of Jesus story in the form of *bios* and employed various life experiences of the characters through extensive use of literary devices.

---

99. Ibid., 219.

100. Ibid., 223.

101. Reading the Gospel of John in its final form, as a finished product, is more appropriate from a literary approach. Cf. Lincoln, "Lazarus Story," 211.

102. John wrote with intention to distribute his writing to the wider community. Olsson also poses that from the study of Johannine literature, including the 1, 2, 3 *John*, the Johannine audience apparently included some who were located at a distance, thus necessitating the writing of letters. By implication, the Gospel of John was also distributed for wider circulation. Cf. Olsson, "All My Teaching," 205.

THE GOSPEL OF JOHN: A TESTIMONY OF JESUS

John lived with, learned from, and remembered Jesus the Teacher. From his own lived faith experiences, he added his learned knowledge of the Scripture, and wrote a *bios* of Jesus.[103] In this process, he has taken stock from his years of accumulated information and turned it into a narrative learning process, thereby presenting a narrative text to his contemporary.

The recognition of John's Gospel as biographical is important as Gamble points out:

> Genre is presupposed in the act of writing and in the act of reading ... though they may not correspond absolutely, the aims of writing and reading can meet only if recognizable generic signs are provided either in the text or in the situation where the text is received and read, or both.... A sense of the genre of any particular text is essential to its comprehension: the reader must be able to judge what sort of writing is being read.[104]

In this *bios*, John uses a host of literary devices to help the audience, either as a reader or a hearer of the words, re-experience the Word revealed. John has chosen to present the works and person of Jesus memorably in an amalgamated form of Greco-Roman biography.

John's Gospel as Bios in Defense of Jesus

David Aune points out that biography with its varied form is hard to define in antiquity. Greek biographical tradition is as old as fifth century BCE; however, the actual term "biography" (Greek *biographia*) first appears a thousand years later. Before that, biography has been referred to as "lives" (Greek *bioi*; Latin *vitae*).[105] As a narrowly defined literary genre, the Greco-Roman biography is "an independent literary composition, usually focused on the character, achievements, and lasting significance of a memorable and exemplary individual from birth to death, with the emphasis on his

---

103. There is recognition of Jesus as a teacher in the Johannine writing. Pryor points out the role of Jesus as teacher to his disciples and the elect covenant community that was "taken after the custom of pupil-teacher relations both in Hellenism and Judaism, a pattern of living and dying which serves as a model for the disciples." Pryor, *John*, 146.

104. Gamble, *Books and Readers*, 38.

105. Aune, *Westminster Dictionary*, 78.

public career."[106] From this perspective, biography is a latecomer in Jewish literature formed under Hellenistic influence during the first century CE.

However, on a broad perspective, a "biographical" interest in the lives of individuals can be seen in various guises throughout the OT and early Jewish literature. The story of people is a common tool in the Bible to bring forth a lesson for the audience. Koester noted that numerous biographical sections are found in the Old Testament: the story of Abraham, Moses, Joshua, David, Solomon and the prophets are but some of the major life stories.[107] There are also other minor episodes of minor characters interjected in these stories and connected to the major figures.

By the time of the New Testament, the literary genre of the biography had entered Greek literature. "The beginnings of Greek biography grew out of an increasing interest in the lives of famous poets and philosophers. Greek biography was born when one began to inquire into the relationship between the works and the life (*bios*) of such persons, and when one began to search for examples for the right conduct of the wise man."[108] The systematic development of these interests "into a systematic literary activity is the achievement of the students of Aristotle, especially of Aristoxenus who wrote biographies of Pythagoras, Socrates, Plato, and others, of which unfortunately nothing is preserved."[109] In the Greco-Roman world most of the biographies were written by scholars and antiquarians with a clear purpose in mind.[110]

The Greek biographies usually aim to "present the principles of philosophical doctrines, conduct of life, and formation of character in the form of a *bios*, as was customary in the school of Aristotle.[111] The Hellenistic biography became a popular expression as they embrace a new appreciation of the human as an individual.[112] With Polybius, the biography also became a standard feature in recording history. Polybius recognized that "one of the important causes for historical developments was the individual as he was shaped by the factors of his *vita*."[113]

106. Ibid., 79.
107. Koester, *History*, 132–33.
108. Ibid., 133.
109. Ibid.
110. Cf. Aune, *Westminster Dictionary*, 79.
111. Koester, *History*, 133.
112. Ibid., 134.
113. Ibid.

Talbert subsumes these classifications of Greco-Roman biography under two principles: (1) the composition of formal elements and (2) the extent to which each is historically reliable.[114] He proposes that Greco-Roman biography be categorized as either didactic or non-didactic *Lives*. Non-didactic lives are unconcerned with moral example. Didactic lives are interested in the propagandistic enterprise of compelling an audience toward or away from the emulation of a certain person (of the hero or avoidance of his example) or state.[115] He subdivides didactic biographies into five possible categories or functions.

> Type 1 biographies function as a pattern of emulation.
>
> Type 2 biographies function to replace a false image of a teacher with a true representation seen as worthy of emulation.
>
> Type 3 biographies function to discredit or expose a teacher or individual as false or flawed.
>
> Type 4 biographies function to indicate where authentic tradition is to be found; to record and establish the true delineation of a particular school or philosophy by documenting the succession of the students from the teacher and thus establishing orthodoxy via succession.
>
> Type 5 biographies function to validate or provide an interpretive key to a teacher's doctrine; to shed understanding on the behavior or teachings of a particular figure especially in stances where the behavior as peculiar, strange, or out of step with social norms.[116]

Aune rightly identifies a great deal of cross-fertilization between various types of biography. He argues that "it is methodologically incorrect to try to link the Gospels rigidly only with that specific type of ancient biography with which they appear to have the closest affinities."[117] The canonical Gospels, he asserts, constitute "a subtype of Hellenistic biography, one that exhibits the syncretistic insertion of a Judaeo-Christian message

---

114. Smith, "About Friends," 53.

115. Ibid.

116. Cf. both Aune, *Westminster Dictionary*, 80, and Smith, "About Friends," 52–53, for their summaries of Talbert's five categories of Greco-Roman biographies.

117. Aune points out that in ancient biographical tradition, there is an extreme flexible and varied literary type. Its literary presentation of the life of a public person could include an account of the person's birth, youth, death, and legacy. Cf. Aune, *Westminster Dictionary*, 81.

in a Hellenistic envelope."[118] John's Gospel is the result of John's knowledge of, interpretation, and re-presentation of the Scripture (OT) message of a right relationship with God and living in light of this renewed relationship through Jesus.

John writing the Gospel is itself an act grounded in his lived experiences and situations. Michael Fishbane reminds us that life itself is alloyed by our various sources (of knowledge, educations, media exposure and the like).[119] He asserts, "theology is a spiritual exercise . . . conditioned by time and place and tradition, and by the differential impact of these factors . . . Each generation produces the expressions appropriate to its conventions and needs."[120] In this sense, educating the people of God to live with adequate faith in God ought to create a fuller understanding of God. It also ensures a continuity of living the faith in God. Yet, within this continuity, there are changes and in some sense, a discontinuity.

Smith identifies the motive of writing a biography as "written by people who had an interest in the subject, either personally or academically."[121] There are reasons as well, for the interest such as wanting to see the subject's portrait remembered by others, to defend (unwarranted and untrue attack) the honor, or to expose the (unethical) moral character and virtue of the subject. They wanted future generations to remember and remember well their subjects, and by remembering, to honor and respect these individuals.[122] A biography is able to attain these goals as it "said more about the individual than statues or portraits. Biographies spoke to the lasting effects and characteristics of the individual honored."[123] Biography is also "transportable": in written form "they were copied, spread, read, and discussed."[124] The genre of biography is a complex category with numerous possibilities for variation.

The Gospel of John is a product of Hellenistic literature syncretism. It is a pedagogical tool that was formed from oral tradition and became a reliable written document. It meets the criteria of a biography in several ways. Ferguson asserts that "Gospels are Hellenistic biographies in form

118. Ibid.
119. Fishbane, *Sacred Attunement*, 10–11.
120. Ibid., 1.
121. Smith, "About Friends," 55.
122. Ibid., 56–58.
123. Ibid., 67.
124. Ibid., 67.

and Jewish in content. The distinctive purpose of the Gospels narrative is to deepen faith (Luke 1:1–4; John 20:30–31)."[125]

Seeing Johannine Christ through Old Testament Narratives

John's presentation of Jesus the Christ hinged on John's interpretive task of the OT. Stanley E. Porter points out the key factor in understanding the NT authors' use of the OT involves identifying the quotes, the version the NT writers used, and the interpretation of the NT writers on the OT text.[126] Steve Moyise identifies three basic types of OT appearances in NT text: quotations, allusions and echoes.[127] Moyise catalogues the NT writers' usage of OT in NT as: typology, allegory, catch-word links, quoting from variant texts, altering the quoted text, reading the text in an unorthodox manner, use of *haggada* legends, and traditional forms of homiletic argumentation.[128] Moyise further recognized three general ways the NT writers interpret the OT: interpretations that emphasize continuity, discontinuity, and both continuity and discontinuity. Interpretations that emphasize continuity focus on the eschatological fulfillment of the OT in the NT, to correct traditional Jewish interpretation, the unity of God's sovereign plan.[129] Discontinuity in interpretation occurs where NT writers manipulate or change the wordings of the text to prove what he wants to prove, or to stress the apologetic nature of the NT use of the OT.[130] Finally, there are others who consider the previous two views limiting and see either the contextual situation, dialogical, or intertextuality in play.[131]

Moyise posits that, "the use of the Old Testament in the New has many similarities with contemporary Jewish exegesis. In particular, the New Testament authors share with the Qumran writings the presupposition that they are living in the age of fulfillment. This means that Scripture can be applied directly to those involved in the final eschatological events."[132] Dennis L. Stamps warns of the need to "recognize that use of the OT in the NT

---

125. Ferguson, *Backgrounds of Early Christianity*, 122.
126. Porter, *Hearing the Old Testament*, 1.
127. Cf. Moyise, *Old Testament in the New*, 5–7.
128. Ibid., 128–31.
129. Ibid., 132–33.
130. Ibid., 133–34.
131. Ibid., 135–37.
132. Ibid., 128.

is not exclusively a study of the influence of Jewish interpretative methods on the NT writers. Rather, the use of the OT in the NT takes place within a clash of cultures, which was primarily between the emerging Christian culture and the Hellenistic world."[133] He further argues that we need to "understand how the diverse ways the NT uses the OT are persuasive in that collision of cultures."[134] He sees persuasion as a force that has "remained central to the history of rhetorical study so that modern studies echo ancient definitions."[135] He stressed that the NT writers quoted the authoritative text from the OT as a means to persuade and to educate: "The practice of collecting excerpts of important writings arranged topically in what are known as anthologies or extract collections was widespread in Greco-Roman literary practice primarily for educational or didactic purposes."[136] Furthermore, "by expanding the understanding of why and how NT writers may have referred to authoritative tradition through such use in Hellenistic culture, scholars may better understand how NT authors, who wrote in a predominately Hellenistic context, used OT references in their texts."[137]

Most NT authors, according to Köstenberger, were Christian Jews. They would more likely "have followed Jewish conventions for citation, allusion, etc., rather than Greco-Roman ones in their use of the OT . . . one may very well continue to look primarily to Jewish models."[138] Köstenberger illustrates his approach by his study on John's use of the OT. He agrees with Pryor that John writes within a scriptural, salvation-historical framework. "In his references to the OT John spans the entire range from explicit quotations to verifiable allusions and thematic connections. In keeping with John's purpose statement, Jesus is identified as the Christ and Son of God and is set in relation to the major figures in Israel's history, whether Abraham, Jacob, or Moses, as well as the Prophet, by citations of or allusions to Scripture."[139] Köstenberger is right to add that the Jewish writers would have interpreted the OT through their Jewish lens. However, would the presentation of their interpretive reading in Greek remain

---

133. Stamps, "Use of the Old Testament," 10.
134. Ibid.
135. Ibid., 26.
136. Ibid., 27.
137. Ibid., 33.
138. Köstenberger, "Hearing the Old Testament in the New," 259.
139. Köstenberger, "John," 415.

unperturbed by the use of a different medium that carries the message? It appears that John's Gospel is Greco-Roman in style and Jewish in content.

Since Jesus taught mostly in Aramaic, and the Gospels were written in Greek, Marshall points out that the Gospel materials would not be transmitted through a word-to-word dictation. Through the process of oral memory to the written composition, changes of wording are inevitable. "Story tellers would naturally vary the wording to emphasize one point or clarify another or extend an application."[140] John is familiar with Jewish exegetical practice that the early Christian exegetes inherited and adapted.[141] For the NT writers who wrote in Greek, the LXX is a handy resource to base their work on, in the case of John, "He quotes often from the Greek, but at least once from the Hebrew against the Greek (19:37), indicating his familiarity with the Hebrew text and his facility in its use."[142] The intermingling of ideas to the conveyance of an idea originated in Jewish thought, and into a common language took place as the NT writers penned their words into phrases, sentences, and books.

The NT writers, as shall be seen later in especially the writer of the Gospel of John, no doubt regarded the use of an authoritative OT text as a necessary component in making powerful persuasion in their particular religious-social setting. Yet one cannot discount the prevalent Hellenistic literary convention they lived in. The prevalence and influence of the Hellenistic influence on the writing of the NT is well documented by David Aune and George Kennedy.[143] It would be fair to say that the mainly Jewish NT writers' interpretive usage of the OT is grounded in Jewish tradition. However, the written presentation is Hellenistic.

Miller asserts that John re-interpreted the Hebrew Scriptures in light of Christ and led to deeper Christological and theological profiles of Jesus.[144] At a time when the Temple is gone, the identity of the Jews in the Greco-Roman world closely related to their religion is challenged. It was

---

140. Marshall, *Concise New Testament Theology*, 17.

141. Miller, "They Saw His Glory," 127.

142. Ibid., 127. Köstenberger also holds a similar view on John's use of the available Greek text, "It therefore appears that John was familiar with both the Hebrew text and the LXX (as well as with Jesus' own use and earlier Christian quotation practices) and thus was able to cite the Scriptures either in the exact or slightly adapted LXX version or to draw on the Hebrew where this suited his purposes or seemed necessary for some reason or another." Köstenberger, "John," 415.

143. Cf. Aune, *Westminster Dictionary*. Also cf. Kennedy, *Classical Rhetoric*.

144. Miller, "They Saw His Glory," 127.

a time the rabbis wanted to use traditions of the Torah to shape Jewish identity and practice. At the same time "Christians wanted to show that Scripture anticipated Jesus, and they used biblical interpretation in their controversy with the synagogue to demonstrate that their claims on behalf of Jesus were supported by the very Word of God."[145] John wrestled with this problem, at the end of the first century, to find the true meaning of the scriptures.

Miller noted the use of introductory formulae as a key to John's appropriation of the OT. Though the use of introductory formulae is widespread in both the OT and the NT, we find in John obvious division of the two types of introductory formulae. There are seven occurrences of "It is written . . . " in the book of signs and seven occurrences of "In order that Scripture might be fulfilled" in the remaining chapters of the book. In the time of Jesus' public ministry where his work is the emphatic message, the biblical quotations are introduced with the words "It is written." During this time, Jesus "performed signs that pointed to his true identity as the revealer of God, the light come into the darkness . . . that confronted the world with a choice whether to receive that light or to reject it. . . . his claim to be the light of the world was being advanced and tested, Scripture itself functions as a kind of sign pointing ahead to the appearance of the Word."[146] After the pivotal statement of John 12:37, "Although he had performed so many signs in their presence, they did not believe in him" the formula changes to "In order that Scripture might be fulfilled." Miller sees this change as the author's deliberate hermeneutical move, here, "Scripture does not only point to Jesus but is fulfilled in two senses: first, its meaning is fully disclosed in Christ; and secondly, it is completed, superseded, and even replaced by the living words of Jesus."[147] Miller also highlights how John uses the quotation formulae in finesse, "each of the relatively small number of explicit quotations in the Fourth Gospel is a tiny window opening onto the vast panorama of the biblical story. John is such a skilled exegete that he can use a mere fragment of biblical texts as a kind of exegetical magnet, attracting whole clusters of other texts and themes to it."[148] We shall later in this paper look at how John uses another one of the magnets, the OT characters to affirm his view of Jesus the Messiah.

145. Ibid., 129.
146. Ibid., 131.
147. Ibid.
148. Ibid., 132.

Furthermore there is enough proof of John's implicit usage of OT in the Gospel of John. Köstenberger listed sixty-five implicit OT usages in the Gospel of John.[149] Köstenberger points out the significance of these OT usages in John, "Together with the direct OT quotations and references to broader OT themes . . . the OT allusions found in John's Gospel create a web of intertextuality that grounds the theology of the Fourth Gospel profoundly in the Hebrew Scriptures, particularly with regard to the person and teaching of Jesus."[150] One obvious observation of these implicit quotations is the bulk of these implicit quotations, fifty-four out of sixty-five, appear in John's book of sign. Also, there is a concentration of both explicit and implicit quotations at the transitional chapter (John 12) between the two major sections of the Gospel. The immediate section (John 12:44–50) is highly charged with a call by Jesus to believe in his testimony. The message is also explicit on the consequence of disbelief. John's message has to be received with the key-unifying theme of the message: the love for God and how the believer responds in entering a loving relationship with God and with one another (John 13:34–35; 14:21, 23–24; 15:9–14; 16:27; 17:22–26). The emphasis of love ties to unity is especially stressed in the concluding sentences of the Farewell discourse. Those who believe will know God, live in his love, and share in his glory. This is the core teaching presented in the lengthy didactic section of the text (John 13–17).

It is apparent that John sees these OT characters as informing and helping the reader see Jesus, recognizing Jesus as the One sent from God, and ultimately seeing him as God. Moses, with all other human being, did not see God in physical form (cf. John 1:18), but he was granted privileged insight and witnessed the signs and wonders that manifested God's working. In a sense, "Moses saw the prefigurations of tabernacle, signs and wonders, manna and water, whose full meaning was made known in Jesus."[151] Moses' raising up of the serpent in the wilderness furnishes not a type of Jesus but echoes of the work of Christ when he was raised up on the cross. God fed the Israelites in the wilderness. This manna made available performed through Moses is inferior to Christ giving the people the true Bread

---

149. For a complete list of OT allusions and verbal parallel in the Gospel of John, and the sources of these implicit usages, cf. Köstenberger, "John," 419–20. Interestingly, the one figure who is conspicuously absent in the Gospel of John is King David, who is not mentioned in an exegetically significant way in at all. Cf. Miller, "They Saw His Glory," 147.

150. Köstenberger, "John," 420.

151. Miller, "They Saw His Glory," 146.

The Narrative World That Shaped John's Gospel

of Life. The act of Moses hitting the rock and bringing forth water is again compared to the greater work of Jesus giving the living water to all who come to him.[152] Those who eat and drink what Jesus provides will not go hungry or thirsty. Therefore, the signs in the Gospel of John are indicative of the glorious work of Jesus that surpassed Moses.[153] Moses is a mere type and, at the same time, one who had witnessed a much smaller portion of the glory of God.

Under the pen of John, Abraham is the source of truth and freedom (John 8:31–47). Those who are true descendants of Abraham know the truth of believing in the one who provides and belongs to the household. As a member of the household, they are no longer subjected to slavery. The theme of household is set in the prologue (John 1:12–13) and permeated throughout the Gospel. Wes Howard-Brook highlighted in the Gospel of John the key to become a family member is intimacy with God. "When the Johannine Jesus and narrator speak of knowledge of people or the things of God, it is always a matter of intimacy and personal connectedness, not of purely intellectual understanding."[154] Abraham, again, did not see Jesus. He saw by faith in the promises of God for his household to be a great nation. In a book with its well-known emphasis on believing, it appears that Abraham, "unlike the Jewish leaders in Jesus' day, showed continual faith by taking the long view of looking forward to Jesus' coming, which is adumbrated in 8:56 by the expression 'seeing Jesus' day.'"[155] The implication here is that Abraham saw Jesus' day by faith and was glad though his family was not perfect. In contrast to the subsequent event in the household of Abraham, the family in the Gospel of John is characterized by unity. John's Jesus presented a better vision of a future filled where the family members are united as one.

John presents the OT as preserving Isaiah's vision of the Logos to whom the prophet bore witness. "John's purpose in using the Abraham tradition is twofold: to prove that true descent from Abraham comes from

---

152. Ibid., 142–44.

153. Pryor also points out that in John's Gospel, Moses is contrasted against Jesus. Jesus is the one who comes and speaks in the name of God, and thus is the true Mosaic prophet. Cf. Pryor, *John*, 118, also 119–22.

154. Howard-Brook, *Becoming the Children of God*, 35.

155. Köstenberger reminds that in the entire Gospel, there are ninety-eight instances of *pisteuein*, including the Prologue (1:12), and the purpose statement (20:30–31) highlights the key theme of believe. Köstenberger, "Hearing the Old Testament in the New," 279.

faith and obedience, not birth; and to show that Abraham saw the future salvation in Christ."[156] The Gospel of John presented Isaiah as the prophet who foretold the coming of the Messiah, and a voice would prepare his coming (John 1:23). By his vision of a coming, Isaiah implied he saw a day when this Messiah would reveal himself. He is another witness in the OT, not only of the glorious work of God, but also the stubbornness of the people of God. The text in which John explicitly states Isaiah's role in seeing and testifying to the Logos is 12:36b–41. It is a passage set at a critical juncture in the Gospel, drawing chapters 2 to 12 to a close and providing a transition to chapters 13 to 20.[157]

John the Baptist comes in between the OT and the NT. He has been portrayed as the intermediate witness and a crucial one. Miller is right in pointing out "John saw Jesus in the flesh, so his testimony bears a special weight."[158] The work of John the Baptist has been variously told in relation to Jesus. John the Baptist is most poignantly described as the witness to the status of Jesus (John 1). Isaiah foretold his work of witnessing for Jesus (John 1:15, 19–23). John the Baptist pointed people to follow Jesus (1:29–37). He baptized and finally gave way to bring the work of Jesus to the forefront (3:22–30). His work is one that helps people to identify Jesus. From John the Baptist, John the author became the latest witness to this Jesus, the Christ. And the audience was further charged as the faithful followers that will continue the witnessing through their way of life.

The OT characters in John are found in the Book of Sign (John 2–12). All except Abraham have an appearance in the first part of the Gospel. They are interpreted in John as sources of comparison and explanation for Jesus' work. The comparisons highlighted the identity of Jesus whose work excels the works of others. The emphasis is especially obvious in the work of Jesus compared to the work of Moses on several instances. Jesus provides water and food that excel what Moses gave to the Israelites. Jesus also provides a family that excels the name of being in the household of Abraham. Because Jesus has seen God, his witness in both showing and telling has the forcefulness that none of these forerunners have in their testimonies of God. In turn, this is also the force of John's witness of Jesus. The witness of John in the Gospel of John is true since he is a live witness. Consequently, when John writes, he is a valid witness in the biography of Jesus that tells the new

---

156. Miller, "They Saw His Glory," 140.
157. Ibid., 138.
158. Ibid., 137.

household that they will know and remember the truth revealed by the true messenger of God.

Now that Jesus had come to reveal God's glory most fully, the OT characters are but indicators of the full revealing. All the prophets and teachers of the old were teaching God's people the way to live. The contemporary state of God's people showed that the past teaching was insufficient. The teaching from Jesus is true, it is the way that leads to a different life (John 3:16), the life in relation to God the Father who lives eternally is life eternal.

There is in John's Gospel an example of reintroducing and transforming a traditional understanding that became rigid and ossified into a fresh presentation: the Law of God that is undergirded by a law of love. John reinterpreted and re-presented to his audience the third commandment.[159] By their obedience to this commandment to love they would live out an authentic relationship not only with God, building on their faith in God, but also with one another in the faith community. In the OT, the first mention of the love of God for his chosen people is through the mouth of Abraham's servant (Gen 19:16, 19; 24:27, 49). Love is not greatly or clearly emphasized in the OT narratives, perhaps due to the cultural habit of the time that does not easily express emotional feelings. But the relational factor is always present in the OT stories (34:6–7; Num 14:18–19), and taught as a way of life (Lev 19:18, 34).

Deuteronomy's covenant of love and obedience in John's Gospel is often echoed in John 14–16. In the covenant God made with Israel's people, the ground for God to give life and all that is necessary to sustain life is to love God and a voluntary obedience to God (Deut 4:37). Where Deuteronomy's command to love was repeated also in the Hebrew Bible through the mouths of prophets (to mention a few, Jeremiah, Hosea), the call came more often as rigid command. The Johannine depiction of love is embodied in the affective story of Jesus' love for the world (3:16). John's love story is more affective than didactic. When Jesus commands the disciples to love, the setting for the command occurs in the context of one who is ready to give up his life out of love for the followers. The theme of love in John's Gospel is also prominent when compared to the legalistic binding Laws the Jewish authority imposed on the life of their adherents. The many narratives (third and fifth signs, and the dialogues in John's Gospel) contested the Jewish authority in observing the Law that has become rigid observance of law, not out of love for God. Thus, in the Farewell Discourse, Jesus

---

159. Exod 20:6; Deut 5:10; 6:5; 7:7–9; 10:12–19; 11:1.

emphatically reminded the Disciples that, to love God is to obey His Word. In this case, it is the imitable Word of God made flesh in Jesus. Jesus' teaching ran against the interpretation of the contemporary Jewish authority. This contest of interpretations continued into the end of first century and separated the Christ followers from "the Jews" in John's Gospel.

In his rendition of the gospel, John's presented a griping version God's love commandment. It is an example of continuity with an element of discontinuity that is always present as a tradition is practiced throughout the generations. His teaching of loving God and one another is faithful to the Jewish tradition. Yet it represents a departure from his contemporary's view of who the best example of this love is. The best representation of the teaching is not the Pharisees teacher or any other human teacher, he is none other than God himself who has revealed and is again revealing, this time fully through Jesus—God *enfleshed*. John tells the rebirth of an authentic life in God is made possible through loving and obeying the members of the household. John also tells of a life that is exemplary, superseding the past, the contemporary, and the future. Jesus is the revealer and embodiment of living in love and in obedience to the Father (15:9–13). John's biographical narrative also gives identity to a group of people—to be the children in a family that is close knitted in a loving relationship (14:15–21, 23–24; 17:25–26).

The Gospel beseeches the audience to listen to Jesus instead of mere tradition; Jesus is the true presentation that superseded all prophets and teachers and his message is genuine. The audience is called to embrace the way of life modeled by Jesus; he shows the way to live life with adequate faith in God that he trusts God with his death. The faith community can also share in this faith and live an authentic life that is a testimony of faith and one their children can imitate, leading others back to God, and for generations to come.

Summary

The aim of John in writing the biography of Jesus is to foster remembrance among his readers who were gradually separated by time from the life story of Jesus. In biographical form, John begins the story of Jesus with his origin—a divine and eternal origin (1:1–2)—foretold by the OT witnesses, and now by him. It teaches the true members of God's household to do the work that glorifies the head of the household. This work is the realization and recovery of the lost love among the family members retold through the life of Jesus who came to manifest this great love of God that the audience ought to imitate.

John uses his unique resources of personal witness of the life and teaching of his teacher—Jesus—as the content of his writing. John compared Jesus to the most respected figures in his community and faith tradition. The personal honor or teaching value of these OT characters are not discounted or denied. Rather, the commonly perceived leadership roles of these leaders are reinterpreted as pointer to the one teacher who brought to completion God's revealing of the appropriate way of life for all people. John used the literary convention of the Hellenistic culture to his benefit as a teacher among a Hellenized generation and wrote a life story of Jesus to show his audience an honorable way of life that would glorify the name of God and His Family. This biography is written not only to show the glory, it also teaches how one can and should respond to the loving God.

CONCLUSION AND IMPLICATION FOR TEACHING THE BIBLE

When we compare the first-century Diaspora and the global Christian community, we can identify similar challenges to their way of living life faithful to their own tradition and religion, for both the Church and the Jews living in Diaspora, they are caught within the contesting value systems, both religion and cultural values. In a similar manner the post-Temple, post-Jerusalem Johannine community in Diaspora was caught in the sphere of Jewish Judaism and the Synagogue, and their newfound faith. Secondly, the cultural influences such as Hellenization and globalization posted challenges to the unique existence of the Johannine and the global Christian community. Both communities faced the necessity to adopt new languages and the cultures that come with them. In the first century Greco-Roman world, Greek had become the dominant language-culture. The Jews were successful in the Hellenistic syncretism, while the Church often resisted the new culture surrounding them, or uncritically embraced new idea.

The religious challenges of the Church and the Johannine community is further complicated by the method of approaching the text. First of all, the Johannine community has the OT stories and a new story handed to them by their beloved Elder to guide them in negotiating these terrains.

They often read the Scripture through midrashic interpretations.[160] The Church faces a similar challenge of reading and interpreting the text in the presence of two traditions. There is the trusted Church tradition. And there is also an academia that at times seems to teach different ways of reading the Scripture. A form of biblical reading and theological reconfiguration took place in the Church that gradually broke away from the current development while it gives the Church a sense of identity and informed their way of living. How would the local church read, interpret, retell, and present the Story to enable a Christian way of living that is adequate to overcome the problems identified so far? This is where recent research in narrative learning is important, as is the task at hand of a biblical narrative learning aids in forming a network of sharing, building bridges among the global Christian community, the past and the present, and among the different churches and people groups.

The fight for survival led the Jewish community in the Diaspora and the Johannine community to gather more adherents and expand their sphere of influences in the late first century, after the destruction of the Temple in 70 CE. This resulted in an increasingly reining-in of the loosening Jewish way of life in the Jewish Christian community. These Christians were challenged in their specific issues, in their beliefs and way of life, much as the Churches are challenged. We have looked at some of the teaching purposes in John's Gospel that point to similar educational, political and social challenges troubling the Church.

Finally, John's Gospel is a narrative learning process in its final form. John had learned from his teachers and after years of showing and telling, written down his lived faith experiences and finalized his version. As a writing that is intended to both create content and preserve memory, John committed the life story of Jesus in a biographical form adapted from his contemporary literary convention. John's characterization of Jesus borrows from the familiar narratives of their great leaders such as Abraham, Moses, and Isaiah. However, John's Jesus is without equal. In John's narrative, he purposefully presented Jesus as one that is unmatched by any character, past, present, or future.

To fully reconstruct with sufficient evidences the lived faith experiences of John himself is not possible. But in the preceding pages, several factors that are involved in his learning brought into focus. What is in view is that narrative learning takes place in communities both past and present.

---

160. Neyrey, *Gospel of John*, 3.

It is available to all people at all levels of education, all places, all cultures, and in all times. The ability of narrative to transcend is the pedagogical tool the two communities shared, and in this way, Johannine pedagogy is deemed more relevant to the Church. Arguably, John's Gospel is rooted in the testimony of Jesus' lived faith experiences and it was later written down as a biographical presentation of the life of Jesus. However, there is a need to always continue this testimony in light of the present. And this is where the contemporary research in narrative learning can contribute to this writer's study on biblical narrative learning as pedagogy.

3

Teaching Faith in John's Gospel

———◆———

The Gospel of John, in the sense of a biblical narrative learning, is a "finished product" presented in a written form. There in John's Gospel is his teaching through using three basic components of narrative learning: event, plot, and character. John's unique contribution to narrative learning lies in his masterful use of literary devices that makes his showing and telling in the Gospel attractive and compelling to the audience. As seen in his presentation of Jesus in the chapter 2, he drew richly on his contemporary Jewish exegetical practices and maintained continuity of the relationship with God in his faith community, albeit a fresh perspective, as he used the love motive as indicative of faith in God through Jesus.

Before proceeding, one must acknowledge one's limitation in exploring John's Gospel as a model of biblical narrative learning. To recover a complete account of how he arrived at writing the lived faith experiences of Jesus as a life story may not be attainable. Access to what went through the author's life experiences of following Jesus and a subsequent showing and telling others how to imitate Jesus' faithfulness to God the Father is limited. However, some insight may be gleamed from his interpretive process, and uncovered through seeing his interpretive exercise of the Scripture—the Laws and the stories of the people's past teachers such as Moses and Abraham. It may be difficult to reconstruct his learning moments and the imagination-inspiration of hearing and learning that took place, and how his personal faith in God was shaped and/or transformed by the many signs he personally experienced when he witnessed Jesus' miraculous healings and deeds. Equally hard to rebuild is the actual teaching and learning moment when he and other disciples learned through the many teachings where Jesus taught them the Scripture and how the Scripture related to their life situations.[1] However, a careful reading of John's Gospel reveals many features that are worthy of our imitation.

The following pages present, first of all, an overview of the narrative content and strategy in John's Gospel. Then, they present a research in John's characterization of the people in his testimony of Jesus and how these characters work to teach adequate faith in his overall narrative strategy. Finally, John's skillful use of the linguistic features is explored. These components are key to the process of narrative learning as John's testimony is both affective and reflective learning, a persuasion for his audience to imitate Jesus, the most complete revelation of God's love for the people.

OVERVIEW OF THE NARRATIVE CONTENT AND STRATEGY IN JOHN'S GOSPEL

This section examines the narrative content and narrative strategy in John's Gospel. The narrative content of John's Gospel displays a well-structured arrangement centered on the Glory of God and how the people live in relation to this glory. The strategy of John's narration is twofold. On the one hand, it involves plot and characterization on the showing level. On the other hand, it also involves the linguistic finesse in the telling and explanation of these sign-events.

The message of John's Gospel is contained in a conspicuous narrative structure of the document. It can be divided into the prologue (1:1–18), the book of signs (1:19—12:31), the book of glory (13–20), and the epilogue (21). Within this narrative structure, the Gospel teaches by showing

1. I believe the Fourth Gospel can be considered a reflection of Jesus' theological interpretative frame. I believe for a teacher who has a vast choice of stories to choose from, she or he (John is included in this category) would have to be selective in using the one relevant to the teaching goal. Where the story's meaning has been obscure, an interpretation, and make fresh the story in the narrative learning. We may assume that John, as a student of Jesus, has in some degree imitated not only the faith of Jesus, but also the teaching skill of Jesus (especially the many parable-stories Jesus used). And John has taken the teaching skill to another level with years of experiences in showing and telling others the Story of God in the life of Jesus. Furthermore, he has the years and the context to formulate and refine his theological stance.

and telling the audience to make choices between life and death, light and darkness, love and hatred, truth and falsehood, believe and un-believe, goodness and evil. The basis on which the Christ following believer could make the right choice between the two ways of living is what the writer poignantly shows and tells through this well-crafted life story. This section shall explore the narrative content and strategy in relationship to the six sign-events in John 2–12.

John has chosen to show the way of living in relationship with Christ Jesus through a series of signs. In John 2–12, he presented six signs to demonstrate how people who encountered and experienced the work of Jesus made a decision or no decision to believe in Jesus.[2] The signs in John's Gospel are revelatory of the glory of God to the Johannine insiders and the community.[3] As a literary tool, these signs function as the analogous showing of faithful responses to Jesus through the characters that had encountered Jesus and witnessed his miraculous work. The audience was invited to respond as they see the responses of the characters that had witnessed these signs. The six signs are constructed in a chiastic structure that places emphasis on the purpose of the showing.[4]

After each sign, the author often presented a didactic section as extensive teaching on it. The didactic sections are the *telling* in John's teaching. In these didactic sections, John used various strategies such as asides to add information for explanation or clarification. They take the form of dialogues between Jesus and his disciples, Jesus and the opponents, or Jesus' monologue. The dialogues can also be a combination of any of the three

---

2. I have identified six signs in John 2–12, contrary to the more popular view that there are seven signs in these chapters. Jesus' supernatural walk on the water is not considered in my analysis for the following reason. First of all, it is not designated as showing and telling. Second and most important, this fifth display of supernatural feat in John's Gospel is not followed by any teaching moment that is present in the other six sign-events. The immediate context after the narration of the walking on the water correlates to the fourth sign events of Jesus feeding the five thousand. Though unattested, I'm not the only one who wrestled with identifying the seventh sign in John 2–12. Köstenberger sees Jesus cleansing the Temple as the seventh sign. For his argument cf. Köstenberger, *Theology of John's Gospel and Letters*, 324–35. I see this six versus the general expectation of seven signs in John 2–12 as another deliberate strange-familiar effect in the emplotment of a well-designed writing. The seventh sign in John's Gospel is Jesus himself—his life and work, culminating in his resurrection from the death.

3. Cf. Smith, *Theology of John*, 135–39.

4. I will later explain the chiasmus structure in John's six signs. For one of the most extensive analysis of the presence of many chiasmi in John's Gospel, cf. Mlakuzhil, *Christocentric Literary*, 125–241.

forms. The major didactic-telling sections are John 3:1—4:42; 5:19-47; 6:22—7:52; 8:12-59; 10:1-42, 12:23-50.[5] In some occasions, there are extended explanations by calling in extra characters such as Nicodemus (3:1-10) and the Samaritan Woman at the well (4:1-42) to illustrate the response and practice of faith and its way of living. These formed the major telling sections that complement the showing through the signs as John teaches faith which is better caught than taught. The telling is necessary so that by hearing the testimony of faith they might grasp the possibility of an adequate faith in Christ Jesus, and in God.

The lengthy speech in John 13–17 is crucial and necessary to complete John's telling of the Logos revealed. It is the telling that precedes the grand sign—Jesus' death and resurrection. Marshall observes that John gives his readers a different set of events and teachings of Jesus. Despite some similarities, John's narration and theological argumentation are distinctive.[6] John introduces Jesus as the Word, but after the prologue, the Word no longer surfaces, instead, the speeches of Jesus, which Bennema describes as the telling portion of Jesus, continues to fulfill the role of the Word. Jesus reveals and communicates life, light, and glory and makes the Father known.[7] More specifically, Jesus reveals not only the person of the Father, but also how a relationship with the Father is lived out, and gives a showing of living life in a highly dualistic world of his audience. In this final lengthy discourse, Jesus talks about his relationship with the Father and how the disciples should relate to this Father through this eldest Son.

The showing and telling in John's Gospel focuses on how the audiences, both the private audience (insiders) and public audience (outsiders), would learn from the narration and make a decision to live Jesus' way of living in the Light, motivated, united as one, and empowered by love of the Father, to the glory of God.

---

5. In some occasions there are some reports of reaction from the audience or narrative to explain the events between the sign event and the didactic telling. Though at times it may be hard to differentiate which event gave rise to the didactic telling, such as in the narrative right after resurrection of Lazarus, there are a few events reported (John 11:45—12:22), which can lead to questioning of which event leads to the didactic telling from 12:23 onward. However, the theme of death (John 12:24-25, 33) does link the didactic telling to the Lazarus event and also leads into the passion of Jesus (13:1).

6. Marshall, *Concise New Testament Theology*, 186.

7. Ibid., 187.

Chart 1. The Structure of John's Gospel

Overarching glory of the Family					
Overarching sign—Life story of Jesus					
	6 lived faith experiences in 6 signs		glory		
insiders	public/outsiders	insider	public	insiders
John 1: To those who know (have adequate faith)[A]	John 2–12: 6 signs (showing) and 6 teachings (telling) presented in chiasmus construction	John 13–17: Teaching the disciple—insiders	John 18–19: The grand sign	John 20–21: To those who know

A. The Johannine's life story of Jesus can also be viewed as having a beginning (John 1), middle (John 2–17), and an end (John 18–21). Paul A. Du Rand offers a similar three-part division of John's Gospel with 1:1–51 as setting (beginning?), 2:1—17:26 as development (middle?), and 18:1—21:25 as conclusion (ending?). Cf. Du Rand, "Creation Motif in the Fourth Gospel," 24. On the chiastic parallel between the prologue and epilogue, Mlakuzhil provides an interesting analysis that shows clearly a historical sign-introduction and sign-conclusion in this pair of parallels. Cf. Mlakuzhil, *Christocentric Literary*, 147.

Showing Biblical Faith through John's Characters

The showing of adequate faith in John's Gospel through the six sign-events is in John 2–12, in addition to the one overarching Jesus event. These sign-events reveal a narrative strategy that builds on characterization of the people involved. These characters are seen in relation to, and support the main character Jesus, that John wrote in the genre of Greco-Roman biography.

The Gospel of John is best analyzed through narrative reading that focuses more on the life story of Jesus in Johannine composition. This reading also benefited from the invaluable contribution of the historical-critical readings. Without the help of the historical-critical approach, some of the linguistic finesse would be lost in translation.[8] Moloney acknowledges that the narrative approach is the most important addition (not a replacement)

8. For example, Jerome T. Walsh points out that the English translation has deserted the term "Behold!" The term is widely used in the Old Testament. In the New Testament and also in the Gospel of John, more recent version of translation have left out this emphasis on the intense sense of a *live* present action the character in the narration perceives, "as though the narrate or reader were perceiving the object through the character's eyes in the same moment that the character does." Walsh, *Old Testament Narrative*, 49.

Teaching Faith in John's Gospel

to the historical-critical approach. He reminds us that the achievements of historical-critical scholarship over the last two hundred years contributed to the rediscovery of the world behind the text so that there will be no abuse of the world in the text. It is an essential part of a sound narrative critical approach to the Fourth Gospel. "Contemporary narrative criticism, starting from the stance that the text is as it came down to us ... claims that it is possible to identify a strong narrative unity across the Fourth Gospel."[9] He further points out, behind each "story" exists a real author who has a definite audience to whom he or she tells the story.[10] The author constructs a narrative as a means to communicate a message to an audience.

The Gospel narrations in each document consist of two basic components: plots and characters. Culpepper notes the relationship of plot and character in a narration: "The interdependence of plot and characterization ... The affective power of the plot pushes the reader toward a response to Jesus. The characters, who illustrate a variety of responses, allow the reader to examine the alternatives. The shape of the narrative and the voice of the narrator lead the reader to identify or interact variously with each character."[11] The plot and characters in a story interact, along a certain time line, through a sequence of events or episodes. In the narration an author devises certain rhetorical features to hold the plot and character together so that the reader will not miss the author's point of view.[12]

The narration is held up by a series of narrative strategies.[13] These narrative strategies include: "the way characters are presented through the position of the narrator or the point of view, the use of space and time in correspondence to the events, and the many linguistic features an author

---

9. Brown, *Introduction to the Gospel of John*, 31.

10. Moloney in Brown, Ibid., 31–32.

11. Culpepper, *Anatomy*, 148. At this juncture, the relationship of plot and character is again set aside. But it is recognized that the plot of the Fourth Gospel is well formed within the context of its implied audience. "The plot of the Gospel of John ... revolves around Jesus' fulfillment of his mission to reveal the Father and authorize the children of God. ... The plot is a plot of action in the sense that Jesus achieves his goals ..." Culpepper, *Anatomy*, 88. Also, "The plot of the gospel is propelled by conflict between belief and unbelief as responses to Jesus. The centrality of this conflict is confirmed by the fact that almost half of the occurrences of the verb "believe" in the New Testament are found in John (98 out of 239). Ibid., 97.

12. Cf. Moloney, *John*, 14.

13. Walsh identifies the narratives strategies as characterization, point of view, manipulation of time, gaps and ambiguities, repetition and variation, and voices of the narrator. Walsh, *Old Testament Narrative*, 10.

would employ to augment the key theme in the narration. These rhetorical features are *in* the narrative."[14] Reading the text as narrative helps us appreciate the linguistic attention the author puts into story telling.

The narrative, as Walsh points out, works to evoke responses from readers, and moves beyond transmission of information, beyond the intellect to the emotions of the readers. We listen or read a story, we grew to like or dislike the character(s) and the story.[15] Karl Allen Kuhn also stresses the importance of recognizing the emotion in the biblical narrative and reader's emotional engagement in the reading process.[16] Stephen Voorwinde also reminds readers that Jesus is full of emotion in John's presentation. Johannine Jesus displayed his emotion evenly throughout John's Gospel.[17] Recognizing the narrative strategy of John's Gospel as presenting to persuade, the author's use of emotion calls for an appropriate affective response in the reading process.

Characterization in John's Gospel

Various biblical scholars had recognized the presence and the role of the various characters in the Gospel of John in the last two decades, albeit with a different level of attention given to them.[18] These scholars include Alan Culpepper, Collen M. Conway, Susan E. Hylen, Sam Tsang, and Cornelius Bennema. The study will also investigate the Gospel writer's intention as he unfolds these characters before his audience or reader and how this study is useful to the contemporary reading and teaching of the Bible.

Alan Culpepper's *Anatomy of the Fourth Gospel* is probably the cornerstone to the study of the characters in the Gospel of John. Culpepper analyzed the Gospel of John as a literary work and presented a chapter on

---

14. Brown, *Introduction to the Gospel of John*, 32. Author's italics.

15. Walsh, *Old Testament Narrative*, xii.

16. Cf. Kuhn, *Heart of Biblical Narrative*, 29–59. In comparison, Stibble probably restricted by his stance as pure literary and narrative approach to the text has chosen to refrain the flow of emotion in storytelling. Cf. Stibble, *John as Storyteller*, 198.

17. There are at least fifteen displays of Jesus' emotions within John's Gospel. The pervasive display of Jesus' human emotion is well documented, for a brief listing cf. Voorwinde, *Jesus' Emotions in the Fourth Gospel*, 81. For comprehensive listings of emotion in John's Gospel see the appendixes, 299–303.

18. Bennema gives a brief account of seventeen previous studies on the characters in the Gospel of John. cf. Bennema, *Encountering Jesus*, 2–10.

the characters in John's Gospel.[19] Culpepper is more interested in the overall literary structure of John's narrative and his analysis of the characters is selective and brief. His work focused on the character of Jesus and the Father, the Disciples, the Jews and the people representing opposition to the Johannine community, and the rest whom he classified as minor characters.[20] Culpepper sees the inclusion of these characters as against conventional presentation of characters in a narrative. However, these characters work under the pen of the author to firstly "draw out various aspects of Jesus' character successively by providing a series of diverse individuals with whom Jesus can interact," and secondly "to represent alternative responses to Jesus so that the reader can see their attendant misunderstandings and consequences."[21] It is key to read these characters in relationship to the central protagonist, Jesus, within the plot of the Gospel of John.

Collen M. Conway undertakes a study of the characters in John's Gospel with her eyes on the presentation of different genders in the Gospel. She analyzed five female and five male characters in the Gospel: the mother of Jesus, the Samaritan woman, Martha and Mary, and Mary Magdalene, Nicodemus, Pilate, Simon Peter and the Beloved Disciple.[22] She came to conclude that the Gospel presented all five female characters in a positive tone while only two of the five male characters in a positive tone. She also noted that the two who are portrayed in a positive characterization remained unnamed as the man born blind and the Beloved Disciple. While she cautions against an anti-male attitude or a gender dualism, she insists the Gospel as "a polemic against the 'world,' not only in the sense of those who reject Jesus, but also of precisely those recognized structures."[23]

Sam Tsang's work on the characters begins with a lengthy coverage of the main character: Jesus. In his studies on Jesus, several characters are mentioned in relation to the characterization of Jesus as light. These include: Nicodemus, the Samaritan woman, and the two men healed by Jesus (John 5, 9).[24] The two characters healed by Jesus are not given further

---

19. Culpepper also presented a study on the role of the narrator, who can also be considered as a character in the Fourth Gospel. However, It is not the intention of this paper to delve into the subject. For more discussion on the role of narrator and the point of view of the narrator or author, cf. Culpepper, *Anatomy*, 15–34.

20. Ibid., 106–44.

21. Ibid., 145.

22. Cf. Conway, *Men and Women*, 69–199.

23. Ibid., 205.

24. Cf. Tsang and Ou, *Eternal Word Spoken*, 25–94.

space in the book. Tsang devotes the next chapter on five disciples that followed Jesus. He gives attention to Simon Peter, the Beloved Disciple, Lazarus, a "certain disciple,"[25] and Judas. In Tsang's book, Nancy Ou writes the chapter on the women in the Gospel of John. She looks at five women in the Gospel: Mary the mother of Jesus, the Samaritan woman, Martha, Mary of Bethany, and Mary Magdalene. Finally, Tsang looks at the characters that represented the old religion. He places Nicodemus in this category with the Jews.[26] Tsang's work highlights the functions of the characters in the Gospel of John. John the writer, Tsang argues, uses these characters to bring out the communication purposes of portraying faith in Jesus: these life stories function as witnesses of faith in Jesus that enable living lives to the fullest.[27]

Susan E Hylen categorizes seven key characters in John's Gospel into two groups. The first group of five includes: Nicodemus, the Samaritan woman, the disciples, Martha and Mary, the Beloved Disciple. The second group has the Jews and Jesus. Her choice and subdivision reflect her conviction that contemporary readers had often misread the characters in the first group as flat. She believes these characters represented some degree of ambiguity and thus they are more round than many interpreters previously perceived.[28] She explores these characters mainly from their reaction to Jesus: whether they believe or disbelieve in him. She suggests that their responses to Jesus are less clear-cut; there remains a certain degree of ambiguity. Her second group is chosen as they both "encompassed virtually the entire Gospel."[29] She asserts that through the many metaphors John uses to present Jesus, even the character Jesus is made ambiguous in the Gospel. She argues that it is this ambiguity that leads the reader into a deeper understanding of Jesus. She concludes, "Ambiguity in the character of Jesus involves the reader in a theological task that does not end when the Gospel closes, but deepens as the reader returns again and again to understand different aspects of his character."[30]

---

25 Tsang cites John 18:15–16; 19:26–27; 20:3, 8 as references. Tsang's identification of that certain disciple is unique and his argument for that nameless disciple is questionable. It seems that he does not delineate the occasion when that disciple was clearly connected to the Beloved Disciple, especially his treatment of John 19:26–27. Ibid., 147–57.

26. Ibid., 101–299.

27. Ibid., 304.

28. Cf. Hylen, *Imperfect Believers*, 1:15–16.

29. Ibid., 16.

30. Ibid., 154.

Teaching Faith in John's Gospel

Cornelius Bennema has the most comprehensive coverage of the characters in the Gospel of John. He lists twenty-three characters in the Gospel of John but leaves out the agents such as the servants of the royal official in 4:51–52, "since they simply fulfill a function in the plot and do not make any response to Jesus."[31] The characters or character groups in his work are:

1. John
2. The World
3. "The Jews"
4. Andrew and Philip
5. Simon Peter
6. Nathanael
7. The mother of Jesus
8. Nicodemus
9. The Samaritan woman
10. The royal official
11. The invalid at the pool
12. The crowd
13. The Twelve
14. Judas Iscariot
15. The man born blind
16. Martha
17. Mary of Bethany
18. Lazarus
19. Thomas
20. The Beloved Disciple
21. Pilate
22. Joseph of Arimathea
23. Mary Magdalene

Bennema studies these characters in the sequence as they appear in the Gospel. He has left out Jesus, the Father, and the Holy Spirit. This choice is

31. Bennema, *Encountering Jesus*, 14.

apparently due to Bennema's choice of characters and his analysis centers on their response or lack of response to Jesus and how all the responses fit into John's dualistic worldview. His analysis also takes into consideration John's literary techniques such as irony, misunderstanding, metaphor, symbolism and double entendre in order to fortify his point of which he addressed in another paper.[32]

At the end of his study Bennema found the characters in various degrees of flatness or roundness.[33] Secondly, he categorized the characters in their responses to Jesus as either adequate or inadequate.[34] The type of adequate responses include acceptance of Jesus and his revelation, bearing fruit as causing others to come to Jesus, belief based on Jesus' word, cooperation, devotion, following Jesus, hearing Jesus' voice, intimate with Jesus, introducing or directing people to Jesus, loyalty or commitment, obedience, open or public confession, persistence, remaining with Jesus, seeking Jesus, servanthood, signs-faith, submitting to Jesus' authority, sympathy, testifying about Jesus, and understanding with or without struggle.[35] The inadequate responses include: alignment with the devil, ambiguity, apostasy, betrayal, compromise, defection or disloyalty, dishonesty, division, fear, hostility, misunderstanding, murder, no open commitment, no response or apathy, opposition, pseudo-belief, pseudo-devotion, rejection, secrecy, signs-faith, thinking "from below," and unbelief.[36] Bennema sees these various responses as representative values of the contemporary readers.[37] He relates the responses of these characters to the possible responses from contemporary readers of the Gospel, thus bridging the Johannine characters to the present.

Johannine characterization is a key component that is crafted to lead the readers into making a decision to believe and follow Jesus, the Son of God who came to reveal God. These characters show their responses so

---

32. Ibid., 12–15, 18–21. Also cf. Bennema, "Theory of Character," 375–421.

33. Bennema uses "type," "personality," and "individual" to distinguish the flatness and roundness of these characters; where "type" represents "flat," "individual" represents "round," and "personality" as in-between. Ibid., 203–4.

34. Cf. Bennema's chart summarizes these responses. Bennema, *Encountering Jesus*, 204–5.

35. Ibid., 205–6.

36. Ibid., 206.

37. Cf. Bennema's detailed chart on the representative value of various characters in the Gospel of John. The chart is an interpretation of an array of human responses to a relationship, positive or negative, to Jesus. Ibid., 209–10.

that the readers can consider their mimesis and respond appropriately as these stories are told. Among the many characters portrayed in the Gospel of John, Culpepper highlights seven types of responses exhibited by them:

1. The first response is rejection, the rejection of the world hostile to Jesus.
2. The second response is acceptance without open commitment. The characters who illustrate this response are the secret disciples
3. The third response is acceptance of Jesus as a worker of signs and wonders.
4. The fourth response is belief in Jesus' words. The Samaritan woman (without a sign) and the royal official and the blind man (for whom a sign is worked by their obedience to Jesus) each eventually find faith because they are ready to trust the words of Jesus.
5. The fifth response is commitment in spite of misunderstandings. The disciples believe, they see Jesus' glory, yet most of them misunderstand in one way or another.
6. The sixth response is paradigmatic discipleship. It blends with the top end of the previous response in that there is no further criticism of those who surmount misunderstandings. Peter will receive a pastoral role and martyrdom. Thomas and Martha offer climactic confessions. Mary Magdalene is allowed to report the resurrection she has misunderstood.
7. The seventh response is defection, and Judas is its infamous paradigm.[38]

In recent studies each of these scholars has presented the characterization in the Gospel of John from his or her perspective and interest. However, there hasn't been a study of the characters with respect to the sign-narrative structure of the Gospel of John. The characters as learner-audience is also lacking. The next chapter focuses on the signs of the Gospel (in John 1–12, part one of the Gospel) and how these characters serve as the key in these sign events as they play the crucial role of portraying their responses in relationship to the main character, Jesus. Their responses act as the agent to challenge the reader to make a decision to believe and follow Jesus. To this purpose, John uses many linguistic devices writing his telling.

---

38. Cf. Culpepper, *Anatomy* 146–48.

TELLING BIBLICAL FAITH THROUGH JOHN'S LINGUISTIC SKILLS

The history of human beings is expressed through words. The basic function of the word is to create understanding and meaning. The Word is to be interpreted in relation to human history, which entails continuity or discontinuity of explaining our existence, often through stories. By contrast, Anderson points out, the animal does not have a history precisely because it does not have a voice. The Word that creates and sustains is the condition of the possibility of a new creation of humans.[39] Human ability to be aware of, to appropriate, and to respond to the Word of God is unique to humanity.[40] Humans possess an inherent capacity of knowing and learning the Word that informed being and doing. However, Christians living in the postmodern period are challenged in their viability of holding to the Truth of the Scripture as the source of meaning and truth. This section will focus mainly on John's highly organized arrangement of the material that is effective in teaching and contributing to remembrance on the part of the hearers or learners.

Harry Y. Gamble reminds us that early Christian literature is steeply grounded in the techniques, forms, and modes of Greek rhetoric. "The Gospels, too, are indebted to rhetorical strategies in their elaboration and use of traditions about Jesus."[41] In the Greco-Roman world "education in rhetoric had become the accepted form of higher education in Roman society; the language of instruction was Greek."[42] This highest form of education at that time "might last as long as five years.... Consist of rhetorical theory, study of the famous classical orators, and practical exercises in public speaking."[43]

The author of John's Gospel obviously employed his rhetorical skill in his writing. Gamble rightly points out: "If in language, style, and genre the earliest Christian writings did not belong to the higher reaches of the literary culture of Greco-Roman society, their authors could not for that reason be said to have lacked all awareness of or approximation toward literary standards."[44] He also sees the potential of the Gospel writers: "These

---

39. Cf. Anderson, *On Being Human*, 34–35.
40. Ibid., 35–43.
41. Gamble, *Books and Readers*, 35.
42. Koester, *History*, 94.
43. Ibid.
44. Gamble, *Books and Readers*, 39.

authors had the benefit of education, for otherwise they could not have written at all. They were not only literate but also literary to a degree . . . that intends to teach and persuade . . . skill that must have been available to Christianity virtually from its birth."[45]

The skillful usage of literary devices in the Gospel of John has been explored and new insights continue to appear. As early as in 1837, Karl August Credner isolated seventy-eight Johannine style characteristics.[46] Julius Wellhausen (1908) noted in the Gospel frequent occurrences of simple sentences, the penchant for parataxis and asyndeton, frequent use of historic presents, and other markers of Johannine idiolect.[47] W. F. Howard observed unique Johannine expressions *pas* ("all" or "every") and *hina* ("so that" or "in order that"); his extensive use of demonstrative pronouns to recall the subject; and his employment of synonyms (ask, say, or speak). Rudolf Schnackenburg noted several indicators of stylistic unity, such as the phrases "prince of this world" and "Spirit of truth," and the use of an initial *pas* followed by a personal pronoun.[48] Marie-Emile Boismard and Arnaud Lamouille (1977) compiled a more extensive list of Johannine style traits. They listed as many as 416 items.[49]

Eugen Ruckstuhl, aided by Peter Dschulnigg, identified 153 style characteristics. They based the identification on four criteria:

(1) A given feature must occur in John at least three times;

(2) It must appear at least twice as often as in Matthew, Mark, or Luke;

---

45. Ibid.

46. "Credner's list included such items as (1) *amen, amen* at the beginning of an utterance; (2) expression of a thought positively and then negatively; (3) frequent parentheses or asides; (4) the extensive use of the word *kosmos* ('world'); (5) the designation 'prince of this world' for Satan; (6) the phrase 'eternal life'; (7) vocabulary associated with judgment (*krisis, krinein*; 'judgment,' 'to judge') and witness (*martyrein, martyria*; 'testify,' 'testimony'); and others." Cf. Köstenberger, *Theology of John's Gospel and Letters*, 130.

47. Ibid., 130–31. Also, "Another remarkable Johannine trait is John's simplicity of style. Nigel Turner observed that John's 'idiom is the very simplest and the vocabulary the poorest in the NT, relatively to the size of the book.' John also reflects Semitic modes of expression. Thus many scholars, including C. H. Dodd, Rudolf Bultmann, and C. K. Barrett, have concluded that John thought in Aramaic but wrote in Greek." Ibid., 132.

48. Ibid., 131.

49. "Among other features, they include (1) *ho pempsas me* ("the one who sent me"); (2) *martyreo peri* ("testify concerning"); (3) *meno en* ("remain in"); (4) *ego eimi* ("I am"); (5) *didomi* ("to give"); (6) *kathos. . .kai* ("just as. . .so") + pronoun; and (7) "Son of Man" plus *hypsoo* ("lift up"), *doxazo* ("glorify"), and *anabaino* ("ascend")." Ibid., 131.

(3) In relative numbers, it must not be found in the rest of the NT as often as in John; and

(4) In relative numbers, it must appear in John at least as often as in a select corpus of extrabiblical Greek writings.[50]

Vern Poythress, Stephen Levinsohn, and Randall Buth, all contributed to better understanding of the sentence structure in John's gospel.[51] In view of the diverse studies conducted over the years, the present studies are more interested in the key literary features of John instead of looking at all the literary objects in the Gospel of John.

Raymond Brown recognized the stylistic features of John primarily as poetic or semi poetic. He regarded that John more solemn than the Synoptic. This solemn portrayal is seen as representing the Jesus in John as a representative from God and "therefore it is appropriate that his words be more solemn and sacral."[52] In addition, over the years, Brown recognized misunderstanding, ambivalence, and or riddles, twofold or double meanings, irony, inclusions and transitions, chiasm or inverted parallelism, parentheses or footnotes or explanatory notes, *relecture* and *réécriture* as literary devices in John.[53] John used these devices to reflect his theology and at the same time evoked responses from his wide-ranging audience situations.

James L. Resseguie gives an in depth study of the various literary features in John. He combines various researches and categorizes these narrative designs in terms of how John uses them to present a different point of view. He argues that the ideology of the Gospel of John is expressed through phraseological, spatial, temporal, and psychological point of view. Resseguie also highlights the use of literary devices such as irony, misunderstandings, and double entendres to achieve his rhetoric purposes. John

---

50. Ibid., 131.

51. Ibid.

52. Brown, *Introduction to the New Testament*, 333. Brown retained his stand on his observation on the quasi-poetic and solemn nature of John. "I do not believe that one can consistently find rhyme, strict parallelism, or exact stress patterns. If the prose is solemn, it is far from lyrical. The language of the discourses achieves a monotonous grandeur by repetition of simple words and not by the use of highly literary vocabulary." Cf. Brown, *Introduction to John*, 286–87.

53. Cf. Brown, *Introduction to the New Testament*, 333–37. Also cf. Brown, *Introduction to John*, 287–92.

added the sense of space within his writing; descriptions of inside and outside, near and far is given for various locations.[54]

Resseguie's starting point is that "the *mode* or *angle of vision* from which characters, dialogue, actions, setting, and events are considered or observed" represents "the narrator's *attitude towards* or *evaluation of* characters, dialogue, actions, setting and events."[55] The narrator "expressed in words and phrases that deliberately modify or even undermine common, everyday perceptions ('born again or anew'; 'living water')."[56] In his thesis, Resseguie provides an insightful argument on how John forcefully tells the Gospel to his audience. In the following paragraphs, the attention is given to linguistic frame that provides the most comprehensive view of John; the three spatial, temporal, and psychological frames subsumed under the phraseological frame, as each is part of, and only possible within, the linguistic endeavor of the narrator.

Köstenberger identifies almost an exhaustive list of linguistic features to date in Johannine writing. First of all, we see that in the Gospel of John there is coherence in themes. The following list gives an overall view of the distinctiveness themes and features in John's writing.

(1) Overall simplicity of expression and use of basic terminology, including verbs of knowing and seeing, basic necessities or realities of life such as water, bread, life and death, light and darkness, etc.

(2) Overall simplicity of sentence structure and frequent juxtaposition of sentences without use of conjunctions (asyndeton)

(3) Double *amen* introducing Jesus' pronouncements

(4) Characteristic address "children" for Jesus' followers

(5) Distinctive phrase "after these things" or "after this" to indicate general time references

(6) Frequent use of preposition *peri*

(7) Frequent use of the conjunction "so, therefore" to continue the narrative

(8) Frequent use of conjunction *hina*

(9) Positive statement followed by converse statement

---

54. Cf. Resseguie, *Strange Gospel*, 27–59, 61–107.
55. Ibid., 1, Author's italics.
56. Ibid.

(10) Back references to characters, sayings, or events previously mentioned in the narrative

(11) Parenthetical statements or asides by the author

(12) Frequent use of historical presents

(13) Frequent use of distinctive terms such as *kosmos, sarx*

(14) Frequent use of double entendre in conjunction with irony and or misunderstanding

(15) Characteristic use of "just as . . . so"

(16) Use of "he, that one" to refer to previous subject

(17) "The word that he had spoken"; "of whom you say that"

(18) "On the last day"

(19) Frequent use of "we know that"; or "know" plus indirect question

(20) Frequent use of "believe that"; and "believe in"

(21) "The one who sent me"

(22) Use of other memorable expressions, such as "the prince of this world," or "the disciple whom Jesus loved."[57]

This list highlights the range of themes that John utilizes in the entire Gospel to convey the Gospel message. The various themes found throughout the Gospel also show the unity of content. The following section shall look at the literary devices that convey these themes and give life to John's storytelling, and how storytelling is animated through recognizing the physiognomic expressions in storytelling. At the same time, these literary devices are active agents that create the familiar-strange effect on the audience and cause them to reflect as the message creates momentary dis-equilibrium.[58]

Spatial

Spatial movements to and from a fixed location underscore a narrative's ideology. The movements are possible from the perspective of inside and outside. From this perspective, Resseguie identifies the setting of sheepfold,

---

57. Cf. Köstenberger, *Theology of John's Gospel and Letters*, 131.

58. I consider the dis-equilibrium "momentary" as the learner will "stabilize" as a new meaning scheme is formed in the process.

garden, courtyard, and praetorium. Within the Gospel of John the narrator is "an invisible, roving narrator"[59] who moves freely from the inside to the outside and back inside.[60] The spatial movement also includes the difference in center and perimeter, where well, temple, and tomb are some of the events took place.[61] Finally, Resseguie named the near and far perception in the narration of spatial movement where the use of sea and mountain communicates estrangement.[62]

Using the spatial setting, "the narrator is able to shape familiar settings to express an unfamiliar, new, or otherwise strange point of view. Inside space is secure space."[63] The narrator uses space to communicate decision-making. The temple as architectural structure is reshaped into a person; in the resurrection narration, the tomb, inside space for dead persons, is depersonalized, ordinary space is transformed into extraordinary space. These temporal moves give the narrator a tool to present a new perspective and to make an offer to his audience as to where they want to stand. "Spatial

---

59. Resseguie points out, "A narrator within a scene may adopt basically two types of narration: 1) A narrator may be a silent, invisible presence who observes characters from a particular spatial stance.... 2) A second type of narrator is not only invisible but is a roving presence within the scene—similar to a moving camera and montage. An invisible, roving narrator has the advantage of moving freely from character to character, glancing at one and then the next, stopping long enough to focus on certain details, ... This technique allows the narrator to present differing and often conflicting points of view with remarkable ease." Resseguie, *Strange Gospel*, 6.

60. Resseguie gives some samples of these movements: "in Jesus' trial before Pilate, for example, the narrator roves freely between what takes place inside the praetorium and the deliberations outside (18:28—19:16). Further, the invisible, roving narrator may easily take note of the spatial stance of characters within a narrative, which in turn provides clues to the ideological perspective of a narrative." Ibid., 6, also see 63–71 for his fuller explanation and examples.

61. In John 4, "the narrator has Jesus remain stationary at the well of Jacob while others—the Samaritan woman and townspeople—travel to and from this fixed location. The spatial arrangement reinforces the narrative's ideology: Jesus is like a well to which the characters come to draw 'living water.'" Ibid., 7 also see 71–95 for his fuller explanation and examples.

62. Resseguie summarizes: "Distance communicates estrangement. And so the disciples' separation from Jesus is a struggle for survival.... survival and struggle are simply human efforts—and somewhat unsuccessful efforts at that—until Jesus enters the scene." Ibid., 107.

63. This idea is "hammered home with unmistakable regularity in the images of the sheepfold and garden." Ibid., 106.

stance defines one's allegiance, or resolve, or even willingness to listen to the voice of truth."[64]

Temporal

The temporal point of view "encompasses two aspects of the narrator's relation to the narrative world: the pace of the narration, and the temporal distance between the moment of telling and when the narrated events take place."[65] Lanser identifies four possible relationships between the moment of telling and when the narrated events take place:

1) *anterior* narration takes place before the events it purports to recount; it therefore most frequently takes the form of plan or prophecy;

2) *simultaneous* narration takes place as the story is itself unfolding in time; this mode uses present-tense narration;

3) *interspersed* narration is the mode of the journal or the epistolary narrative; here actions happen between (and during) the moments of narration;

4) *posterior* narration, the most common form, in which the events recounted have been wholly completed.[66]

The narrator of John frequently uses posterior narration to recount events that are viewed from a post-resurrection perspective.[67] John also varies the pace of the narrative as an important indicator of what is ideologically significant. A slow-down in narrative pace draws attention to what is taking place.[68] By contrast, the narrative of the empty tomb in John 20 accelerates the movements with the disciples and other characters in "a racy, hot-off-the-press account with one event after another recorded in rapid-fire succession. Characters come and go to the tomb, run to others and report each new discovery. The superfluity of parataxis augments the frantic pace, isolating and magnifying each discovery at the tomb."[69]

64. Ibid., 106.
65. Lanser, quoted in ibid., 8.
66. Ibid., 8.
67. Resseguie gives these illustrations of posterior narration: John 2:22; 7:39; 12:16; 20:9. Ibid., 8 also see 71–95 for his fuller explanation and examples.
68. For example, the narrative pace slows down after chapter 13 "until it virtually grinds to a halt at the climactic day." Ibid., 8–9.
69. Resseguie further explains, "Thus, the ponderous narration allows the drama

Psychological

Psychological point of view elaborates and develops the point of view that is expressed through behaviors of the characters. There are two ways in which the narrator may observe human behavior. "A narrator may take the point of view of an outside observer; he or she is restricted to what can be materially or objectively observed... Or the narrator may look inside the consciousness of a character and describes the feelings, motivations, and thoughts of a character; or the point of view may be described from the point of view of the person himself or herself."[70] In telling the life story of Jesus, the narrator of the Fourth Gospel "adopts an internal stance,[71] providing insight that is unavailable to a narrator who adopts solely an external stance."[72]

Resseguie again describes the narrator of the Fourth Gospel as "an invisible, roving narrator who has privileged access to the inner consciousness of characters. He knows their beliefs, emotions, and motivations... making his point of view congruent with the point of view of the main character, Jesus."[73] The narrator "makes no pretense at producing an impartial report. He states his ideological perspective outright: to persuade the reader to believe in his testimony and proclaims his purpose of writing the Gospel (20:31)."[74]

The Gospel writer presented four categories of character to "elaborate, reinforce, or in some way highlight ideological perspectives of the gospel."[75] The first is Jesus the main character. The presentation of Jesus, Resseguie argues, is four-fold: through the mouth of the narrator, what others characters

---

to build slowly to a dramatic climax. The four-day delay, the separate interviews with the sisters, the cumbersome narration, and the intensification of emotions all heighten death's impact in the narrative." Ibid., 9.

70. Ibid., 16.

71. If Ehrman is right, John is a radical departure from Greco-Roman's understanding of human development which saw personhood as static and, "Greco-Roman biography does not generally deal with the inner life, and especially does not do so in the sense of what we would call character formation.... A person's experiences were opportunities to demonstrate what those traits were, rather than occasions for those traits to develop." Ehrman, *New Testament*, 57.

72. Resseguie, *Strange Gospel*, 16.

73. Ibid., 21–22.

74. Ibid., 22.

75. Ibid., 109.

say about Jesus, Jesus' own speech, and Jesus' actions.[76] The second group consists of some dominant characters that include Nicodemus, the Jews, the world, and the royal officials.[77] The third group are the marginalized characters such as the people Jesus healed.[78] Resseguie names the disciples as the fourth groups of character in John. In the characters that failed to see Jesus, Resseguie finds their perspective often tainted by the materialistic world. He contrasts the perspectives of these characters,

> The lame man and the blind man represent the marginalized that are victimized by material point of view. . . . Nicodemus and the royal official are denizens of the dominant culture that abandon their material perspective for a nonliteral, spiritual way of thinking. . . . The world and Jewish authorities represent that segment of the dominant culture that remains unconverted, ensconced in a "below" point of view.[79]

Resseguie further points out:

> The disciples may also represent material perspectives, but they are awakened . . . Mary Magdalene adopts a material point of view until she is awakened to a new point of view. Peter represents the disciple who exegetes at a superficial level, interpreting extravagance as discipleship. . . . Thomas exegetes at a literal, concrete level, insisting on material evidence of the resurrection. Judas represents a material point of view that resists grace, and is not persuaded by an above point of view. The beloved disciple represents a correct, nonmaterial point of view that is able to see beyond the literal to a spiritual interpretation. His point of view stands apart from others even in the way that he is introduced in the gospel. He enjoys an intimacy with Jesus that no other disciple has, and therefore can interpret an above point of view to others. He is the reliable witness in the gospel narrative.[80]

Byrne posits out that the later believers cannot share the experiences of Jesus as Mary, Thomas and the disciples had. But they believe in him through the records in the Fourth Gospel, just as the Beloved Disciple

---

76. Ibid., 110–20.

77. Ibid., 120–34.

78. The two men Jesus healed (John 5:1–18; 9:1–41), and Mary Magdalene. Ibid., 134–49.

79. Ibid., 167.

80. Ibid., 168.

came to believe through the experience of seeing the empty tomb. They can also be included in the community of faith because "a deeper, more creative faith is going to be drawn from their hearts ... the historical Jesus of Nazareth remains for all generations of mankind the abiding and saving revelation of God."[81]

Phraseological

The phraseological point of view in the Gospel of John is probably the most studied Johannine literary devices. This section will see more of the work of other researchers adding onto the work of Resseguie. Resseguie talks of the phraseological point of view in terms of the linguistic devices within the language of estrangement: irony, ambiguities or misunderstanding, and double entendres. He emphasizes the narrator's usage of these three literary devices "to make familiar points of view seem strange."[82] Köstenberger's survey highlights the use of asides and symbolism in the Gospel of John.

Irony

Köstenberger defines irony as "the comic effect created by a character's lack of awareness of a disparity between appearance and reality."[83] He adds, "in many instances, irony takes the form of a declaration as a question."[84] Resseguie points out that as a making-strange device, "Irony plays upon an incongruity, contradiction, or incompatibility between the literal and the intended meaning; between appearance and reality; between vehicle and tenor; or between two points of view—an upper, superior level and a lower, victimized level.... irony opens a window to view the unfamiliar with a sensation of freshness."[85] It "brings out the superficial, exposes the material, highlights appearances."[86] Paul D. Duke studies the irony in the

---

81. Byrne, "Faith of the Beloved Disciple," 94.

82. Resseguie, *Strange Gospel*, 10.

83. He also lists the passages in John's gospel in narrative sequence that may be classified under the rubric of irony. For a complete list Cf. Köstenberger, *Theology of John's Gospel and Letters*, 153–55.

84. Ibid., 153.

85. Resseguie, *Strange Gospel*, 30, 28.

86. Ibid., 198. Also see Duke, *Irony*, 95–100, where Duke highlighted how some characters, especially Peter and Judas Iscariot, in the Gospel of John are characterized in

Johannine context and argues that irony in the Gospel is deeply related to the techniques of Greek drama.[87] He places irony as a pointer to something beyond the surface reading of the text, "It is mystery, height, depth-hidden significance in need of crucial illumination ... an invitation to abide 'above,' in the presence of him who is the revealing and penetrating light of the world."[88] He also claims that while "irony does exist in oral settings, it is only in milieu conditioned by the controlled distance of writing that irony can take on the kind of sustained subtlety that it does in the Fourth Gospel."[89] With its multiple effects, irony "so forcefully engages us in what we read. Instead of setting out propositional arguments, it jolts us with incongruity or nudges us with possibilities—then grew suddenly silent, leaving us to choose a meaning or a value or a commitment."[90] It is among the most powerful literary devices.

Misunderstanding or Ambiguity

Resseguie asserts, "Ambiguity is a portal to see through the blur of the everyday so that the reader never settles 'for less than reality.'"[91] It is a "common estranging device is to use ambiguous words, phrases, and concepts to retard the hearer or reader's facile assimilation of new concepts and ideas. Ambiguity forces the hearer or reader to slow down and puzzle over what is being said, thereby stumbling over the new and *really seeing* the unfamiliar."[92] R. Alan Culpepper identifies three elements that characterize misunderstandings in John:

---

an ironic manner.

87 Ibid., 140.

88. Ibid., 146–47.

89. Ibid., 148.

90. Ibid., 155.

91. Resseguie, *Strange Gospel*, 43, 143 Köstenberger adds: "Misunderstandings include a certain amount of hyperbole, exaggerating the degree of misunderstanding and thus accentuating it even more keenly, as well as a dimension of irony, highlighting the at times almost comical nature of a given person's incomprehension. The misunderstandings also help the reader appreciate the spiritual nature of Jesus' words and his mission, ... they are suitable for sharpening readers' perception of spiritual truth, helping them to identify the significance of Jesus' words and serving as a fitting vehicle for conveying the Johannine worldview." Köstenberger, *Theology of John's Gospel and Letters*, 143.

92. Resseguie, *Strange Gospel*, 41. In terms of their effect on the reader, Köstenberger points out, "the misunderstandings keep readers' interest by presenting them with riddles they must solve in order to progress to a fuller spiritual understanding of various aspects

(1) Jesus makes a statement which is ambiguous, metaphorical, or contains a double-entendre;

(2) his dialogue partner responds either in terms of the literal meaning of Jesus' statement or by a question or protest which shows that he or she has missed the higher meaning of Jesus' words;

(3) in most instances an explanation is then offered by Jesus or (less frequently) the narrator.[93]

Culpepper concludes that the function of misunderstandings is "to enforce a marked distinction between 'insiders' and 'outsiders,' between those who understand Jesus and those who do not." Resseguie adds, "the most important function of misunderstandings is to teach the reader how to read the gospel."[94]

Köstenberger defines Johannine misunderstandings as "a statement, normally involving ambiguity, metaphor, or double entendre, whose intended meaning is not properly identified by the original audience of the statement, which typically leads to a subsequent explication of its proper meaning by the person making the statement (most frequently Jesus) or the narrator."[95] On the phraseological level "Johannine misunderstandings develop, elaborate, or reinforce new ideological points of view."[96]

---

of Jesus' mission. . . . Similar in effect to parables, as mentioned, misunderstandings draw a line between 'insiders,' who understand a given spiritual truth, once explicated, and 'outsiders,' who do not." Ibid., 143.

93. Culpepper, *Anatomy*, 164–65.

94. Furthermore, the reader "learns to rule out 'literal, material, worldly, or general meanings' and to avoid the trap of John's befuddled characters. . . . misunderstandings make strange the reader's stale perception of reality and open up a fresh perspective on the world." Resseguie, *Strange Gospel*, 43.

95. For the list of twenty-five Johannine misunderstandings, cf. Köstenberger, *Theology of John's Gospel and Letters*, 143–44. "The most common type of misunderstanding pertains to Jesus' death and resurrection (his 'glorification')." Ibid., 144–45.

96. Resseguie, *Strange Gospel*, 11. Also for further insight on the dynamic of misunderstanding, cf. Köstenberger, *Theology of John's Gospel and Letters*, 141. Duke adds on the relationship between misunderstanding and irony: "while some misunderstandings are presented ironically, many function without irony yet with an effect similar to irony." Cf. Duke, *Irony*, 146.

Double Entendres

Double entendres are words that have twofold meanings and both meanings are intended. The reader selects one meaning, which he or she believes exhausts the meaning of the vehicle, while on further reflection, a second meaning surfaces. The two meanings mutually illuminate each other making strange common, everyday assumptions, or the one adds an additional dimension to the other that is not immediately apparent.[97] The use of double entendre often involves misunderstanding and taking a word's figurative meaning literally. Johannine "double meaning" encompasses the notions of misunderstanding, irony, and symbolic or allusive ambiguity.[98]

Narrative "Asides"

Köstenberger rightly included John's usage of literary device, "asides" or parenthetical remarks for the purpose of orienting his readers and misunderstandings that normally occur in conjunction with double entendre. To him, the narrative "asides" are used more frequently in John than in the other gospels. One of the major functions of these "asides" is that "they enable the narrator to steer his readers to his desired conclusion. . . . The narrative 'asides' thus bear witness to the way in which the fourth evangelist carefully crafted his narrative with a view toward communicating his message to his first readers."[99] The Johannine parentheses aid the audience in following the Gospel narrative through these bits and pieces of relevant information. They fulfill an important narratological function in "facilitating an informed reading of the Gospel and preventing the reader from being sidelined because of missing data required for a successful decoding of the narrative."[100] Köstenberger offers a rather comprehensive list of these asides that help to clarify issues such as translations of Aramaic or Hebrew terms, explanations of Palestinian topography and Jewish customs, references to issues his audience may be unfamiliar with, and clarifications of sayings.[101]

---

97. Cf. Resseguie, *Strange Gospel*, 51.

98. Köstenberger points out that ambiguities leading to misunderstanding are found in pericopae such as John 2:19-22 and 14:4-10. Symbolic expressions in John include "night," "light," "darkness," and "water." Paradox attaches to the Johannine treatment of "seeing and not seeing." Cf. Köstenberger, *Theology of John's Gospel and Letters*, 132.

99. Ibid., 135-36.

100. Ibid., 140.

101. For the complete list of these asides and functions, see ibid., 136-40.

Symbolism

Because of his particular cosmology and worldview, John necessitates the usage of rich symbolism to communicate spiritual realities. Köstenberger differentiates the general and specific symbolism. In the most general sense, a symbol is something that stands for something else.[102] When it is more specific, "a symbol is an image, an action, or a person that is understood to have transcendent significance."[103] As Culpepper notes,

> the meaning of a given symbol, cannot be reduced to a one-to-one correspondence and usually yields a "surplus of meaning" or "semantic energy" that derives from past associations of a given word or concept, which may evoke different nuances of meaning in various contexts.... symbols provide a suitable vehicle for conveying spiritual truth, opening a window, as it were, to a world of mystery and transcendent reality and providing a place where the finite and the infinite can meet.[104]

Köstenberger asserts, "It is virtually impossible to understand John's gospel without appreciating the meaning of the symbols it contains, and the gospel's 'symbolic universe' renders it virtually impenetrable to outsiders who fail to grasp it."[105] The water, bread, and light symbolisms in John "illustrate the foundational nature played by symbolism in conveying John's theology, especially with regard to Jesus' messianic mission and the benefits it bestows on those who believe in him."[106]

Resseguie adequately observed that the linguistic tools that John richly employs to "invert the human propensity to view the world as a patina of the ordinary and thereby to miss the spiritual side of life. The reader who thinks in terms of the quotidian, the ordinary, the material, the earthly is confronted with a new way of thinking that sees the spiritual, the new, the

---

102. Symbolism thus typically involves the use of metaphor, a procedure that may be defined as "a device which speaks of one thing (tenor) in terms which are appropriate to another (vehicle), with the vehicle serving as the source of traits to be transferred to the tenor. While a metaphor thus expresses the tenor by means of a given vehicle, the symbol conveys information regarding the nature of the vehicle." Ibid., 157.

103. Koester quoted in Köstenberger, ibid., 157.

104. Ibid., 157–58.

105. Ibid., 167.

106. Ibid. He discusses three key symbolisms in John: water, bread, and light symbolism, 162–67.

unfamiliar, the defamiliarized."[107] These devices are helpful in communicating the teaching of John and at the same time devices that foster memory of the audience. However, there is another aspect of John's presentation that Resseguie misses.

In the performance of the Gospel, the literary devices functions together to teach, to delight, and to move the audience.[108] In Resseguie's words:

> The narrator of the gospel uses every aspect of point of view to make strange common, everyday perspectives. He slows the narrative pace down to force the reader to ponder new, strange ways of thinking or uncomfortable views. He throws double entendres to cause the reader to stumble over habitualized perspectives. He creates misunderstandings to bring to the surface routinized perceptions. He rearranges furniture—settings—to catch the reader's attention and to reinforce ideological patterns. Characters voice material perspectives to underscore the strangeness of common norms and practices, and the marginalized dismantle the thinking of the dominant culture. He creates positive primacy effects to overturn accepted, natural points of view, and he makes a below point of view seem strange while an above point of view is made to seem natural. The shape of the plot creates a positive primacy effect that overcomes and defeats the recency effect of opposing points of view.[109]

The writing of John is both didactic in content and mnemonic in presentation, which helps the audience to learn. Bauckham affirms the relationship between remembering and transmission of the gospels. He writes: "Memorization was universal in education in the ancient world."[110] These devices are helpful in communicating the teaching of John and at the same time act as devices that foster the memory of the audience.

Summary

The literary devices are tools that John placed strategically in John's Gospel for their various functions. Putting these devices together, John sought to

---

107. Resseguie, *Strange Gospel*, 58–59.

108. I am remotely linking here to the Aristotle's classical tradition of teaching. Cf. Cunningham, *To Teach, to Delight, and to Move*, 16–34.

109. Resseguie, *Strange Gospel*, 197.

110. Bauckham, *Jesus and the Eyewitnesses*, 280.

maximize the showing and telling effect that clarifies a way of authentic living for Jesus' followers. He also sought to use these mnemonic devices to foster memory on his audience. John's overall strategy is not only teaching as a telling, the usage of these literary devices within the content structure of John's Gospel can be a most vivid form of memory reinforcement in a time no other media was available. The next section, it is to be seen that, though at a limited level when compared to real life, the teaching strategy in John's Gospel is effective and vivid. The Johannine life story is further animated when the audience participated in its physiognomic expressions.

Teaching the community a new way of exemplifying their faith is a complex matter. John uses careful literary construction to teach and help them both learn and remember. For a faith community in need of a wholistic engagement in their faith living, John employs a host of literary devices and uses them to show and tell. Dorothy Lee explores the physiognomic expressions in John and adds to the wider possibility of teaching the Bible beside the "standard-traditional" approaches such as lecture.[111] In John's Gospel, we can appreciate the impact of the narrative when audience uses their senses of sight, smell, touch, hearing, and taste to "perceive" the impact of the storytelling. One of such example is the Lazarus narrative (John 11). Another narrative filled the senses of the audience is at the scene of Jesus crucifixion, where the smell and taste of the vinegar and blood, the sound of the whippings and cries of the people are made vivid.[112] The end result is stronger impact and memory of the message on the audience. The next chapter shall examine how a narrative reading of John's Gospel as life story provides possibility in a lively, relevant reading of the Bible to animate our faith in God.

CONCLUSION AND IMPLICATION FOR TEACHING THE BIBLE

In this chapter, what have been presented are the components of narrative learning found in John's Gospel and how John teaches faith in the Gospel. John's teaching strategy involves a well-structured characterization and skillful use of the language. John, a learner-turned-teacher re-presents his personal experiences of believing in Jesus, remembers, interprets, and

---

111. Lee, "John and the Five Senses," 115–25. Also see Ha, "Familiar-Strange," 168–69.

112. For further descriptions of feeling the narrative with our senses in these scenes in John's Gospel, see Ha, "Familiar-Strange," 169.

teaches his community a way of life through a showing and telling of faith in Jesus.

John's teaching model will be informative especially in teaching adequate faith, an elusive lesson that at times, can be taught, but often is caught more than taught. And as demonstrated above in John's Gospel, there are rich presentations of authentic lived faith-testimonies worthy of our imitation. This example calls in the aid of literary devices, making the showing as real as possible, injecting the element of strange-familiar, showing the audience the "live" scenes of the lived experience, making the stories memorable and teachable.

The media John used to teach his audience is crucial to his teaching approach. John crafted his Jesus Story using popular sources familiar to his audience helps in teaching them to have adequate faith in Jesus. His creative and affective narration of the Jesus Story utilizes both the Jewish and Greco-Roman tradition and context. The effective use of language is the foundation of good storytelling that captivates the audience and enables transformation of lives. The recognition and utilization of physiognomic expressions in John further enhances the teaching effect of storytelling. For the Church, the practice of storytelling is not a new concept, but these skills are not always recognized or articulated, far less taught to the teachers. Most teachers tell stories intuitively.

The finesse in the use of literary devices in John's Gospel creates a most realistic representation of lived events, showing the audience the reality of human faith experiences that creates affective learning. This may be named as the *showing* of lived faith experience that a narrative learner can imitate. At the same time, John's writing includes the telling, or teaching through explanations or didactic instructions to ensure clarity in the message. Storytelling and teaching the meaning of the story goes side by side. Gudmundsdottir sees the functional relationship of the story and discourse in forming an organized text.[113] With the written form of John's Gospel, it is easy for one to see the Gospel as a written discourse and miss seeing its nature as a showing, rooted in lived faith experience.

In terms of his literary skill as a storyteller, John uses the Greek language to present an accurate Jesus *live* to his audience. He constructed a biography using a tight structure to integrate 1) storytelling through showing, and 2) teaching through telling. As he presents a model for a Christian way of life, he also presented a model of teaching through rich use of

---

113. Gudmundsdottir, "Narrative Nature," 25.

narrative components: event, plot, and character. John's teaching model is not just imparting some information, but giving an authentic testimony of lived faith experience that affectively invites the audience to respond and imitate. His showing is focused on telling the main character Jesus, aided by the various supporting stories of the characters in the sign-events. His characterization within the plot is a powerful presentation that addressed and challenged his audience to choose and live faithful to God in a dualistic worldview.

At appropriate point after his showing, John offers a discourse of telling-teaching that explains or clarifies his showings. He used a wide variety of literary devices in his writing to teach them and elicit decision. The literary devices also serve as tools to make his showing as lively as possible. The skillful presentation draws the attention of the audience, brings the past into the present, connects the audience with the character's lived faith experience, elicits affective response from the audience, and reinforces lasting memory in his audience. John's narrative fully engages and challenges the emotion of the hearer. Karl Allan Kuhn argues for greater attention to the emotion of biblical narrative to capture the affective element in a narrative. An author projects the emotion of the narrated event through the skillful rhetoric and stylistic arrangement.[114] Furthermore, strong emotional interface with the narrative is capable of reinforcing lasting memory of the message.

The work of John skillfully weaves the two elements of showing and telling to present a most powerful narrative experience for the audience. It embodies both affective and active learning. The present readers of John's Gospel would benefit from learning to use both the showing and telling to adequately teach faith as this is borne out as part of the Johannine contribution in teaching faith in this and the next chapter. For the Church, the language challenge will benefit from the reminder that it is pertinent in our testimony telling to be attentive to cultivating fine literature as in John's writing. A fine presentation will create much more forceful message in awakening the people of the realistic problems challenging the Church.

The skillful use of literary devices, and with the ongoing development of languages, is key to learning faith in the whole presentation process as the teacher teaches either by showing and/or telling. The language facilitates the creation of striking images of lived faith experiences and relays to the audience an authentic, thus by association, an imitable faith life. The role of

---

114. Kuhn, *Heart of Biblical Narrative*, 1.

language and literary devices in offering an imitable lived faith experience will be further explored in chapter 5. Here, I would like to briefly point out the implication on the teacher. The demand on the teacher and the person sharing the lived faith experience would be to expand her or his fluency of the language and skills of the language usage to recreate *live* these scenes of lived faith experiences.

In chapter 4, it shall be apparent a narrative learning in its completed form is the production of a stable form, most commonly as a written text. As Maynes and others rightly claim that oral historians have learned, "until a story is committed to the tape recorder or the written page, it is a living text that changes with circumstances and the audience, "always a work in progress."[115] The written form is also a tool for preservation and transmission, for its reach occurs both in time and space. Thus aiming for a written account of lived faith-testimonies is useful not only for the Johannine community; it is also an important aim of the biblical narrative learning in the Church. The model of narrative learning identified in John's Gospel will inform the Church both the form and the skill of their biblical narrative learning practices in sharing lived faith-testimonies. The Church practices sharing lived faith-testimonies in various church settings, but not many narrators are well organized with sensitivity to the narrative components. Few are consciously aware of the educational properties of biblical narrative learning. And rarely the lived faith-testimonies are written for an educational purpose.

---

115. Maynes et al., *Telling Stories*, 119. Also, "Writing up analyses based on personal narrative evidence also presents particular methodological and rhetorical challenges to social scientists and historians." Ibid., 11.

4

Learning Faith in John's Gospel

The Johannine community had waited a few decades longer than the Matthean or Markan communities for the second coming of Jesus. While waiting, various issues arose about the way to live in the midst of their faith tradition, and especially the kind of living as it related to God and to others. How should the Johannine community anticipate life as they await the eschaton? John wrote to teach faith as an obedient to God through consummation of love. He presented the stories of the characters, centering on Jesus, the main character, in order to teach adequate faith. He aimed to edify the community for its prosperous survival as they journeyed on. This chapter will present a learning process that emphasizes living with adequate faith so as not to waver in their following while the journey continues. The learning goal of John's audience-students is the focus here: seeing, knowing, learning and remembering how faith is lived out in the life stories of real people.

This chapter will take three readings of faith taught by John through the characters in the six signs in John 2–12 and the life of faith of the main character Jesus. The first reading will focus on the characters and their responses to their encounters with Jesus.[1] The second reading will focus on

---

1. In John's storytelling he used many literary devices. In this reading it would not be feasible to try to apply every literary device he used. This reading of John 2–12 is a selected reading of John's showing and teaching faith.

the temporal aspect in John's narration. The second reading will highlight this unique teaching element in John's Gospel and how it reinforced the core theme of living a way of life by faith. This faith, as the six signs highlighted, is one that entails waiting in suspense for God's action to be realized.

The third reading reflects a narrative reading of Jesus' life story. Besides the commonly acknowledged teaching of Jesus, it is also the plot of John's Gospel to present the main character Jesus who lived faith in suspense. The faith of Jesus, as emphasized in Johannine Jesus, is living in close relationship to the Father. Jesus is the core imitative reference for the Johannine audience. As examined in chapter 3, John's showing and telling of Jesus' crucifixion help facilitate a teaching through rich engagement of the audience in various sensory faculties. Here, the narrative reading of Jesus' life story reveals his ultimate faith in the Father as Jesus approached his crucifixion. John's narration portrays Jesus as exemplar of living faith-in-suspense, and Jesus is the grand sign-event of the Gospel. Jesus was able to obey in extreme condition because of his deep love for the Father and vice versa. From these three readings of faith-in-suspense, one could discern the application in biblical education among the contemporary Christians living under constant and increasing double threat of the racial and religious extremists.

LEARNING BIBLICAL FAITH THROUGH SEEING ADEQUATE FAITH IN JOHN 2–12

Let's look at the characters in the John 2–12 and how they responded to their encounters with Jesus in the six signs. The section will begin with a narrative reading of the plot of John's Gospel, followed by a survey of the recent studies on the characters in the Gospel of John. This will open the way to an analysis of the characters in the six signs (John 2–12), and will help us see how they responded to Jesus. It also reflects the understanding of the OT, especially how the Laws is re-interpreted through these events.

Narrative Analysis of John's Gospel

The primary purpose of John's Gospel is the strengthening of the believers' faith while they anticipated the coming of the Lord as they endured the various challenges in life. For them, coming to faith and holding on to faith was an ongoing process of navigating a way of life challenged by the environment. John's Gospel provides the example in this two-tier development of coming to faith and solidifying the faith. This is recognized as showing and telling in narrative criticism. James L. Resseguie reiterates the dual mechanisms of showing and telling in narrative characterization. Showing is the dramatic method or indirect presentation whereby the author presents the characters "talking and acting and leaves the reader to infer the motives and dispositions that lie behind what they say and do."[2] Showing demands greater involvement from the reader who must make judgments about the characters as he or she "actively collaborates with the narrator" in construing the characters and the primary world they inhabited.[3]

Telling is a direct presentation where the narrator intervenes to explicitly tell us something about a character or the plot in the narration. The readers receive the message directly, sometimes as instruction, and they are not required to guess the character's traits or motivations as in showing.[4] This is the least commonly used technique of characterization, as it is the least powerful in terms of its effect on the reader.[5] In the Gospel of John, the narrative consists of both showing and telling. Compared to the Synoptic, John has more telling in the form of narratives asides and explanatory notes.

The narration of John also uses a narrative time or gap to create effects on the reader's experience of the story time. The manipulation of time can take two forms, tempo or order of events. In the tempo changes, the narration might prolong the events, longer than to read about it or the reverse, where the events take less time to transpire than to recount. Or, the event and recital take approximately equal lengths of time.[6] The changes in the narrated order of events include use of flashback and foreshadowing.[7] These are also common in the Gospel of John. In the following, the combination of the narrative time effect will be seen in the analysis of the faith experiences of the characters in John 2–12. It will examines the effect of showing and telling working hand in hand within the manipulated narrative time as John presents a perspective on faith.

2. Resseguie, *Narrative Criticism*, 127.

3. Walsh, *Old Testament Narrative*, 37–38.

4. Resseguie, *Narrative Criticism*, 127. Also cf. Walsh, *Old Testament Narrative*, 35–37.

5. Walsh, *Old Testament Narrative*, 35.

6. Ibid., 53–58.

7. Ibid., 58–62.

Analysis of the Characters in the Six Signs in John 2–12

The attention is given to the six signs and explores how the characters in these signs displayed adequate or inadequate faith to follow Jesus.[8] Bracketed within these signs are the encounters between Jesus and several key "supporting" characters. Who are the recipients of the sign-acts in each of these events? Who saw the sign, believed and followed, and who failed to do the same? This study will focus on the key supporting characters. The following outline attempts to position these signs and characters in the overall narrative of the Book of Signs in the Gospel of John.

First of all, these six signs are bracketed by the narration of some insiders who see Jesus, believe and follow him. In the call story (1:19–44) the disciples came to see Jesus and believed. They immediately followed Jesus. There is little explanation for their action except for Nathaniel who seems to be convinced by Jesus' proclamation and recognition of Nathaniel's inner thought (1:45–51).[9] But at this stage, did these disciples have adequate faith? This is the question or the suspense that John's Gospel has woven into his narration. The insider move is again introduced in John 13–17 when the disciples were given an exclusive session of teaching. Of course, in the course of writing out these teachings of Jesus, those who read John's Gospel now also has access to be insiders.

---

8. Fortna pointed out the pejorative use of signs in Synoptic and to some extent also in Johannine redaction. Cf. Fortna, *Fourth Gospel*, 48. Von Wahlde instead argues for a more positive use of signs in John such as in John 2:23; 4:39, 53b; 7:31; 11:45, etc. Cf. von Wahlde, *Gospel and Letters of John*, 2:132.

9. The doubting of Nathaniel at John 1 and the doubt of Thomas at John 21 seem to bracket the "doubt" versus the "adequate faith" motive in John's Gospel. The two disciples of John the Baptist believed and followed through the testimony of people they knew and trust. Peter and Andrew seemed to have seen something. The calling of Philip is not so clear on how he came to believe. I believe the author glosses over the matter here, as it is not the key point he was trying to tell. These are the insiders in the story. Their stories were probably well known to the community thus does not need to tell their call story in detail. Furthermore, other Gospel writers have told their call stories (Matt 4:18–22; Mark 1:16–20; Luke 5:1–11). On this matter, Luke probably provided the most in-depth offering of how the disciples were called and left all that they were doing to follow Jesus.

The First Sign: Changing Water into Wine at Cana during a Wedding (2:1–11)

Characters involved in the event: Jesus, the mother of Jesus, the Disciples, the servants, the headwaiter, the bridegroom, and presumably the guests at the wedding. A conversation took place between Jesus, his mother and the servants. Here the faith of Jesus' mother provides a positive model for both the disciples and the readers.[10] The other characters such as the bridegroom, the guests, are flat in this event as they obviously are not the key characters in the narration. The monologue of the headwaiter is obviously representing an outsider whose words used as an emphatic narrative to highlight Jesus' miracles exceeded normal human capacity.

An allusion to Moses beating the rock and gushing of drinking water is possible here. By comparison, Jesus performed a miracle one notch above the plain drinking water by turning the water into wine. The teaching significance is the superiority of Jesus over Moses as revealer of God and his provision for those who obey him. This allusion is later fully explained in the fourth sign (6:22–71) where Jesus is depicted as one who gives sustenance that will nourish the partakers into eternal life. In comparison, those who ate the food of Moses died (6:49).

In response to this event, the Disciples believed in him (John 2:11). The primary role of the first sign is to enable people to recognize Jesus for who he is—as readers are guided by the Prologue (1:1–18). He is the One from God to reveal God. But how much did they believe at that point in time? Probably not that much.[11] Immediately following this event, Jesus, his mother, his brothers, and his disciples went down to Capernaum. Having stayed there for a few days, Jesus went up to Jerusalem for Passover. There he was enraged with the inglorious way the people turned the temple for commercial gain. Jesus made a scourge of rope and cleansed the temple.[12]

---

10. Cf. Keener, *John*, 1:504.

11. Fortna pointed out that, "We are not actually told that in this particular deed the disciples recognized Jesus specifically as Messiah. But that is clear from what precedes in the source.... It is the only conclusion to be drawn from the series of miracles that Jesus has now embarked upon and that will follow one another in the source." Fortna, *Fourth Gospel*, 51.

12. Köstenberger argues that the cleansing of the temple fits the criteria of a sign in the Gospel of John and sees this as the seventh sign in the book. Cf. Köstenberger, *Theology of John's Gospel and Letters*, 324–35. However, this argument comes short as the narrator specifically designated the healing of the healing of the official son as the second sign (John 4:45). Also, for the placement of the Jerusalem event after the first

The cleansing of the Temple is closely linked to the purification of the jars in Cana and teaches a necessary cleansing of the place or vessel,[13] implicating the people whose act is the cause of impurity, enabled a an intimacy with God.

It is significant to see the author's explanation that when the people *remembered*, after the resurrection of Jesus, they came around in their understanding of the event and the Scripture and the word of Jesus (John 2:22).[14] Here, John seems to draw the word of Jesus to same level of authority with the Scripture (v. 22b). In the narrator's concluding remark on the whole events, Jesus is portrayed as skeptical of the people (2:24–25). However, in the subsequent encounters, it's the people who turned their skepticism on Jesus. This negative perception will endure till the end of the whole drama, when the disciples will represent the audience and acknowledge Jesus in the final affirmation (John 20).[15]

In the first sign, the author has brought out the challenge of showing and teaching faith, and that it takes time and further seeing and teaching moment, coupled with crucial remembrance for understanding. Thus in the teaching section John 13–17, one of the key workings of the Spirit in teaching the people of faith in Jesus is to help learners *remember*. And this

---

sign, Keener sees the unit as addressing the purification of the Temple much the same way as the purification of the pots in the act of turning the water into wine. Cf. Keener, *John*, 1:492–95.

13. Loader points out that "The six stone jars at the Cana wedding need no explanation for John's readers. We may assume they would have recognized their use for purifying hands before the meal and respected the practice." Loader, "Jesus and the Law in John," 140.

14. Also see Michaels, *John*, 170.

15. The narrative inserted two main episodes of Jesus' encounters with Nicodemus (John 3) and the Samaritan Woman (John 4). The encounters and the discourse that follow each are significant pieces of Johannine teaching. However, they do not fall within the sign-showing-telling focus in this research. The role of John 3:1—4:42 can be discussed separately as a unique and well-developed Johannine characters. For the possible explanations of these digressions cf. Michaels, *John*, 240-41. In these two discourses, their presence set up a contrast between Nicodemus the rich and powerful, educated social elite who came in the night, with the poor of the society, a woman of lowly status, whom Jesus approached in bright day light. The setting is itself indicative of the outcome of the encounter: the one who should have seen the Light, came in the dark did not see the light; the one who did not seems to live in the Light, she walked into the bright sun and saw the Light. Both events introduce a major teaching session (3:3–21; 4:10–26). For the rhetorical importance of John's pejorative usage of the "night" to represent a limitation on doing God's work, cf. ibid., 178.

first sign reinforces the aim of John's writing: that the readers remember who Jesus really is.

The Second Sign: Healing the Royal Official's Son while Jesus Was on a Journey Back to Cana (4:43–47 // Matt 8:5–13; Luke 7:1–10)

Characters involved: Jesus, the royal official and his slave, his son and his whole household, and Galileans. Jesus came back to Cana of Galilee from his journey through Jerusalem, and Samaria. A father who is a royal official in Capernaum came to beg Jesus to heal his dying son. The royal official apparently had heard about the miracles Jesus performed or as others (the Galileans) had seen them (John 4:45b). He came to seek help from Jesus.[16] Though Jesus critiqued those who believed through seeing miracles (John 4:48), the role of sign in this occasion is a positive one. Michaels is right to point out that here, Jesus' critique of believing through seeing signs is "not all bad . . . not so much a rebuke or an insult as a simple fact."[17] He further pointed out that at the end of the Gospel, exactly the same grammatical structure is used in Thomas' doubting. Human learning of faith has always depended on our sight and hearing. The narrative of John's Gospel has thus far taken this cue: from the calling of the first disciples (1:39). Nathaniel (1:46), the Samaritans (4:29), the audience were invited to "come and see." Each time, the seeing leads to believing and following.[18]

Jesus proclaimed the healing of the sick son and asked the man to go home (John 4:50). The official believed the word that Jesus spoke to him and went off, towards his home, "Having believed without verification."[19] The response is one of adequate faith in the word of Jesus. On his way home, he met his slaves who came to report the good news of his son's healing and verified his adequate faith to move forth. In the questioning of the slave, the man found out that his son was healed at the moment Jesus proclaimed the healing (John 4:51–52). Schnackenburg pointed out that the official comes

---

16. Michaels pointed out that the official "is not said to have remember the miracle at Cana, nor would we expect him to, given only Jesus' disciples and a few servants knew what had happened there. That memory is for the reader alone (v. 46)." Ibid., 277.

17. Ibid., 278.

18. Ibid.

19. Michaels, *John*, 271.

to full faith (*pisteuein* used absolutely, v. 53b) only after the verification of his child healing.[20]

The restoration of life for the son helped the father to come to greater maturity in faith and eventually led his whole family to become people of faith. This second sign confirms the effectiveness of sign in leading an outsider (the official) who experienced the sign came to adequate faith, just as the insiders (in the first sign) came to believe and followed. The official and his household are now a part of God's Family.[21] As members of the Family, there are roles and responsibilities, and benefits.[22] On the other side, the others—the family of Satan—bring harm to the well-being of God's family members.[23] The end of the Cana cycle in John's Gospel also signals a shift in the narration. Though the next sign shares the experience of seeing a restoration of a wrecked life to its fullness, the main character or recipient of the third sign exhibits a different response.[24] Also different is the location of event—the next sign took place in Jerusalem and is called a "work" of Jesus instead of a sign.[25]

The Third Sign: Healing the Lame at Bethesda Pool on Sabbath (5:1–15)

Characters involved: Jesus, a man ill for thirty-eight years, and a multitude of people sick, blind, lame, and withered waiting to be healed, and the Jews. Jesus singled out the lame man from a crowd of sick people at Bethesda pool. Jesus offered and initiated the healing.[26] The power of healing lies in

---

20. Cf. Schnackenburg, *St John*, 1:468.

21. For Johannine motive of believers as member of God's family, see the work of van der Watt, *Family of the King*, especially 178–88. Seeing John community as a family, also cf. Howard-Brook, *Becoming Children of God*, 55–58.

22. Van der Watt gives a convincing reading of the family metaphor in John's Gospel. The education and ethic are key communication within the family of God. In the family, knowing of God and the Son is communicated. The love for one another also call for sharing the honor of the family, giving care and protection to one another. These are basic to the members of a family. Cf. van der Watt, *Family of the King*, 264–357.

23. Ibid., 357–59.

24. "The notion of restoring to life gives a connection not merely with ch. 5, but with all that Jesus says and does." Schnackenburg, *St John*, 1:477.

25. Ibid., 476.

26. Michaels compared the differences of this healing with other similar events in the Synoptic and pointed out the straightforward approach taken by Jesus in this incident. Cf. Michaels, *John*, 292.

the efficacy of Christ's own words. At the spoken words of Jesus "Get up, pick up your mat and walk" the man was healed immediately and walked.[27] There was no indication that this sign helped the healed man to believe in Jesus. In fact, this man later reported Jesus' work of healing on a Sabbath to the Jews resulting in a confrontation between the Jews and Jesus (John 5:16–17).

It is notable that this is the first occurrence of the verb "to sin" in John's Gospel. "Neither the first disciples, nor Nathaniel, nor Nicodemus, nor even the Samaritan woman (despite 4:18), were said to have 'sinned.'"[28] The healed man did not show any word of appreciation, or any commitment to stop sinning.[29] This is the first sign that does not generate faith in the direct recipient and who personally experienced the work of Jesus. The sign, instead, generated hostility from the Jewish authority that failed to see the authority of Jesus. The non-recognition of Jesus for who he is, the one from God, logically leads to diminished authority. To the Jews, Jesus apparently encroached into their way of living a life in obedience to God, as the people of God.

The characterization of the people who recognize-believe or fail to recognize-believe Jesus continues in the subsequent encounters with the potential disciples. However, from John 5 onward, there is a more mix-bag of characters arriving on the scenes. The Jews and others who subscribed to their authority continuously failed to recognize Jesus.

The Fourth Sign: Feeding the Five Thousand at the End of a Teaching Session (6:1–14 // Matt 14:15–21; Mark 6:35–44)

Characters involved: Jesus, a large crowd, his disciples, Philip, Andrew, and a child. Jesus multiplied the five loaves and two fish of the child and fed a multitude of five thousand. The scene of fourth sign reverts back to Galilee. A huge crowd followed Jesus. The author explained that the huge crowd was following out of an interest in Jesus healing the sick. The setting of John's Gospel differs from the Synoptic. While in the Synoptic, the need to feed

---

27. Michaels noted the inclusion of the mat in the narrative as an added emphasis to highlight the drama of the man's restoration to health and able to leave the place, needless to return to it. The carrying of the mat is also intentional as a challenge to the religious authorities in Jerusalem and their Sabbath laws. Ibid., 294–95.

28. Ibid., 297.

29. Ibid., 299.

the crowd was because the crowd had been with Jesus for a long time, and it was late in the evening (Matthew 14:13–21; Mark 6:30–44; Luke 9:10–17). In John's Gospel, none of these is mentioned. Instead, Jesus saw the huge crowd coming to him and initiated to get bread, offered to feed the crowd. This sets a very different context that links well to the telling section that follows the showing of the sign, while none of the Synoptic made specific teaching in reference to the event.

The event, through the narrator's asides, was also linked to the approaching Passover. Michaels pointed out, this inclusion functions to "evokes Moses, keeping alive in the reader's mind the conclusion of the preceding discourse (5:45–57; also 5:37–40), and anticipating further controversy over Moses and the provision of manna in the desert."[30] The showing (vv. 1–15) in John's Gospel facilitates a lengthy teaching session that follows (John 6:16–71). By contrast, the Synoptic recorded the miracle as an event with no teaching session attached. In John's Gospel, every feeding-sign correlates to a teaching session. In the following chart, we can see the literary set-up of John 6. John 6 features all elements of a narrative: beginning, middle, and ending. The beginning comes as a preamble or prologue (vv.1–2), and scene setting (vv. 3–4). The middle section (5–11) narrates the miracle and an ending (12–15) that gives the result of the miracle. The ending is given in two parts: the physical leftover of the food, and the personal reaction of the people. Similarly, there are corresponding sections in the teaching-telling section (vv. 16–71). Apparently John is not unintentional in any of his narrative. He shows with the intention to tell.

Chart 2. Literary Set-up of John 6: Showing and Telling

6:1–15	Showing: 4th Sign—Jesus Fed the five thousand	6:16–71	Telling: Teaching Sessions on the real food for living
1–2	Narrator gives the reason of the crowd following Jesus	25–27	Jesus offers an appropriate reason for them to seek him
3–4	Set-up—link to Passover	16–25, 59	Set-up—link to teaching in a synagogue[A]
5	Jesus initiated an offer to feed the crowd	28–34	The better food is offered to the crowd
6–7	Phillip's answer—human's way to get food	35–40	Jesus' answer—God's way

30. Ibid., 343.

8–9	Andrew's solution in a dialogue set-up	41–42, 52, 60	Three reactions from the crowd in a dialogue set up
10–11	Jesus give them food	43–51, 53–58, 61–63	Jesus gives three teachings sessions on his sufficiency and the permanence of his food
12–13	The leftover—proof of abundance		
14–15	The crowd's response to the sign	64–71	The crowd and the disciples' responses contrasted

A. I don't want to stretch the setting too far, but I see here a contrast and deliberate move in moving the location of teaching to a synagogue (compare to the Synoptic where the teaching took place on the mount or wilderness). It reflects the narrator's point of view to highlight or a reminder that Jesus taught in synagogue. This is particularly relevant for the Johannine community that lived with the synagogues as centers of teaching and learning.

The end-result in this sign is that the people saw Jesus as the prophet that is to come. However, they did not come to perceive Jesus as the Son of God, nor did they wanted to follow Jesus, but the narrator told us that the crowd perceived wrongly, and if they had followed Jesus, they would be coming to him for the wrong reason. Their desired relationship is for him to be their earthly king (John 6:15) that solely satisfies their physical needs, not to be related to the Father through a loving relationship. The consequence of the people's expectation, if realized, would be a repetition of the Israelites erroneous request for a king in 1 Samuel. The true relationship of living by faith in love with the Father would be gravely missed-out. Thus the narrator's explanation sets up the teaching session that subverted the old way of life where the people adhered to a conception of God deduced from the miracles brought by Moses, and misconstrued with the Gentiles God as mere supplier of their military strength.

The second and third signs focus on the restoration of life. The fourth signs proceeds to tell of the food that is needed for the life restored. The man in the third sign, and the crowd in the fourth sign, either failed to make a commitment to follow, or followed for the wrong motive—getting physical benefit without seeing what Jesus was really offering them—the Word of Life, the food that would sustained them into living eternally with God. This telling section of the fourth sign points out that the food of their ancestor is insufficient to maintain their living (v. 49). In line with the theme of eternal life, the people need the food that gives life (v. 48, v. 51). Those who do not receive this food will not have life (vv. 53–58). At the end of explaining the fourth sign, Peter emerged as an insider to reaffirm the status of Jesus as the One who has the Word of Life (6:68) and declared his devotion to follow Jesus, the Holy One of God (6:69). In contrast, the lack of faith among the outsiders continued and is presented in a long discourse (John 7–8) that detailed further disputes and growing hostility against Jesus. How do the two signs, where the characters did not respond with adequate faith, function in his narration? This relates to John's literary intention of these two signs when all the signs are considered in John 2–12.

The Fifth Sign: Healing a Man Born Blind at Galilee on Sabbath (9:1–41)

Character involved: Jesus, his disciples, a man born blind and his parents and his neighbors, the Pharisees, and the Jews. In this episode, similar in the construction of the third and fourth sign, Jesus took the initiative to heal. By these emphasis on Jesus' taking the initiative, the presentation of God as one who comes and seeks his people is obvious. The presentation of Jesus as the one who come seeking his people also stands out in the allusion of Jesus to the shepherd who opened the door for his sheep, and led his sheep (John 10:3).

There were also a few rounds of conversation in which the narrator re-enacts a much talked about event: a man born blind was healed. The event again took place on Sabbath and generated considerable amount of argument presented in six dialogues. The first "argument" occurred between the disciple and Jesus (9:2–5). The second argument was between the neighbors of the blind man (9:8–9). The third round of argument was between the neighbors and the blind man (9:10–12). The fourth round of argument was between the Pharisees and the blind man (9:13–17). The fifth confrontation was between the Jews and the parents of the blind man (9:18–23). The longest and final argument was the second confrontation between the Pharisees and the blind man (9:24–34). These arguments took place in a context where the narrator had just "provided a grim example of aborted faith" (8:30–59); John added "a case study in genuine faith."[31] At the end of this confrontation, the healed blind man was caste out of the Jewish community.[32] In these dialogues, it is obvious that the author portrays the

---

31. Michaels, *John*, 539.

32. Those who advocate the separation of Johannine community from the Jewish synagogue in John's Gospel would easily identify this as a sign that teaches the reality of expulsion and how they can choose to become followers of Jesus with a commission to confess Jesus is Lord and worship him (9:38).

character of the blind man as an antithesis to those who have sight but failed to see Jesus.

In comparison, the blind man healed by Jesus (9:1–41) contrasted the man at Bethesda. After the healing of the blind man became apparent to all, a debate started among the neighbors. They were surprised by the event and the matter was brought before the Pharisees. The healing recurred on a Sabbath and raised more contempt among the Pharisees. The blind man stood by his claim, though he was yet to know the identity of this man, although he knew that the man who healed him could not be a sinner. He also stood to proclaim that only the one who came from God is able to perform such healing. He was caste out by the Sanhedrin. In contrast, the lame man healed by Jesus was probably living in sin, while the Pharisees accused the blind man of living in sin. The subsequent encounter of this man with Jesus attested his faith and proves it to be contrary to the judgment of the Pharisees. The Pharisees turned out to be the sinners (9:41).

When the Jews expelled the healed blind man, Jesus went searching for him (9:35). When the healed blind man met Jesus for a second time, Jesus again took the initiative and asked the healed blind man if he believes in the Son of Man. The conversation led the healed blind man to identify Jesus as the Son of Man and proclaimed his belief in Jesus (9:35–38). In this act, Jesus showed himself to the man and declared his identity as the Son of Man. This sign further corresponds with the shepherd section (9:39–10:21) where Jesus presented himself as the shepherd who calls and protects his sheep versus the blind guide. The ability of his flock to recognize Jesus is highlighted (10:2–5). His sheep will recognize his voice (the tone, loudness etc), the sound of the gate opening, the speed of the gate opening (not violent), his smell as he walks toward and with them, the sight and smell of the food he offers, the touch of the shepherd's staff, the patience of the shepherd standing there waiting for each one to pass through the gate into the safety of the compound, the closing of the gate for protection, and the security of the sheep fold as they lay down to rest, though it is dark in the night. The healed blind man recognized his shepherd, immediately believed in Jesus, and worshiped him.[33] Jesus further declared his love for his flock that he would willingly lay down his life for them.

---

33. Michaels points out that in Jesus' second encounter with the blind man, Jesus also used the emphatic "You" to ask him "do you believe in the Son of Man?" (v. 35) The emphatic *you* is all too familiar to the man (vv. 28, 34), "but now he is hearing it not from an accuser but from someone who cares about him." Ibid., 565.

John highlighted the healed blind man as the example par excellence in successful seeing of Jesus and grasping adequate faith to proclaim Jesus as the Son of Man (9:35–38). Jesus then condemned those who have sight but were blind to his identity and power. The unbelieving were condemned in comparison to the blind man's decision and action. In a closing remark, the narration turned to commentary in the form of a conversation that condemned the Pharisees for their failure to recognize Jesus while Jesus reiterates his mission in the midst of threat on his life (10:19–42).

In this sign, the focus again points to the need to see Jesus, and the story shows that the character is able to pinpoint the status of Jesus as the One sent by God. In Johannine's narrative structure, the healing of the blind man unmistakably assured the audience of the possibility to see and identify Jesus as the Son of God. This seeing resulted in the blind man's ability to recognize Jesus as the One. Consequently, the encounter ended with the healed blind man worshipping Jesus.[34] The sign again subverted the traditional concept of relationship between God and his people. While in John 4, the encounter of the Samaritan Woman led to a discussion about the place of worship, this encounter led to a direct act of worship. The ability to recognize Jesus and to have adequate faith in Jesus is more prominently displayed in the next sign.

The Sixth Sign: Raising Lazarus from Death at a Grave Site, Four Days Later (11:1–57)

Characters involved: Jesus the Teacher, the disciples, Thomas, Lazarus and his sisters Martha and Mary, the Jews, the chief priest, the Pharisees. The familiar (to contemporary readers) event of the raising of Lazarus contains a few unusual features. First of all, the description of the character is rich in this event and the characterization of many characters is round. The sisters are well described in this narration. Martha and Mary are described at length (John 11:1–2.). Mary is introduced as the one who anointed the

---

34. The relationship between people and God is in focus in John's Gospel. "When the Johannine Jesus and narrator speak of knowledge of people or of the things of God, it is always a matter of intimacy and personal connectedness, not of purely intellectual understanding." Howard-Brook, *Becoming Children of God*, 35. Koester also sees that in John's Gospel the Jesus-God Father relationship is central to the act of belief. "Throughout John's Gospel, Jesus refers to God as 'my Father' or 'the Father' and to himself as 'the Son,' disclosing the unique relationship between them." Koester, "Jesus as the Way," 120–21.

Lord with ointment and wiped his feet with her hair. Lazarus is repeatedly described as a close friend whom Jesus loves (11:3, 5, 11, 33, 36), and the sisters are also significantly close to Jesus. Secondly, we see a rich display of emotion.[35] The sadness of the sisters is also repeatedly reported to highlight the intensity of their suffering at the loss of their brother (11:19, 29–33a). The narration displays a sadness that should affect all readers. Those who came to comfort the sisters are also drawn into this event emotionally (11:33b). Even Jesus was affected by the whole display of sadness. He was publicly emotional; he cried though he knew the outcome is not hopeless as the others saw it (11:35). Following the show of emotion by Jesus, an interesting portrayal of the Jews took place. Here the Jews were seen as emotive and made positive comments on Jesus (11:36) and suggests the power of emotion in transformation of audience.[36]

Thirdly, the plot and narration thickness increase with the importance of the sign events as it comes to a climax of all six sign events.[37] The amount of details the narrator put into these signs is similar to the previous sign (John 9) but far exceeded the earliest four events. The purpose of this sign is interwoven into the dialogue between Jesus and his disciples, the sisters, and his proclamation in front of the crowd. It is interesting to note one of the dialogues between Jesus and Martha.

The conversation between Jesus and Martha, and Jesus and Mary presented two perspectives. Martha seems to be representing a faith that is rational while Mary represents one who is bold to question the why when tragedy happens (11:21, 24, 27, 32b). How the author intends to present different faith encounters through the two sisters is open to discussion. Though Martha seems to have said the right thing and affirms that Jesus is the giver of life eternal, she appears to be making rationalistic statements of what she thinks is the right thing to believe. Her comment made in front of his brother's gravestone suggests otherwise. At the moment Jesus commanded the bystanders to remove the gravestone, Martha interrupted and said, "Lord, already there is a stench because he has been dead four days"

---

35. There is also Jesus' emotion of anger in this event (John 11:33, 38). For the meaning and possible reason of his anger, cf. Michaels, *John*, 636–42.

36. This is one of the incidents where we can see that "the Jews" in the Gospel of John does not necessarily point to a definite opposition group. It is also used to refer to the crowd in general.

37. Köstenberger sees the first three signs as inaugural signs and three further signs characterized by mounting controversy. Köstenberger, *Theology of John's Gospel and Letters*, 334.

(11:39). To Martha's objection, Jesus replies, "Did I not tell you that if you believe you will see the glory of God?" (v. 40) While Jesus did not say so to Martha, the narrator had Jesus explain earlier (in 11:4) the purpose of this sign-event is for the glory of God. Furthermore, the sign reinforced the many occasions when Jesus declared that he is the Resurrection and the Life that everyone who lives and believes in him will live (11:25–26).[38] Martha's apparent contradiction of faith is representative of faith learned through propositional learning and is the dilemma of many Christian through the ages. In a sense, at this stage, her faith is inadequate.

The act of raising Lazarus is a well-dramatized narrative piece that proclaims freedom for those who believe in Jesus. The event is animated with the reminder of the smell of death, a dramatic prologue to Jesus' instruction to move the stone (11:38–40), the loud proclamation, declared to those present, his work is in line with his status as the Son working according to the will of God and to reveal the glory of God (11:40, 41–42), the final commands for Lazarus to come out of the tomb and be released (11:43c, 44d), and the dramatic scene of Lazarus walking out, more likely groped his way, into the presence of the waiting crowd. Lazarus wrapped –including his face—in clothes is a huge visual impact on the onlookers. The final command of Jesus in this event is to the crowd standing around, "Loosen him, and let him go" (v. 44) is astounding. The command to loosen again acts as affective and mnemonic tool that link to many occasions that Jesus taught about how to live free, "Freedom and eternal life were synonymous in that setting."[39] The audience is reminded, in Christ Jesus, they are freed from the prospect of dying in their sins (8:21, 24), freed from falsehood (8:44, false leadership as seen in the shepherd discourse following the fourth sign), and free from the problematic and narrow sight of the old system (explicated in fifth sign) that limited their freedom to practice their new found faith.[40]

Fourthly, in the meetings of the sisters and Jesus, and the conversation that ensued consistently show the sisters' sufficient knowledge of Jesus and affirmations of their beliefs in what Jesus could have done if he was there earlier (11:17–32), but lack of adequate faith that led to their emotional

---

38. Cf. Michaels, *John*, 642.

39. Ibid., 647.

40. William points out the reference to Abraham in John 8:31–59 as a reminder of true freedom in Christ as compared to a deceptive perception that they were not slave to anyone. Cf. William, "Abraham," 212–16.

struggle when hardship hit. Finally, the faith response to this sign event is further explicated in the lengthy closing of the part one of the Gospel (11:47—12:50). In the ending of signs section, there appears a mixed report of some in the audience came to believe in Jesus, while others obviously did not and instead went to the Pharisees to report on Jesus (11:45-6). The Sanhedrin condemned Jesus to death (11:47-53), and restricted the work of Jesus (11:54-57). There is also a report of others coming to seek Jesus (12:20-22). All these happened in a chaotic narrative rush in the shadows of Jesus' imminent death. Yet the narration took another long delay (Jesus taught the insiders 13:31—17:26, with Judas excluded, 13:30) as audience was put in suspense for the fate of Jesus. The final sign in John's book of signs (John 2-12) is indeed a combination of the various elements in the previous signs. It is also another story filled with the uses of literary devices that created tension, suspense, and delivered a solution to the audience—a full manifestation of Jesus the Son's interaction with people through his active participation with God the Father.

Summary

Characters in the Gospel of John are presented in a well-structured manner, and with a careful attention to the chiastic arrangement. In the first sign-events the disciples are the one who believed and became insider to the narration; thereafter, their responses to the signs are no longer necessary. From this point onward, they are characterized more frequently as those who know and eventually are able to affirm and declare the status of Jesus. In the second sign-event, the royal official and his whole household believed in Jesus, but there was no indication that he understood the person of Jesus and his relationship to God. However, in whatever he had come to experience, he and his family believed in this Jesus. Though it is not the part of John's narration, it is safe to assume that he would later learn the way of life in Jesus. In the third and fourth sign-event, there is no adequate faith response from the beneficiary of the signs. In fact, both recipients of the signs failed to recognize Jesus as the Son of God.

In the fifth sign-event, the man born blind was healed and his response is a positive faith response to Jesus. He too, though not yet on the same level as Martha and the Disciples, became a knowledgeable insider who recognized Jesus—by his work—as someone from God (9:30-33). In the sixth sign-event, Martha readily acknowledged Jesus as Lord (11:27), though in a limited fashion. The climax of the revealing is the public proclamation by Jesus himself that he is closely related to God and sent by God (11:42). The responses from the vast audience who witnessed the raising of Lazarus are split between belief and disbelief. This prepares the upcoming final challenge, when after the explanation and teaching (13–17), the audience is given a chance to make a faith response to Jesus and the final grand sign is revealed.

The responses of the people in these six signs exhibit a chiastic construction:

> The First Sign: adequate response to Jesus
> > The Second Sign: adequate response to Jesus
> > > The Third Sign: inadequate response to Jesus
> > > The Fourth Sign: inadequate response to Jesus
> > The Fifth Sign: adequate response to Jesus
> The Sixth Sign: adequate response to Jesus

The six sign-events in the Gospel of John are chiastic and emphasized the responses of the characters who had experienced the signs, or the works of Jesus. In this chiastic construction, there is no center point (an *epanodos*), thus the prominence is given to what comes first and last.[41] From the chiastic structure of the six sign-events, the author's intention of showing and telling the audience to see the signs and learn to have adequate faith response is made known. Where the characters failed to learn adequate faith, the telling section that immediately follows the sign emphasizes the ability of the disciples to affirm their recognition of Jesus.

The signs progress from showing and teaching that Jesus is the Messiah (first sign). He comes to save life. His salvific act is three-folds: first by restoring damaged or broken life (second and third signs), second by feeding (fourth sign), and finally have sufficient faith to recognize and acknowledge him, and point out to others that Jesus is the One (fifth signs). Finally, the saving of life is ultimately manifested by his ability to give life, even when one has been dead well over any hope of coming back to life (sixth sign). And integrated in the sixth sign is the repeated affirmation of Jesus as the One sent from God, as it shows that the followers knew who he was; even some among the Jews also came to acknowledge Jesus for who he was through his work.

---

41. Talbert, *Reading John*, 130. Also, Howard-Brook explained the role of chiasm and identified the numerous chiastic constructions in John's Gospel. Cf. Howard-Brook, *Becoming Children of God*, 38–40, and his entire commentary on John's Gospel employ literary analysis in chiastic construction.

Moving through the six signs, other characters are gradually included as the insiders (blind man, Martha and Mary) who declared their knowledge of and faith in Jesus. Yet they were unable to comprehend the mystery of eternal life. Similarly, when the grand sign-event of Jesus' passion drew near, there were signals of confusion such as the disciples' failure to understand Jesus' authority over death (11:12–13), Thomas' comment (11:16), and Jesus reiteration of their need to believe (11:14b–15). The confusion is expected as the Disciples (and the audience) were yet to witness the definitive event that show once and for all the reality of eternal life: the resurrection. The next section offers a view on learning faith in John's Gospel through emplotment in the narrative, especially through the narrative time in the storytelling.

LEARNING FAITH IN SUSPENSE THROUGH THE SIX SIGNS IN JOHN 2–12

It is always a challenge to explain to someone what it means to believe or trust in something beyond the normal perception of human understanding. John presents what it means to have adequate faith in Jesus—the Son of God, through the responses of the characters in the six sign events. The afore-examined six signs in John 2–12 is constructed as a chiasm that highlights those with adequate faith in following Jesus. The six signs in John's Gospel involve provision for human consumption (the first and fourth signs), three healings (the second, third, and fifth signs), and one resuscitation (the resurrection of Lazarus).[42] In John's Gospel there is no mention of exorcism performed by Jesus, while in the Synoptic, it counts for more than half of the healing events. John has chosen these sign events in a structured manner to show and tell what faith is in a vivid manner. This section shall examine the presentation of Johannine teaching on faith through looking at the narrative time in these signs. It shall also compare, where applicable, these Johannine signs to similar miracles in the Synoptic to highlight the Johannine angle of teaching through these faith stories.

In the first sign, the author prolonged the waiting time for the outcome of the deed of Jesus. There are some details on the temporal and spatial setting (John 2:1–2). The author added a little "jabbing" between Jesus and his mother Mary (2:3–5). The narration continued with the instruction

---

42. For the categories of the miracles in the four Gospels, cf. Powell, *Introducing the New Testament*, 88.

from the mother to the servant that seems to portray that Mary knew the capacity of Jesus to perform miracles. The servant obeyed at the utterance of Jesus. Here the narrative time quickened while in real time, there would be some time spent for the servants to fill up the six hundred-liter (26 gallons) jars to the brim (John 2:6–7). There was another real time waiting as the servant obeyed Jesus' instruction to draw out the wine, bring it to the chief steward who tasted it. There was a time of confusion and questioning and finally they called the bridegroom. The narrative revealed the miracle performed by Jesus. The revealing was through an indirect statement as the headwaiter accused the bridegroom of doing something unconventional (2:8–10). The narration concluded with a declaration by the narrator that this is Jesus' first sign. The name of the place was recorded. The purpose was declared: to reveal his glory. The result of the sign was also announced: Jesus' disciples believed in him (2:11). The declaration affirmed the positive effect of the sign and inducted the disciple into the faith community and they, Jesus' mother, his brothers, and his disciples, embarked on the journey to accomplish his mission in his public ministry.[43]

The narration of the second sign begins again with the temporal and space (4:46a), the key character, and why he came (4:46b–47). The movement of the royal official coming to see, and the meeting with Jesus (4:48–50a) is quickening as the narration obviously focuses on the outcome after his encounter with Jesus. The narration immediately reveals that the man believed the word that Jesus spoke to him and started on his way home. However, the narrative time slows down somewhat to portray his meeting with his servant who was on the way to meet him to report the good news of his son's recovery (4:50b–51). In real time, a day has passed from the man's encounter with Jesus and his hearing the confirmation from the servant (4:52–53a). The result is presented through the narrator: the man himself believed, along with his whole household, which obviously took place at a later time (4:53b–54). The play of narrative time and actual time when the reader pauses to reflect on the event would certainly reveal again a time of waiting while the man took faith in the word of Jesus. The sign event again closes with reaffirmation of the location where this took place (4:54).

---

43. I have adopted the view that the first part of the Gospel of John is as much a focus on Jesus' public ministry while it is also recognized as the book of signs. Cf. also Lincoln, *Saint John*, 3–14.

The third sign begins with a description of time (5:1) and space (5:2), the setting (5:3), and a description of the character (5:5). The encounter between Jesus and the lame man is different from other signs. There is a quick exchange of words, and at Jesus' spoken word, the man was healed. The event does not exhibit any faith on the part of the man healed in this sign. Nor does he show any intention to believe or follow Jesus after his second encounter with Jesus. Neyrey pointed out that Jesus went to find him. While in normal "finding" of someone always indicated recruitment, in this case, Jesus gave a warning instead, the man was warned not to sin again.[44] The statement by Jesus implies that the man is a sinner with a certain past. The man healed did not have adequate faith response. In this sign-event the man was healed without any tension of waiting in suspense, either in actual time or narrative time, for the healing to take place.

The fourth sign begins with the introduction of space (6:1–3), and time (6:4). The conversation of Jesus asking his disciples was on pace with actual time. Finding the five loaves and two fish was told at a quickened narrative time. This reflects that finding them is not the focus of the story (6:5–10). The pace of narrative time quickened as the five loaves and two fish were distributed to the five thousand, while there are plenty that can be said if approached from a different point of view.[45] In precise moment of the event, the deed of Jesus multiplying the food took a while as he handed out as much as they wanted (6:11), with twelve baskets of leftover (6:12–13). The response of the people is mixed. The people who had witnessed this sign-event identified Jesus as the prophet and wanted to enthrone him as their king (6:14–15). At this point the narrator steps in to explain that the people were wrong in their understanding of Jesus (6:15). Later when these people were running after Jesus, Jesus also declared their erroneous understanding (6:26). In this sign-event, again the people who benefited in their encounter with Jesus did not display adequate faith. To be more specific, they had the wrong faith by desiring for instant gratification of their physical need.

The fifth sign has no temporal and spatial introduction at the beginning of the narration. It is simply that as Jesus was walking along with the Disciples, they saw a man born blind (9:1). The disciple made a theological enquiry to why the man was born blind (9:2). To Jesus, this is to reveal

---

44. Cf. Neyrey, *Gospel of John*, 104.

45. Every individual encountering this distribution of food is a story. The Johannine narrative not intended to bring out all these "minor" stories.

the work of God (9:3). Jesus then turned the conversation into telling the disciples the importance of recognizing the dualism of light and darkness and that they should heed this urgency to work while there is light (9:4–5). The blind man was mute at this point of narration. Instead of instant healing, Jesus told the blind to go, wash at the Siloam pool. He went, washed, came back and regained his sight (9:6–7). The narrative time is short here, while the real time is longer and the endeavor of the blind man needed much more effort. With the mud on his eye, he needed adequate faith to take the journey to the pool, to wash, and apparently he only regained his sight when he came back.

In this lengthy narration of sign event, the blind man was healed, but the healing did not come instantly. The blind went through a process that took time and experienced his faith as the event unfolded. He was in suspense as he moved his feet and groped his way to the pool, found a spot to wash, and waited for his sight to return. He did all these while he believed the word of Jesus. His faith is again one that has him waiting in suspense. A further show of his faith is that though he did not fully understand his benefactor, he stood by his faith that the man who healed him is not a sinner. And when he met Jesus for the second time, he immediately responded in faith to the invitation of Jesus (9:38).

The outcome of the signs so far had the outsiders hanging in suspense and wonder about the identity of Jesus. After the telling section in 10:1–18, the Jews were divided in their opinions of Jesus. A group surrounded Jesus and sought clarification, "How long will you *take away our life*? It you are the Christ, tell us plainly" (10:24), emphasis mine.[46] The translation of "take away our life" is a strange Greek construction. It is most often rendered "keep us in suspense" (RSV, CUV).[47] It stresses the intensity of anxiety in the hearts of these Jews. It also contrasts the serendipity for those in the know—those who believe and follow Jesus the good shepherd.

The sixth sign tells the story of Jesus raising Lazarus from death at a grave site in Bethany, Judah. It took place four days after the death of Lazarus. The narration of this sign-event has a few locations mentioned: Bethany (11:1, 18), location of Jesus and the land he would travel to reach Bethany (11:6–7), the village where Martha and Mary greeted and met

---

46. Translation of v. 24 is taken from Michaels, *John*, 593.

47. Keener sees this construction as another one of John's wordplay: "though Jesus lays down his life for his followers (10:11–15), he will take it from the hands of those who think they have killed him (10:18)." Keener, *Gospel of John*, 1:824.

Jesus (11:30), and the grave site (11:17, 38). These locations give a sense of distance as the event unfolds. Distance also acts as a pointer of time, as travel across distance requires time. However, the narrator again stretched and squeezed the narrative time to emphasize his point.

The event narrated reveals an extended time of waiting on the part of Martha and Mary.[48] There is considerable time of waiting in real life when the two sisters sent their servant to seek and inform Jesus that Lazarus is sick (11:3). Jesus' reply to the servant is reminiscence of the opening conversation with his disciples in the fifth sign event. He further delayed the journey to Bethany for two days (11:6b). The next conversation again takes on a similar content as in the fifth sign-event when Jesus explained his intention to work within the urgency of time, and the contest of light and darkness (11:9–10). Here, the narrative added the precarious situation as the disciples reminded Jesus the danger of stoning by the Jews (11:8). The narrative time was manipulated by the additional conversation that reveals the disciples' confusion on the matter of death (11:11–16).

The narrative provides extensive pointers to the time involved in the event (11:17, 21, 24, and 39). When Jesus arrived at Bethany, Lazarus has been dead for four days (11:39). Then Jesus proceeded to make a public declaration and explained the purpose as he spoke out, "that they may believe that you sent me" (11:42). The conversation again places a narrative pause before the outcome of the event: Would the audience smell a stench of decayed flesh when they removed the tombstone?

After this Jesus cried out in a loud voice for the benefit of the crowd that was present, "Lazarus, come out." The dead man came out, his hands and feet bound with strips of cloth, and face wrapped in a cloth. The scene held the crowd in suspense, as they would still wonder, was his flesh deformed in the four days? While the people were held in awe as Jesus gave another command to loosen the resurrected man. The crowd fixed their eyes on Lazarus as someone unwound the burial clothes and the living flesh was revealed. Lazarus certainly walked and talked, maybe a bit dazed? But the narrative leaves out the details. The equally dazed crowd witnessed an unprecedented event—one that they could not possibly forget. Later, there were still others who came to see this man who came back to life (12:9). Many of the Jews, who had seen what Jesus did, believed in him (11:45).

---

48. In this sign event, Lazarus is a flat character. There is no revealing of his thought, emotion, or faith. Thus the focus is not Lazarus, but the faith responses of his sisters and the spectators.

The author also tells us that some of the Jews went to the Pharisees and told them what happened (11:46), leaving the event open for the later development where the persecution against Jesus grew (11:47–54a).

Overall, in the sixth and final signs, there is an obvious deliberate stretch of time and delay, both in precise moment of the event and narrative time. This happens in arguably the most significant sign event in the book of sign to dramatize the agony of waiting in a crisis situation. It brings to the forefront a faith in suspense that manifests the work of Jesus. In addition, it glorifies the Father through the Son of God. This is also fitting in the narration to bring forth the next portion of John's Gospel: the book of glory where the grand sign-event of living faith in suspense is revealed where Jesus himself is the subject matter.

The emphasis of John's Gospel is different from the Synoptic.[49] Where there is a similar case of someone with a prolonged illness, the woman with hemorrhage for twelve years touched the cloak of Jesus and was instantly healed (Matt 9:20–22, instantly; Mark 5:25–34, immediately; Luke 8:43–48, immediately). Where the several occasions of healing the blind men were told in the Synoptic, the healing occurred immediately (Matt 20:34b; Mark 10:52). The narrative in the Synoptic also lacks the dramatic temporal and spatial effect that leaves the reader in suspense, or portrays the actual time of waiting for the healed person. The Synoptic authors all attribute their healing to their faith, in a way different from John's. The faith in the Synoptic characters more often involved the personal effort or persistent request of the person in need of healing. The woman with hemorrhage had to squeeze through the crowd and reached out to touch the cloak of Jesus. The two blind men at Jericho had to keep on shouting to get the attention of Jesus.

There is a healing in Mark that has some resemblance to the healing in John 9. In the Markan narrative of the blind man at Bethesda, the healing took longer than the other healing events in the Synoptic. Jesus took the hand of the blind man and led him out of the village, put saliva on his eyes and laid hands on him, then a second time when the blind man fully regain his sight (Mark 8:22–26). However, the Markan narrative lacks the

---

49. Powell points out that the basic story in the Gospel of John "is congruent with that of the Synoptic on all essential points: Jesus is the Messiah and son of God; his life and teachings reveal God's character and will for humanity; his death and resurrection bring forgiveness of sins; salvation is found through faith in him; and a godly life is obtained through obedience to his commandments." Powell, *Introducing the New Testament*, 177–78.

frame that John uses to tell what adequate faith is. In Mark, there isn't any report of the faith response of this healed blind man. In other instances of healings, the healing effects have been instantaneous.[50]

Summary

In four of the six sign-events, there are adequate responses from the characters when some form of waiting was involved. In the first sign, the disciples did not know what would happen until the servant had gone for the water, poured and filled the six containers with water and served it to the headwaiter. The disciples had to wait till they heard the headwaiter proclaimed the drink was wine of superior quality. In the second sign-event, the royal official had to embark on the return journey and it appears to be almost a day time when he finally met up with his slaves to find out his son had recovered (4:52–53). In the fifth sign, the man born blind had to take a walk of faith, found his way to the Siloam pool, reached the water, washed off the mud before he regained his sight.

The key to adequate faith response involves a certain degree of waiting. The waiting allows the character time to reflect. The reflection entails pre-understanding, adequate data or knowledge of lived faith experiences of others and possibly of oneself, or for later reader, included adequate faith in John's stories. McDrury and Alterio posit that personal reflection is intuitive and it processes what Polanyi called "tacit knowledge." The "consequence of reflection is a changed conceptual viewpoint."[51] In John's sign-events, this reflection is a process of drawing on a personal remembered resource of understanding about God that shapes the faith of the person. There is no further "crush course" at that moment of decision-making. This understanding is built on the person's data bank of the faith stories (others and or the person's own lived faith experience), and interpreted them in light of the experience that she or he is facing. In the reflection, one reexamines her or his personal relationship with God, imagines possible outcomes, and allows the Spirit to baptize them into imitating the faithful, and finally, a decision and an act of faith. These cases of the sign-events, where God's supernatural interventions were experienced, showed how people's

---

50. The healing of Peter's mother-in-law was immediate and the report was brief without relationship to the faith of the healed person (Matt 8:14–15; Mark 1:30–31; 4:38–39). Mark was probably missing a point here.

51. McDrury and Alterio, *Learning Through Storytelling*, 20.

lives can be changed, or restored. Within this process of experiencing and telling (the character), hearing (audience-learner), the imagination-inspiration leads to imitation. The learners who read or hear these lived faith experience, in turn, imitate these characters.

In the third and fourth signs that do not produce adequate faith response, the miraculous events happened instantly for the audience. In these passive (on the part of the recipients, but not passive on the part of Jesus who acted out of compassion for the people) encounters, the recipients of the miraculous acts were lacking several elements. They were not perceptually or spiritually challenged. They lacked the spiritual perspective in the sense of relating their lives to the lived faith experience of the others, and the love of God that generated these divine acts. Furthermore, their interpretation frame for the event failed to see the significance of the act. They have simply lost (under the influence of the pervasive public opinion?) the vision of love that can help them see the act as one of compassion similarly repeating the mistake of the ancestor. Their interpretation of the act was, in a sense, literal and rigid. For example, the unbelieving recipients of the fish and bread were not relating the event to the event of God feeding the ancestors in the wilderness as an act of love. Their understanding was still shrouded in the miscarried entitlement perspective, as was the ancestor who misinterpreted God's love and murmured in the wilderness and suffered loses. Their failure to learn adequate faith is possibly due to a lack of reflection (the lame man), lack of the perception of God's love, which is largely due to a misguided reading of the past events, and unaware of an equivalent lived faith experience. The work of Jesus was thus misinterpreted, that there was no connection of the act to the work of God that could have been if they had the stories of faith from the past and a right frame of interpretation (God's love permeates his acts) as the reference Story to interact with the experience of the present.

In the sixth sign, the raising of Lazarus from death is the greatest of the six in terms of the magnitude of faith involved, and the time of waiting. The sisters of Lazarus repeated a verbal affirmation of the possibility with Jesus while recognizing that their brother had been dead for four days. The excruciating waiting had been most rewarding in this case: the amount of glory is greater, relative to the length of waiting. So should it be for the disciples as they waited for their teacher-friend Jesus who lied in the tomb? And so should it be for us as we wait for the coming of the Lord and his many promises? The arrangement of the characters' responses to Jesus in

Learning Faith in John's Gospel

John 2–12 points us to a faith response that can be adequate as we learn to see, believe, receive Jesus and his word, and wait and walk in faith. The author of John's Gospel further combined the showing with many literary devices to reinforce the telling to the audience.

The six sign-events are representatives of how to live life believing in Jesus. In the first, second, fifth and sixth sign, all these characters who exhibited adequate faith had experienced faith through a certain amount of waiting before they saw the outcome of their faith commitment. The characters in the third and fourth sign events who instantaneously received their healing or provision did not exhibit adequate faith response. In a chiastic arrangement, the two-sign events placed at the center show inadequate faith, while the remaining pairs shows an adequate faith response.

> The First Sign: waiting involved—adequate faith response
> The Second Sign: waiting involved—adequate faith response
>   The Third Sign: immediate help—no faith response
>   The Fourth Sign: immediate help—inadequate faith response
> The Fifth Sign: waiting involved—adequate faith response
> The Sixth Sign: waiting involved—adequate faith response

The signs in the Gospel of John exemplify what faith is: faith is more than rational acknowledgement. Faith is not a human invention—it is a divine gift, thus shown to us through the lives of those who honor God and His servants. Rational thinking asks for quantitative evidence to verify. Faith is not a quantifiable item. Learning to live in faith is acting based on our learning through the Story and the stories of others. On one can see all aspects of an event or life. None can know everything, nor wait till one knows everything in order to come to a decision and action. One learns, decides, and acts within a person's limitations. One does not wait for full knowledge or she will forever procrastinate. One acts in the "best" knowledge possible, but never fully, because knowledge can never come to a standstill. The knowing is constantly moving and changing as one experienced the ever-changing elements that surround us. However, it does not mean that learning such as memorization of Bible verses is redundant, or negates the necessity to study the background of the biblical books. Quite contrary to this, the events warn us not to be ignorant of the many faith stories and teaching in the Bible. One needs to have as many resources as are available, to draw on, and to interact with, in the moment of decision. It would be crucial to be able to remember them, to recall them. Thus, it is significant to be able to present the lived faith experiences and teach in a memorable manner, calling into use of the many literary devices as John did. Most of all, being finite, one must invite and allow the Spirit to consume one's being so that she may live and act with "adequate" faith in God's guidance given through his Word. That's closer to the reality in life.

Acting in faith is more than seeking instant solutions and gratification. A show of adequate faith involves living in suspense while one is committed to read, believe, and remember the word of Jesus. The six signs are not all that there are to tell about the person of Jesus and his work. As John explicitly stated, there are too many stories to tell (20:30). The selections in John's Gospel are specific and relevant to reveal who Jesus is. They teach how one should respond to an invitation to faith, and to build stronger members in God's Family as they learned to wait and live out faith—always in suspense—imitating Jesus, our eldest brother in the Family.

LEARNING FAITH FROM THE STORY OF JESUS

Most biblical scholars view John's Gospel in terms of Jesus' work and teaching with little or no attention to the life story of Jesus himself as the main character that shows us how to live out faith in God the Father.[52] John's Gospel shows faith to the reader through the person of Jesus and his intimate communion with the Father. If one considers the death and resurrection of Jesus as the overarching grand sign of the book that gives substance to all the other signs, then, this sign is indeed the most provocative show of what it means for those who believe in Jesus and whose living faith is in suspense. This grand sign involves, in terms of narrative time and order of events, the longest waiting in the narrative time of John. Built into part two of the book is a four chapter's length of waiting before the passion narration. That is a lengthy narrative time for the readers as they were held in suspense on the outcome of the one who claimed to have been sent by God, and hinted that he would die, but live again.

As early as in John 2:22, and again in John 3:14, suspense has been created by the anticipation of the cross-event.[53] Jesus' crucifixion is progressively revealed in John 6:70–71 when the betrayal of Judas is previewed to

---

52. For a typical reading of John's Gospel in terms of Jesus' work and teaching, cf. Dunn, "John's Gospel and the Oral Gospel Tradition," 166–85.

53. Labahn suggests that as early as in John 2:17 a hint of Jesus' death on the cross is dropped into the narration. Cf. Labahn, "Scripture Talks," 145.

the audience. A foreshadowing in John 7:32 further revealed the plan of the Pharisees to arrest Jesus. Jesus himself also added the urgency of the matter and hastened the narrative time when he said, "I will be with you a little while longer, and then I am going to him who sent me" (7:33). The plan to arrest Jesus escalated into the opponent's plan to kill him (8:37, 40). The plan to harm Jesus then became acts of violence as the opponent attempted to stone Jesus (8:59; 10:31).[54] The frequency of the opponent to arrest/stone/kill Jesus intensified in the narrative with another attempt to arrest him (10:39). The narrator's report of the plan to arrest and kill Jesus resumes and hastened in speed (11:49–53, 57).

The imminent arrest and death of Jesus in John 12 (vv. 1–11, 23–26, 32–33) is postponed with Jesus entering Jerusalem (12:12–19) and his final addresses to the public: the conversations with the public audience (12:20–30) and exhortation (12:34–50). All these temporal pauses created suspense as the readers waited. This is significant as the readers anticipated together with Jesus as he faced his imminent suffering: the shame of nakedness, the pain of crucifixion and physical abuse, the humiliation of being deserted, and the fearsome isolation in the darkness of death, which descended upon Jesus and his followers for three days.

All anticipation of Jesus' imminent death (and resurrection) is further delayed in narrative time as the didactic section (John 13:31b—17:26) serves as a slow-down in narrative. The author created a great pause with this lengthy farewell discourse. The farewell discourse once again projects the audience into an insider mode where Jesus' teaching is targeted at his true followers. Judah had gone out "immediately, and it was dark." (John 13:30b). "After Judah left" (John 13:31a), Jesus began a lengthy teaching to his inner circle of disciples. On the reader's level, they are taught and challenged by a telling of how to be a follower with adequate faith, living as honorable and fruitful members of God's Family. The presence of teaching an inner circle is worth consideration for planning the contemporary curriculum. It reminds us the need to make the curriculum suitable to members of different level of understanding and commitment to the faith.

The key teaching of the lengthy John 13–17 is to exhort the disciples to remain in Jesus. In a series of teaching on love and unity, Jesus groomed them to wait in the greatest suspense and taught them in this didactic

---

54. While the opponents recede into the background, and the sign event of healing the man born blind emerges in John 9. Similarly, the opponents again recede into the background for the sign event of resurrecting Lazarus in John 11.

telling. This is the moment that Jesus reminded his disciples to live by faith through remembering his word. John's readers are similarly reminded of the various discourses already told as series of teaching that follow the various sign events. Jesus emphasized the purpose of his telling, that when the hour comes, the followers will remember what he had taught them (John 16:4). Jesus encourages the readers who doubt his word to at least consider what they have seen in his deeds (the sign-events), so that they may know and understand that he is the one sent by God and truly with God (taught earlier in John 10:38). Jesus gives an additional help in promising the coming of the Paraclete who will remind (*hupomnēsei*, John 14:26) them what he has taught. They are to live in loving relationship, and to obey his command is living in his love, just as he obeys the Father (John 15:4, 9–12).

Craig Koester rightly points out that John's Gospel "presents Jesus as the way, using language that had wide currency, but it recasts this common imagery in a distinctive manner, applying it primarily to the person of Jesus . . . Jesus himself is the way; he not only offers teaching about a way . . . but reveals the way by embodying it."[55] John shows the readers that Jesus' faith is seen in his staunch commitment to do the will of the Father (John 5:19b, 36; 6:38, 57; 8:28–29) at all cost, even unto death (10:18). Jesus is able to remain in this faith because he knows the Father loves him (John 3:35; 5:20a; 10:14–15) and will resurrect him (John 5:21a) and will give him life (5:26). And the secret to sustain this kind of adequate faith that enables Jesus, and by implication, the readers, is to listen to the voice of the Father (5:37), and let his word remain (5:38). The more we hear the voice of God, remember the word and willing to obey out of love of God, the more we can plunge into the Way of life, while we recognize the reality of unknowable future events in life.

Jesus knew his future challenges more than any living being. In fact, the emplotment of John's narration shows and explains that the life of Jesus would be filled with challenges. Jesus is the example of living faith in suspense precisely magnified by the fact that he is courageous and never wavered in obeying and living out the will of the Father. He also taught his disciples how to live in obedience to the will of God. The ability to abide in the Father is grounded in a close relationship bound by love. Jesus explained to his disciples the dynamic of love and obedience in his Farewell Discourse (John 15:9–10). And he urged the disciples to live out this dynamic of love that will unify them and sustain them in the threat of unfair

---

55. Koester, "Jesus as the Way," 129.

persecution (15:11–25). This life of living in love results in unity among fellow members of the household (17:6–23). This unity will bring honor to the name of God's Family (17:1–5, 24), and they will become fruitful witness (15:27) of the way of life as people obedient to the will of God. John is the representative of the disciples to pass on the teaching and in this light the recognition of him as the Beloved Disciple and a reliable eyewitness become significant. He is the most appropriate storyteller with a valid claim to what he narrates. The community came to trust his story, imitated, and lived on in faith though there were challenges.

Summary

This faith in suspense is shown not only through the stories of the six signs; it is the message of the whole Gospel seen through the life of Jesus. The life story of an honorable Jesus is also a teaching in itself as the audience sees and experiences the person of Jesus, not his words of teaching alone. The Johannine Jesus is the living example of how to live out faith in suspense. It is a life informed by the possibilities to live and be held up by promises. The promises are from God and attested by the Story that includes the tradition, the Scripture, and the reflections from stories of the individuals—the community of faith.

Living faith in suspense is not living in ignorance. The example of Jesus as one whose life is utterly committed to doing God's will through full obedience is not a life lived in ignorance, but lived by faith while he awaited the life events unfolded one by one. The faith of Jesus in the Father as he awaited each challenge in life and his eventual suffering is a mirror for every generation, past, present, and future. It enables the readers to remain faithful to the Word and the Way in the face of imminent threat to life, instead of murmuring, blame, rejection, or apostasy. In a contemporary application of the pain and suffering, Jesus endured while he painfully anticipated them, Paul Louis Metzger points out that the hurt and pain in life is not something to wish away, but to live and handle them in a way that glorify God. Metzger mindfully concludes, "*I feel pain; therefore I am.*"[56]

---

56. Metzger, *John*, 241. Author's italics. From Jesus to John, there is also practical implication for church leadership. "John himself did not lead a charmed life—the exact opposite of some founding leaders of ministers . . . John was imprisoned in exile on the island of Patmos as an elderly man" for the testimony of Jesus (cf. Rev 1:9). Ibid., 266. John *felt* what Jesus felt.

Jesus is the exemplar par excellence of what it means to live in faith buoyed by a loving relationship with the Father.

Living and waiting in suspense without knowing the next event and outcome is congruent to the situation of the Johannine community. The early church lived in the midst of uncertainty about their future. Their religious position, social status, influence in the community, and ultimately in defining a way of life were in the balance as they lived each day and continued to inform one another through a core story. The core story of Jesus illustrated by these personal stories in the signs formed the core reference to their way of life—teaching them how to hang-on to faith in a loving God while they engaged and participated in these stories.

IMPLICATIONS FOR LEARNING THE BIBLE THROUGH NARRATIVE LEARNING

The Gospel of John teaches a way to live by faith in God through narrative. Its storytelling gives the learners six signs—six stories of characters who encountered Jesus—and related explanation as narrative learning content. These signs are told in relation to the main character—the Story of Jesus—to whom all these signs related. The learning process shows the audience what faith is and tells them how to live by faith. John's Gospel gives contemporary learners an example of what to acquire and expect in a biblical narrative learning on living by faith in the Word of God. Abiding in these narratives are three core tasks of education in the Gospel: showing, telling, and faith.

The Learning Content

The written form or every act of narrative is selective in its content. There were many complex interactions that took place at the same time: both visible and invisible. A witness of the event can only see the visible from his vantage point. He could possibly penetrate into the invisible from his perceived conception of the scene. This is one of the presentations that John's Gospel emphasizes when Jesus on several occasions is depicted as able to "see" the mind of individuals (Nathaniel, 1:47; the crowd, 2:25; 6:15). The point of view and limitation of the narrator and audience are active in determining the outcome of the narration and learning. The composition (what to include and what to exclude in the presence of other Gospels) and technique (literary finesse) in writing this Gospel further contribute to the success of John's Gospel as a major force in the continuity of the Story.

The written Gospel of John is an end product. From a writer of integrity, the written end product is handed on to the audience. It teaches a way of life espoused by not only how it interpreted the Hebrew Scripture and how it is presented in written form; it also contains the very personal experiences of the author and the others in this legacy—his personal contact with Jesus, and the many people who he interacted with in his life. In another word, the existence and continuity of John's Gospel is a complex matter.

The ideal way of living espoused in John's Gospel is also interpreted to receive acceptance within the religious tradition and capable of addressing the issues troubling the audience. It first of all points the reader to learn what faith is. The characters in the six signs show the audience two responses: adequate faith and inadequate faith. The ability to live by faith is first of all through an interpretive exercise of the ancient tradition that the community learned about life. Adequate faith is in conjunction with waiting in hope while the outlook is not clear that help from God is imminent, but help would definitely come. In Johannine signs, adequate faith is always related to a certain amount of waiting time. Those who wait would have no murmuring, or demand instant gratification as it was in the story of the Jews under the leadership of Moses while they were in the wilderness. The ability to endure in the face of challenge helps affirm an understanding of who Jesus truly is, and the purpose of his mission—to bring eternal life to all believers.

Jesus himself exemplifies the reality of living by faith in the Father, and shows the audience the real presence of eternal life. John's Jesus lived among them and interpreted through both their ancestors and contemporaries. It is a life committed to do God's will through full obedience. It is not a life without challenge. In fact, the life of Jesus is filled with challenges. He stays in his faithfulness to do the will of the Father because of the loving relationship between them.[57] Jesus emphatically taught the disciples to do the same: love God, love him, and love one another.[58] Johannine interpretation of the Third Commandment (Exod 20:6; Deut 5:10) drives at a more affective presentation than the Hebrew Scripture. In the OT, the first explicit mention of God's love for his chosen people is through the mouth of Abraham's servant

---

57. Some of the incidents where Jesus explained his loving relationship with God: John 3:35; 5:20; 10:17; 14:31.

58. On loving God, and one another: John 13:34–35; 14:21–24; 15:9–10, 17.

(Gen 19:16, 19; 24:27, 49). God's love for the people is not often affectively emphasized in the OT. Rather the order to obey God is often presented as a hard rule to the ears of the audience.[59] This less emotional appeal to obey was perhaps due to the cultural habit of the time that did not encourage emotive expression of feelings. But the relational factor is always present in the OT stories (Exod 34:6–7; Numbers 14:18–19), and taught as a way of life (Levites 19:18, 34).

By contrast, in John's Gospel, Jesus expressively elaborated God's passionate love for the all people (3:16; 16:27; 17:23–24, 26). Jesus also emphasized the extent of God's (and his) love for his people (8:42)—it's forever (13:1, echoing Jer 31:3 whose message was delivered at a time of distress), and it is the greatest love possible (15:13). Jesus' love for his people was also expressed in the sixth sign where his love is apparent to all, even those bystanders testified to his great love for friends (11:3, 5, 36). This great love was also taught in his teaching discourse (15:13). In contrast, human love is for own selfish gain or narrow scope of things in the world (12:25, 43). John personally testified his loving relationship with Jesus as the one designated as "the one loved by Jesus" (13:23; 19:26; 20:2; 21:7; 21:20). A reinterpretation of God's love for his people is one of the key themes that are woven into the narrative plot of John's Gospel. It espouses a life lived in love that will ensure lasting unity among fellow members of the household. This is a forceful reminder for every community of faith living according to the Way of the Word incarnated.

The final chapter of John's Gospel further addressed the way the story of faith is to be continued by succeeding generations and also aimed at the leadership of the Church. In its second conclusion (John 21) Peter was recognized as the leader of the church.[60] Bauckham points out that though in this concluding chapter in John's Gospel, the Beloved Disciple appears to hold a lower position than Peter in the church leadership, "BD's special role as a witness to Jesus . . . now becomes a role of witness to the whole church

---

59. For example in Deut 6:5; 7:7–9; 10:12–19; 11:1, the context to obey and even to love is due to a fear of God, told in contrast to the punishment laid on the Egyptians.

60. John's Gospel is careful to include a reconciliation of the Petrine community and Johannine community. For a suggestion of John 21 as an addendum to this effect, cf. Howard-Brook, *Becoming Children of God*, 475–81. Staley goes further in the argument and states, "when BD appears on the scene in the Farewell, Peter can get to Jesus only by talking to the one who reclines on Jesus breast (13:23–25). Similarly, at John 21:7 it is BD's recognition of Jesus ('It is the Lord') that motivates Peter's early morning plunge into the Sea of Galilee." Staley, "Postmodern Approach to the Fourth Gospel," 53.

Learning Faith in John's Gospel

as BD writes his testimony for the whole church to read (21:24)."[61] In John 21, the rhetoric is again set within the theme of love. If there was fraction between Peter's and John's communities, the three "love" questions are a reminder that whoever assumes leadership must act only on the basis of love for the faith community. On the part of the Beloved Disciple, the rhetoric of the final chapter is the Beloved Disciple's imitation and teaching of Jesus' love and unity principle—an echo of Jesus' teaching of love (John 15) and prayer of unity (John 17). Just as Jesus loves the Father and submits to the Father, so also the Beloved Disciple imitates in his submission to his fellow family member (Peter), and similarly, fellow Family members imitate the Beloved Disciple.

The Christian story is too rich and complex to tell all and to pass on. A life lived is not often a life narrated. Not every life story of Christian individual is passed on, though each is instructive for learning about the way of Christian living, and each in its own way is a learning experience for others, regardless of its breath and depth of living. We need to affirm that every life is instructive to someone—who has the opportunity to witness, or come to see and or hear, and learn about this life. Similarly, our task of teaching is more than the act of teaching in home, church, or the classroom. It also includes the showing of life of lived by faith. The survival of John's Gospel points to the existence of a major narrative text that is recognized by the community who share the ideology. At the same time, it enables recognition of many individuals who shared in living this ideal.

The Learning Process

It's always a challenge to learn and live out something as conceptual as faith is. Learning faith differs from merely learning a skill that can be taught in defined steps. It involves much more to be a person of faith in God. It is a non-quantifiable essential essence in life without which our lives will be impossible. Learning to live by faith is difficult to quantify. It is easier shown. Most of it are learned through observation and imitation. Testimony of lived faith experience is the most efficacious vehicle to pass on faith as it offers a learning moment that the audience catches and imitates.

---

61. Bauckham, "Audience of the Fourth Gospel," 111. Bauckham also sees the higher authority attributed to Peter. For more on the life of BD Thatcher gives six biographical details. Cf. Thatcher, "Legend," 97–99.

According to what has been seen in John's Gospel, the learning process involves experiencing or having an encounter with Jesus which entails hearing or seeing the story. In this faith encounter, the moment of waiting in suspense (for both the characters and audience) allows a process of reflection to take place. In this process of reflection, the character or audience interprets and imagines possible outcome as the Holy Spirit inspires the learner into taking mimetic act of faith. In John's Gospel, this learning process, the presence of literary devices in the learning content facilitated the learner's re-experiencing a lived faith experience. The many literary devices in John's Gospel aided in making the familiar story of Jesus fresh to the audience, that is, to make the familiar strange. Yet the mnemonic effect of these devices helps the audience to remember the strange by making them familiar and understandable in real life. John does this through the spatial movements, temporal effect, psychological presentation of the characters, and phraseological skills.[62]

The affective showing of the lived faith experiences is persuasive for the audience to imitate the characters in John's Gospel who were able to reflect and took on the challenge before them. For the case of the blind man (John 9), should the blind man submit and do what Jesus instructed him to, even if it sounded unnatural? The time required for the blind man's response and obedience to follow Jesus' instruction gives the blind man an opportunity to reflect on the stories he knew about God's love and deeds. His subsequent replies to the repeated questionings obviously reflect his adequate knowledge of God's love and deed for the people.[63] This event also reminds us of the necessity to possess a good knowledge for a biblical narrative learning to successfully imagine and allows the Holy Spirit to inspire the learner into imitating as an adequate faith response.

The further telling in John's Gospel explains to the audience how the disciples' personal encounters with Christ renewed their understanding of living in relation with God, which eventually led them to transformation. The first level of encounter occurs in the form of visual perception, some of which may have been misleading and insufficient when the learners view them with their old meaning perspective, such as Nathaniel (John 1:45–51),

---

62. Kasper Bro Larsen also points out the employment of non-linguistic signs in the showing by the performer. He states, "This mode of revealing the information . . . is in fact the only mode available in the iconic, nonverbal semiotics of figurative painting . . . true identity is merely communicable by means of *showing*." Larsen, *Recognizing the Stranger*, 49. Author's italics.

63. Cf. John 9:17, 25, 30–33, 35–38.

the Samaritan woman by the well (John 4), and in fact the same applies to all the disciples. The narrator explained in many occasions that they did not fully understand until they came to the ending of the story—saw the risen Lord. The resurrection event led to a crucial perception experience that led to transformation and empowered the community to continue in faith.

John's Gospel is not so much a refutation or critique of a stale tradition. It is a book about a refreshed approach to living adequate faith in God. While faith is an elusive matter that is hard to define by mere propositional instructions, the Johannine community learned from the characters that lived by faith or otherwise. Ultimately Jesus, the ultimate revealer, showed them how to live by faith through reconnecting them to God's love. The life depicted in John's Gospel is set in the backdrop of the political and religious challenges that enticed them to follow the world instead of the Way. The main character and supporting characters in it lived by faith that is powered by authentic loving relationship with God and with one another. We learn the "how to" of living by faith through their lived faith experiences. Their lived faith experiences invite us to live love according the revealed Way. Chapter 5 further explores how the movements of a biblical narrative learning help us to catch, and move us to faith.

Following the Way of Jesus demands that the Johannine community possess adequate *faith* in Jesus and his words. They are to adhere to a set of guides that differs from the conventional way of life. The Johannine faith community was taught to heed, hear, discern, recognize, believe and follow the Hard Way the hard way. Those who followed are given life eternal and taught to face and survive numerous challenges that befall them. They were shown and explained the way to live in the Way from the characters who portrayed following the Way by faith. Jesus further instructed them by telling them (especially John 13–17) how to live by faith as a community united by a loving relationship fashioned by the Father and the Son.

The Gospel of John is written to help the readers and listeners encounter Christ as the faith community of John did. In these encounters the old understanding and presentation of the relationship between God and his people are re-presented through the life of Jesus. "This is so important that the author is at pains to prove continuity. The old has now been superseded by Christ's revelation which, far from abandoning the past, catches it up and fulfils it at a higher level."[64] As the stories of the members of this

---

64. Loader. "Jesus and the Law," 151. Menken added, "If God reveals himself exclusively in Jesus, what value does the OT retain as revelation? . . . John evidently ascribes

new faith community were told, the listeners and readers again see Christ though the narration while without seeing him physically. Their meaning perspectives are given a new input and understanding. They made a transition in their decision-making that led to transformations that are visible to the community, whose transformations impact those who see, inquire, learn, and are drawn into the kingdom of God.

The readers learn when a reading is able to bring them back to the scene—the act of an animated reading of the text presented before us. It is an act to experience again the events narrated, and as much as possible, to realize the impact felt by the first experience, as of John, his community, and each time a new reading takes place. The interacting of strange and familiar creates the stimulus for the mind to reexamine the knowledge base and elicit rejection or imitation, modifying the meaning scheme of the learner.

A life or an experience itself is complex with many variables. The act of seeing the act again is a combination of multiple sensory and intellectual activities, resulting in a vast possibility of outcomes. The outcome of an encounter between the story and the audience is almost impossible to predict without a fuller understanding of the pre-understandings of the audience. In the act of reading the Bible, either reading alone or as a group where there is a teacher or leader guiding or explaining the text, their theological perspective or orientation, their present life situation, their location in the narration, and their language capacity are alive. The knowing and learning from a narrative is not limited to receiving instruction or even a set of wisdom teachings or stories. The complexity of reading, knowing, and learning often surrounded readers past and present.

A biblical narrative learning environment, where the presentation is as close as possible to the original event, best encourages learning among adult learners. Presentation of the life events have progressed from oral tradition to written document, the capturing of life through drawings on the wall to paintings on the canvas, to capture images on film and digital files, the re-enacting through dramas, from the black and white, then color movies, high definition videos, and now the pursuit of three-dimensional realistic representation. There is a progression in telling the original story in high fidelity. Though it is difficult to re-present all the senses (such as taste and smell) in a narrative, one can work to the best of ones' capacity to bring the past back to life—to make these stories worth re-seeing,

---

to the text of Scripture, to the words that have been written down," Menken, "Observations," 156.

re-experiencing and letting them teach us what it means to be a people and how to live as this people. Narrative learning is the process where the Story and stories are re-presented and seen in best clarity to inform our living. A biblical narrative learning is further accentuated by the priority it places on the centrality of the Bible Story as the anchor of interpretation to view life.

The biblical narrative requires the anchor from which people will examine their narration, reflect and learn about their lives, appreciate or find necessity to change the course of life, find content to teach others as they continue to live by faith in the face of normalcy or uncertainty. In each reading of the Gospel, the "new audience may apply to themselves the conclusions of the model reader."[65] Without the Gospel of John, we would struggle much more on what kind of faith, or how much faith is needed to receive an eternal life. But the Johannine audience would have known what is meant by adequate faith through the showing and telling of Jesus and his disciples. In the Gospel of John the act of following Jesus demonstrates the faith of the believers. Jesus' overarching story of faith shows what it means to follow the Father. He demonstrates the meaning of living in close relationship with the Father by his open proclamation when he deliberately says, "do this so that they will know" (John 11:42). He further demonstrates this by his obedience, even unto death. The apostle Peter also exemplifies his following as the Johannine preview of his following unto death (21:19). The characterization of Judas Iscariot and other such as Nicodemus exhibited what is not adequate faith. They came in the dark, walked into the dark. The stories give audience a mimetic choice: to walk in the light or into the darkness.

The Learning Goal

Storytelling is the process of using words constructed in a fashion to achieve the goal of the narration. The Gospel of John is a well-organized document and exhibits a high level of literary design that aims to re-present a gospel tradition that is familiar to the general audience that already has at least three other versions of Jesus story: namely the Gospel of Mark, Matthew, and Luke. In this process John differs from the Synoptic as he reinterpreted the message of God in Jesus through a reading of the Old Testament as lived experiences and re-presented his reading as a fresh embodiment of these OT teachings in the life story of Jesus. Jesus is the fullest revealing and

---

65. Labahn, "Scripture Talks," 153.

completion of God's self-revealing. In its finished form the Gospel becomes the authoritative witness of Jesus as the One sent by and from God.[66] The aim of John's Gospel as has been examined in the above study, is a pedagogical model that caters to three core tasks in John's teaching ministry: showing, telling, and adequate faith.

i. *Showing adequate faith through personal testimonies of our relationship with God in his community.* God sent Jesus to reveal in a showing of faith through incarnation. Jesus shows us what faith is through a *self-showing* (the Incarnation). This showing is animated as the story is read through physiognomic representations that stimulate our five senses. While Jesus (and John) reminded his followers to remember his verbal teaching, the sign-events are the most audio-visual emotional means of engaging the learners that enable learning and remembrance.

ii. *Teaching adequate faith through structured teaching in our curriculum.* Secondly, John's Gospel as a text is an authoritative telling of faith through Jesus' *self-saying* (the Logos). John has carefully and thoughtfully wrote the telling through semantic representation that creates various teaching effects through emplotment and various literary devices. The most significant teaching effect is probably the creative interchange of the familiar and the strange for the learner. Another strong teaching effect is the play of understanding and misunderstanding. Labahn points out that the use of Scripture in Johannine narrative is "an act of teaching on God's side and an act of hearing on people's side. The latter could be best understood as an act of understanding or *ad malum parte*, an act of misunderstanding."[67] These teaching-learning experiences create a strong impact on the learners' cognition as they hear or read the Bible.

iii. *Showing and telling in Johannine narrative arrive at building adequate faith as its audiences live lives from day to day and seek to glorify the Family Name.* Adequate faith is generated as one sees Jesus' *self-sacrifice* (the Endurance) and imitates his sacrificial love acted out in his endurance in suffering, both the physical and psychological pain. The imitation is a continuous act through the generations of a faith community. Staley points

---

66. Menken concludes, "To John, Jesus is legitimated as God's envoy by the Scriptures. Such legitimation is necessary, not only because the Johannine Christians have to defend their belief in Jesus against Jewish opponents who read the same Scriptures in a different way (see, e.g., 9:28–29), but also and primarily because to the evangelist, Jesus is essentially, and not just accidentally, the climax of God's involvement with Israel." Menken, "Observations," 173.

67. Labahn, "Scripture Talks," 149.

out that, "Throughout FG, no one comes to Jesus without the assistance of another person."[68] The notion of believers coming to believe through their live encounter with another is a constant patent in John's Gospel and is an insightful observation that enables us to rethink the role of personal testimonies as the bases of showing and telling adequate faith in the church's congregational education. These three core tasks of education in the Gospel will inform the narrative learning of the Bible as I shall attempt to integrate the contemporary narrative learning with a biblical emphasis.

CONCLUSION

From Teacher Jesus to Student John, the role of Student John shifted after the departure of the Teacher Jesus; Student John became Teacher John of the Johannine community. John was more than a teacher passing on facts and propositional statements. He "became a symbol for the Johannine Jesus tradition itself, embodying everything that Johannine storytellers judged to be most important about their craft."[69] John learned from the life experiences, undergoes a process of remembering, reflecting, interpreting, teaching and telling, and writing the story. At the same time, the life of John as a respected figure in his community is recognized as he lived with them and continually interacted with them. However, the writing has to come at a point in life where he decided what to include and when to stop further processing of his knowledge on the subject matter. Here, the implication for the narrative learning is the relevance of a narrator—any living person—as one examines life lived, reflects on it in light of the Story, and plans or acts on the next course of action.

Obedience to the Word begins with the recognition of the messenger. John recognized Jesus as the ultimate messenger. The message he proclaimed is from God. The generation after the passing of the earliest witnesses very much imitated the Disciples that "hear Jesus' voice (10:3–5), accept his teachings (12:23–26), are instructed in his secrets (15:15), and imitate his behavior (13:12–17)."[70] The teachers of the Bible in the church are similarly imitative messengers who interpret the message, though with limitations.

---

68. Staley, "Postmodern Approach to the Fourth Gospel," 54.
69. Thatcher, "Legend," 95.
70. Neyrey, *Gospel of John*, 7.

Biblical Narrative Learning

As earlier pointed out, the practices of narrative learning in Christian education have focused mainly on the storytelling and utilizing the stories of the church. There is insufficient effort given to the discovery of the stories. The lack of narrative inquiry as both gathering of witnesses and a learning experience for the researched and the researcher needs to be addressed. The lacking in written, and thus loss of, Christian life stories is another area that requires attention. Presently, most of the written stories are of significant people in faith. Though the great voices of stories showed us what is adequate and significant faith, the small stories of the ordinary people are equally important. The stories of the ordinary are closer to the lives and hearts of the ordinary while the successes of the pillars of faith can be intimidating for the ordinary who rarely envision themselves in the same league.

From many pulpits, the Christian stories are often dated and ossified. We need to hear the voices of the contemporaries instead of relying on some archaic stories. More importantly, one should pay more attention to presentation that makes a story alive. This is exactly how the Story of Jesus is re-presented in John's Gospel. In a biblical narrative learning, it is crucial to place both the Story and our stories on the same plate as we savor the taste of these stories. It is also pertinent that the stories, grand and minor, old and new, are timely and well-dressed when they are presented to the table. John presented the Story-stories in John's Gospel and offers his audience a comprehensive combination of both—the example of the main character and the follower-examples. The Jesus Story and the people's stories tell the Family's Story.

John was teaching his community how to continue a religious living within the OT and other contemporary writings (such as the Synoptic, the Pauline writings). The Church also seeks to continue the Story. Within the changing pedagogical context and other challenges, teachers tell the Story *and* the stories to teach us in what to follow and how to follow a way of life called Christian. There are many lived faith experiences around us worthy of telling, and capable of teaching one another. A suggestion for the Church is to make conscious effort and take steps to engage in a narrative learning that will bring in the voices of the ordinary people, anchored in the Story of the Lord and his church. Their stories will be the catalyst to animate the biblical teaching. The three fold model of showing, telling, and living faith in John's Gospel will inform the three movements of a biblical narrative learning. The next chapter will consolidate and offer a biblical narrative learning that integrates the contemporary narrative learning and biblical faith testimonies.

5

Practicing Biblical Narrative Learning

In a narrative learning process, the task of inquiry and storytelling coexist and rely on each other to be the learning content and educational process. Together, they lead us to a destination. In a biblical narrative learning, the aim is to acquire adequate faith in Christ and a way of living that embodies that faith. This chapter will offer a balanced track that fellow pilgrims travel on with a tour guide on a journey of faith to the eternal home.

The previous chapters have looked into the components and functions of narrative learning in contemporary research on narrative learning (chapter 1), and the context of John's Gospel for narrative learning (chapter 2). We have further identified John's Gospel as a sample of narrative learning in written form. The Gospel of John as a narrative learning-teaching reveals an emphasis on the creative use of tradition, context, and language to teach adequate faith (chapter 3 and 4). Using these findings on narrative learning, we come to a combination of the contemporary research and the Johannine sample on narrative learning in the Church that emphatically teaches adequate faith. Together, narrative learning and Johannine pedagogy formed a three-movement biblical narrative learning built on three sets of key components.

A biblical narrative learning is grounded in three sets of components that are identified in John's Gospel in light of the current research in narrative learning.

Practicing Biblical Narrative Learning

a. Components of narrative learning—the learner, the narrator and researcher who are also possible learners in the process of inquiry, and the existence of plot and characters.

b. The media of narrative presentation—include the literary devices in each language form that create physiognomic expressions for realism of the presentation, in either oral or written form. This includes the full use of literary skill to an optimum presentation and expression that is capable of a lively and realistic recreation of an experience or lived event. The use of media aims to stir the mind of the audience as real life is represented, and to foster remembrance.

c. The anchor Faith Story of Jesus and the faith stories of the individuals—here the learning process of referencing our stories to Jesus' Story is taken in the fashion of Groome's shared praxis.

These three sets of biblical narrative components undergird the process of biblical narrative learning. The three movements in biblical narrative learning are pairs of inter-related movements: inquire and invent, interpret and imagine-inspire, and imitate and impart. Each movement is a pair of intertwined elements from both the contemporary narrative learning and the educational practice identified in John's Gospel. The final movement also incorporates a possibility of imparting their learning that leads to the next cycle of the spiraling narrative learning—a new sharing of faith testimonies with different setting, plot, and character. Here is an overview of the three movements that will be further explicated in the coming pages.

1. Inquire and Invent (literally *a creative finding*)—This movement involves the act of narrative inquiry. This is the building up of the knowledge base that shows adequate faith. The movement encourages skillful use of literary devices in either oral or written form to create maximum showing and teaching. The element "showing" deals with how the life stories are presented and it goes hand-in-hand with the narrative telling process. In John's Gospel, the author has set the example of seeking out both the oral and written tradition plus his personal experiences of faith, putting them into a written document for lasting remembrance. The author of John's Gospel uses the literary devices to their best and to show and tell the characters' adequate faith which his audience may imitate. The Johannine narrative is especially useful for teaching abstract ideas such as faith. This inquire and invent movement is fundamental and accessible to a wide audience as biblical

narrative learning in the Church. This movement is most practical to the Church with its emphasis on the faith community to seek out and make available the faith stories for the community.

2. Interpret and Imagine-Inspire—Interpretation is the necessary and natural move in the process of narrative learning. As it is in John's Gospel and every subsequent generation, one learns faith by imitating the Faith of Jesus, and this imitation always undergoes a process of interpretation. This interpretation is treated variously as one chooses or subconsciously interprets under the influences of the "norm" in her or his interpretive community. This sensitivity to interpretation will be explored, emphasized, and applied when we teach faith in the Church setting. The act of interpretation and imagination is difficult to separate from one another as this movement prepares the learner for imitation. The acts of interpretation and imagine-inspire are often simultaneous and thus gathered here in the second set of biblical narrative learning. The intricate presence of the work of the Holy Spirit adds the element of "inspire" into the midst of human imagination. Again the complicated relationship within imagine-inspire is almost impossible to delineate: when and where a human imagination ends and the Spirit inspires will be beyond our observation.

3. Imitate and Impart—The act of imitation is key to a biblical narrative learning. The invitation to imitate is always suggested by the decision and way of life displayed by the character in a story. Furthermore, it would be a natural outgrowth of imitation for one to impart this transformation in faith leading to a new cycle of narrative telling and learning.[1] As we have seen in John's Gospel, faith is visible to others when one deliberately makes it visible through narrative showing and telling. Or, one may disguise or hide the act of inadequate faith when an imitation failed to occur. In the example of Nicodemus, his lack of adequate faith response is a sample of anti-imitation.

A successful and satisfied imitation will lead to ownership of adequate faith and confidence that further lead to impart. The purpose of re-telling is to continue educating and encouraging the community of faith to live and fulfill to greater extant the command to love one another as God loves. The

---

1. If the result of the imitation is not satisfactory, further quest or cessation of quest in the same plane occurs. This research is an example of one initiated by a sense of lacking in something, a desire to improve the present state or condition.

Practicing Biblical Narrative Learning

process of impartation may take on the form of sharing or teaching faith in either oral, written or other media. In the process of teaching adequate faith, the impartation depends on the production of a written script or text. The written form is the most accessible medium to the Church, and a stable medium can be easily transferred into other media and supports multiple narrative formats. Here, imitation is beyond the way of learning and living adequate faith; it is also applicable to usage of the languages in showing and telling faith.

The following sections will discuss each of these movements from the reading of John's Gospel and research in narrative learning. As John took the effort to write down his lived faith experiences addressing the issues in his time, the Church is also in need of the re-presentation of faith in real life. Thus, the first movement is a concerted effort of the Church to inquire, in a creative manner, and collect the accounts of her members' lived faith experiences. This process will be informed by research in narrative inquiry. The collected stories of faith will give the church a relevant resource as the Story of God's love continues to be interpreted.

As John drew on the tradition he lived in to interpret both the past and the present, the church shall similarly utilize the contemporary research in biblical interpretation within the framework of narrative learning. In the second movement of biblical narrative learning, the move to a relational approach to the interpretation of our lived faith experiences and the reading of the Bible is helpful to make the ancient message relevant and yet not an unrestrained interpretation dictated sometimes by tendency of human experiences to err in its carnal biases.

John learned intuitively as a human, and instinctively every individual has the capacity to do the same. Thus, the third move requires the church intuitive imitation in biblical narrative learning that is reflective in nature. This allows the Spirit to play its role as the learner surrendered more fully to the Spirit animated moments in life. And finally, as John used the conventional resources in literary devices to present a teachable and memorable lived faith experience, the teachers of the Bible should be attentive to the language(s) available at their disposal and augment their mastery of the language(s) to impart their new lived-faith-experiences, with the view to make these stories available to wider audiences. The end result envisioned is the spiral increment in telling of lived faith experiences in the church setting that provides a growing learning resource that is sensitive to its unique position and tradition, encourage and assist in the reading of the Bible that speaks to the reality of the daily challenges in life.

THE COMPONENTS OF BIBLICAL NARRATIVE LEARNING

In the previous chapters, we have identified three sets of interlocking components in a biblical narrative and contemporary narrative learning. This section will briefly summarize and connect these components. This will set the foundation of a biblical narrative learning process in the Church.

Components of Narrative Learning

There are eight components of narrative learning: setting, character, plot, causality, style, point of view, narrative presence, and hermeneutic and proairectic codes. However on a simpler scale, the first three components are what most un-sophisticated storytellers follow and give attention to. In the setting of a church gathering, where the person gives an impromptu testimony, the teller may not always be thinking in these frames. This is the intention of this paper that the testimonies are given better shape through paying more attention to the elements involved. And it is helpful for the congregation to learn the basic, eventually acquire better skill and presentation of their faith testimonies. This would in turn create more teachable moment as the narrator produces testimony that incorporates full components of a quality narrative.

The Media of Presentation

The one component that influences the effectiveness of telling lived faith experience in a narrative learning is the media of presentation. For practical reasons such as accessibility in the church that has limited resources, I have chosen the oral and written form as the main media for presentation, making the narrative more accessible and transportable. The chosen media are the basic platforms for other forms of media such as drama. They are adequate in presenting a clear and affective testimony that interacts with the audience or reader. The effect of the text to convey a persuasive message is at its best when, as in John's Gospel, the many literary devices recreate a most realistic re-presentation of the life story of Jesus and the followers. John's "enfleshment" of the characters through linguistic art elicits the human senses to see and "feel" the events in a lively form that reminds the reader of what is real and *flesh*.

The creative effect of the narrative is enhanced with the use of familiar-strange in the testimony telling. This effect of familiar-strange can be created through the use of linguistic devices such as double entendre, or making the scene fresh with lively description. John's Gospel offers many examples of the skillful usage of literary devices to this effect. The familiar-strange in telling can also be imparted through masterful design of plot in testimony telling. The creation of familiar-strange in testimonies telling provokes the mind through creation of dis-equilibrium that upsets normal expectation and causes rethinking of one's meaning scheme. A good combination of literary devices and plot will draw the audience's attention and at the same time create a lasting memory that helps to continue the teaching even after the teacher has left the podium.

The Anchor Faith Story and Our Faith Stories

A biblical narrative learning aims to build adequate faith in the learner through a process of hearing and telling life stories, and engaging the fullness of human senses. It is a process of education that is based on method we have identified in the Gospel of John and within its context. It aims at teaching the audience to live a life of faith in God. The learning of this faith is through imitating the biblical characters, first and foremost imitating Jesus the exemplar of living his faith in the Father. Secondly, imitating those who responded positively, or de-imitate those who responded negatively to the call of Jesus narrated in Gospel. Thirdly, the call to imitate goes out to the audience to imitate fellow believers, past and present. In this constant hearing-sharing of faith stories, believers grow in practicing adequate faith and work together to bring honor into the Family. In this process, they accumulate and enlarge the faith stories, and many others can hear, consider, and imitate their faith. They continue and expand the spiral of adequate faith that originated from the Faith Story of Jesus.

Reading the Bible as a source of faith learning is an act of constantly going back to the anchor of this faith in God. It is an act grounded in the trustworthiness of the Bible as the key to the past, with a lesson not only worthy of our mimesis, but also as the anchor that defines our direction to the future. The long criticized dull reading of an ancient text in the community can be remedied when they more actively bridge the Story with the stories. This approach also affirms the voices of the individual Christian, in sync with the faith stories of their local fellow believers and the tradition they share. It also seeks to take a deeper look and greater appreciation of their contribution to the understanding of the biblical faith in a changing world as we learn more about other perspectives of living faith. Thus this approach is both a rediscovery of the Christian faith and at the same time propelling them forward as they face new challenges in the eventual encounter of their belief and the beliefs of people from all over the world.

THREE MOVEMENTS OF BIBLICAL NARRATIVE LEARNING

There are many possibilities in the process of biblical narrative learning. I have identified three movements. Each of the three movements can occur as an independent unit by itself and/or interact with other movement(s).[2] For example, a narrative learning moment can take place at the time of the subject telling or writing her or his life experience. At the same time, learning can also take place for the audience hearing or reading the testimony. This is the fluidity of narrative learning. Cortazzi and Lin pointed out the way story works in a learning experience, "The telling of personal experience and other narratives involves *memory* and *imagination* in the recall of what happened and, at deeper levels, the *evaluation* of what happened (why it is interesting, important or meaningful) and *a point of view, voice* or *identity* of the teller (whether the teller directly represented in the story or indirectly represented in the style of telling it)."[3] Within this time space, the interpretation and appropriating can occur depending on the imagination-inspiration state of the participant.

The movements of biblical narrative learning informed by the contemporary narrative research entail fluidity. However, it is not without a clear focus or meaning. It is a process of telling lived faith experiences anchored

---

2. Goodson and Gill see the five stages in a spiral process of narrative learning as consisting of narration, collaboration, location, theorization/meaning making, and direction. The five stages in this case is similar to what I'm proposing but lacking in how should we confirm and preserve the memory, providing inspiration for future generation. Cf. Goodson and Gill, *Narrative Pedagogy*, 102, 118–21, 125–30.

3. Cortazzi and Lin, "Narrative Learning," 651–52. Authors' emphasis.

Practicing Biblical Narrative Learning

in the Faith Story of Jesus. For a biblical narrative learning process that is firmly rooted in the story of God and the stories of his people, the act of finding the stories is crucial and contributing to the educational process of reading the Bible. It represents the contemporary reiteration of faith in God, and forms a knowledge base that is reliable and learners can draw on as real life models of imitation. These faith testimonies also give voices to the faith community and its practice.

The process of a narrative inquiry could produce new telling when a new learner is capable and comfortable to share the new experience as a continuity of the faith Story. The retelling of a new story is more likely with encouragement from the community or the teacher. The interaction of the individuals and community also played to shape the interpretive process and reflected in the lived faith experiences. This does not mean that we are encouraging uniformity or seek control over the reading of the Bible, though some form of control is always in place to prevent deviation from the Story.

The first movement, finding the faith testimonies, will receive more attention. This is the foundation movement on which successive movements develop from. This is also the most obvious initial focus for the church and it requires less academic training to make it accessible to a general audience. Much as the Gospel of John is made educative and accessible to a wide audience of various levels of education sophistication, the biblical narrative learning aims to be user-friendly with minimal instruction. Thus, this is immediately functional in the church. At the same time, the Gospel of John is also one of the New Testament books that require elaborated commentaries.[4] Biblical narrative learning can similarly be a process that requires substantial investment of time and learning.

Practicing these movements involves what Groome practices in *shared praxis*. Where I differ from Groome is my emphatic attention on the person in narrative learning. I place greater emphasis on the role of the narrator and audience on top of the interaction of the Story-stories/Vision-vision in Groome's model. This attention is informed by the research in narrative inquiry and narrative learning. Whereas in Groome's *shared praxis*, and similarly Wimberly's, the focus is more on using the stories as a platform for engaging the Story, in my proposal of biblical narrative learning, I see a

---

4. A quick survey of the many multi-volumes commentaries on the Gospel of John by Brown, Schnackenburg, Keener, and von Wahlde sufficiently proves the possibilities of in-depth studies in this Gospel.

need for dedicated attention to the built-up of a knowledge base from the contemporary faith stories. Not only does this bank of faith narratives give the learner ownership of the faith Story through their contributions, but also, it is a source of learning closest to the learning community. It is easier for the learners to understand as they share the same or similar context, and it gains acceptance of the learners.

Learning can take place at any one of the three movements, and at varied settings and time. A spontaneous learning is possible for both the one sharing the testimony and the researcher or audience. A possible improvement on the Church's present practice of sharing testimony is having a trained teacher in the midst to hear the testimony in its entirety. That is, the teacher will be able to help identify the plot of the testimony, interpret the message, and appropriate the testimony in light of the Jesus Story. The audience's participation in the story with the teacher, and the one sharing may have a moment of reflection, and share or respond to the testimony. The reflection and sharing will be an act of reaffirmation, imitation, and impartation. However, for the teacher to be able to practice these principals, it will take time to cultivate this culture of learning. The Church will need to train the teachers, and most appropriately, through narrative learning. It will be a tedious and ongoing long process of reflection and reshaping the education leadership through stories. Courses at seminary level and also in local churches will be helpful to this effect.

A narrative learning event is never completed in a classroom setting or by the mere process of completing an assignment entailed in a curriculum. Learning and engaging the learner is extended into the future. Thus, the ability to create remembrance is an important part of biblical narrative learning. This is useful especially for biblical narrative learning as the Story and stories may be recalled at any time. Decision and course of action in real life is not always something that one can pause to research and retrieve. Thus an emphasis of biblical narrative learning is on the creation of remembrance. And as a result, in a performance of storytelling it is important to consider the skillful use of physiognomic presentations that create vivid and strong image(s) that can instill lasting memory in the audience.

The process of teaching in John's writing exemplifies skillful use of many literary devices that fully express realism of the stories and engage the audience's full senses of understanding. The process of writing the life stories involves the remembrance of the lived experiences. It further requires the author's selection and interpretation of these experiences and putting them down into organized structure. The written form can be read to various settings and groups. A lived faith testimony is at its best when performed to fully engage the audience and foster remembrance. The stories remembered continue to be a source of imagination for the audience who seek to own adequate faith and make the best decision in life while they face their daily challenges. Living this faith becomes new lived faith experiences that are prime for continuation of the faith Story. A continual spiral of faith stories, anchored in the Story, unfolds as each learner become teacher through her or his lived faith experiences.

There are lessons that are better caught than taught. There are messages best presented through stories than propositional statement. There is always a suitable place for a suitable story in ministry. The role of a researcher may be akin to a physician with a syringe and needle that reaches beyond the skin to draw out the elements, analyze, prepare the report, and present the report to both the clients and the people who will learn from it. The syringe and needle analogy implies that the process may cause pain to some people, but the researcher would offer at the same time the bandage to help heal the cut of the incision, while recognizing the real power of healing is the body itself.[5]

Inquire and Invent

First, on the term "invent." By invention, it refers to the act of finding testimonies. It follows the tradition of ancient Greek literary devices, *inventio* (literally *"finding"*). It is "the first of five parts of an orator that focuses on finding and elaborating arguments and whether the argument should be epideictic, deliberative, or juridical."[6] More specifically applicable to telling lived faith testimonies, the function of *inventio* is to list "a series of topic, with examples, that could suggest things to be said in the exposition of a subject and in support of an argument."[7] The practice of *inventio* has not been, nor meant to be, rigid.[8] The use of *inventio* here is an opening to possibilities in arrangement of topics and themes that would help in the

---

5. Cf. McAdams, *Stories*, 252. Also, Stephen Tyler pointed out that ethnography is potentially therapeutic. Cf. Lawless, *Holy Women, Wholly Women*, 58–59.

6. Aune, *Westminster Dictionary*, 234.

7. Kennedy, *Invention and Method*, xiii.

8. A study on Greek usage of *inventio* centuries later reveals that there were radical differences from the early day of using it, and created new usage. Ibid., xvii.

remembrance and teaching faith through a wide ranging faith narratives. Here, *inventio* is the attention to the finding and categorizing of faith stories from the congregations.

Practicing biblical narrative learning in the church first of all involves narrative inquiry. Here, narrative inquiry is seen as a process of finding and recognizing faith stories. Storytelling has been part and parcel of human progression and their civilization. People are stories, and stories give meaning to the existence and way of life. Stories are lived and told, continually providing guidance for our being. These stories are more powerful in forming the development of individuals and their community than most people consciously acknowledged.

The selection and use of lived faith testimonies have often been seen as chance-happenings in the life of many. We assume that people know what has been heard and remembered through a rather random process in daily lives. Most people come to know some stories through their parents and family members, teachers and peers, colleagues and partners, associates and other social contacts. They may also absorb the meaning-making values of many stories through various media: oral telling, books, audio-visual, and the internet. The overflowing media have made these stories more available and to more people at various places in the world, reaching people in places, even where the culture and social setting may not be compatible to receive the influences of these narratives.

The possibility of learning is wide and at the same time uncertain in the contemporary sea of stories. Theoretically, the chance of learning some stories from different people increases with the widespread of information technology. On the web "small" stories are now more readily available to audience previously unreachable. However, with the increasing numbers of stories, the chances of the voices getting noticed do not necessarily increase. In fact, they may become lost in a sea of stories. Or the user of the stories simply is lost at what is needed and how to locate one when a story is needed for mimesis. The stories of biblical narrative learning is sought to help us organize and make sense of the many imitative possibilities out there. The deliberated search for the appropriate lived faith testimonies is necessary in order to find and identify the voices. This helps to reduce the probability of narratives being ignored or lost in the sea of stories and to help user appropriates the suitable narratives. The search involves the people who have learned and lived faith—both the teacher and the learner.

Challenges in Narrative Telling

The difficulties in researching lived faith testimonies can be caused by one or more of these reasons. The lack of adequate faith on the part of the congregation, the lack of guidance from the leadership which often translates into lack of example or learning model, the lack of skill in articulating their faith experiences, the lack of encouragement from the church leadership, and the failure to provide a safe environment for the members to share their stories. The last one is particularly damaging for some who shared and found themselves victim of back slashing or ill critique toward their testimonies. There are also realistic practical reasons that prohibited sharing of more life experiences in the Church. These included the inadequate education, limited language power, the lack of understanding in narrative components, and cultural factors.

Elana Michelson points out, "not every student succeeds in creating this narrative of self. . . . Some students cannot or choose not to create these narratives because they simply can't find themselves in the plot."[9] Polkinghorne also points out "Narrative studies of lives do not always produce descriptions of functioning emplotted stories that can serve as interpretive scaffolding for subjects' lives."[10] This is possibly due to "a person's prenarrative experiences [that] may be so fragmented and disjointed that no plot can authentically join them together and the life telling does not coalesce into an emplotted story."[11] An untrained individual's failure to see a narrative within the structure of a plot would result in difficulties in meaningful self-narrative.

People do not always realize that they have a story worth telling. Furthermore, given the chance to tell their story, many would not know how to start. Van Schalkwyk confirmed this problem and highlighted some of the issues in narrative inquiry. In her collecting of life stories and analyzing the content of self-defining memories, obstacles to narrative inquiry include,

a. Difficulties some clients have with life story remembering either due to time or emotional reasons. They either failed to remember or not able to organize life events in a chronological or thematic way.

b. For some of the interviewees "it is anomalous to the spirit of the dialectic self and the intrinsic relational focus of their culture." She

---

9. Michelson, "Autobiography and Selfhood," 15.
10. Polkinghorne, "Narrative Knowing and Study of Lives," 96.
11. Ibid.

cites example of adolescents' inability to talk about their life either in conversation or writing. This presents some difficulties on the interviewees as talking about oneself "is inconsistent with the cognitive processes that preclude such self-descriptions."[12]

c. Others "lack the discursive modes of expression and have difficulty expressing themselves in self-expression and seeing themselves in light of the surrounding world."[13]

The lacking in understanding the structure and component of a narrative in effect produces stories or testimonies that could lack a clear focus, without plot, poor characterization, and leave the audience unaffected by the storytelling. The ill effect of an un-composed random testimony can be educative, but the result would be left to chance. Therefore, to promote narrative learning, the storyteller or Christian giving a testimony would be more effective in producing a learning moment when he or she is trained in utilizing the components of narrative. The benefit would be on both the narrative learning of the storyteller and the audience in the process of narrative learning, as they hear a better presentation of a lived faith testimony.

The difficulty in telling our testimonies is also partially due to Christian's emphasis on humility that downplays the importance of self. Whenever there is implication of aggrandizing the self, a sharing could be frowned upon. An indirect effect of this opinion of oneself is the personal refrain to tell significant achievements in life, less one is seen to be bragging and glorifying the self. This obstacle to sharing testimony needs to be informed by a different view—being able to see the sharing not as self-serving but to glorify God and His Family.

The Christian culture of humility would see even fewer people wanting to write a biography. Writing is often reserved for the rich and powerful, or someone who lived an extra-ordinary life. Thus, it is important that we 1) initiate the search for faith testimonies, 2) through this inquiry contribute and teach to liberate the unconsciously suppressed voices, 3) introduce the biblical anchor into the stories to avoid a loss of adequate faith in God. On a similar note, even with the purportedly wide availability of information, Bible study is still more accessible to the "afford-able" groups with financial and academic privilege.

---

12. Van Schalkwyk, "Collage Life Story," 676.
13. Ibid.

Practicing Biblical Narrative Learning

One other obstacle in sharing personal testimony is probably the need for one to admit one's own weakness and failure in these sharing. The confession of one's weakness could have implication of one's integrity when there are past life events that reveal sinfulness, immorality, or painful hurt. This obstacle could see some relief when a safe sharing environment is in place and trust is established among the members.

In order for the practice to gain acceptance, the whole idea of narrative learning through Christian faith testimonies needs to be affirmed as a valid form of learning experience. There are several factors to this recognition. First of all, the Christian community would benefit from an affirmation of their biblical reading through recognition of their unique situations. Secondly, the church needs educational leadership to establish themselves as people of integrity. A story's authenticity is inevitably tied to the narrator's integrity. A story or testimony that is determined authentic favors its reception by the audience. This is very similar to the role of John the Author in the Gospel of John. He had been received by his community and further endorsed by subsequent faith communities as a person of good standing. The endowment of "Beloved Disciple" on the author is crucial as he wrote a Gospel that is radically different from the three previous versions of the Synoptic. The audiences do not always possess the necessary tools to sufficiently investigate and differentiate truth claims, establishment of integrity is crucial as they rely often on the narrator for their reception of the witnessing. Thus, the person giving the testimony and the teacher or the community that endorse the testimony, together, they count as a reliable witness.

To build up the relationship of trust, interviewing and writing life story in a closely knitted global community, there are issues to consider in terms of their consent to the interview. First of all, any story told has the potential of bringing out some aspects of a family member, or friend, church member, organization, or other community that may not be well received. Elaine Lawless realized that when the interviewee is easily recognizable due to her or his position, it is not hard for others to guess who the story is about, even when the real name is not used.[14] However, in the case of lived faith testimonies, anonymity should not be a major issue. In telling lived faith testimonies, the authenticity of the testimony rests on

---

14. Elaine Lawless was against the use of photograph, as it would be too revealing for her interviewees who were too easily identifiable by the reader. Cf. Lawless, *Holy Women, Wholly Women*, 283–84.

the real existence of the storyteller. However, there is a possibility that the interviewees can be very too generous, eager to please the interviewer they know and respect, and ignorant of the impact they may have on the lives and feelings of their family members.

The lack of adequate faith is a conundrum in the whole process of learning adequate faith; the lack of adequate faith is a direct result of lack of sharing-learning experiences. But it does not point to a lack of learning from a life changing Christian faith testimony in the church, more likely, the learning was not conscious or structured. The testimonies are out there waiting to be found. Therefore, to begin the process of generating testimonies that produce fruitful educative biblical narrative learning, the first movement is to initiate and find these stories.

Practicing Testimonies Sharing as Telling Lived Faith Experiences

The practice of sharing testimonies, though, is an accepted form of encouraging one another in living the Christian faith; it needs more encouragement and educated moves to accomplish greater educational result. The testimonies share in the church are often short and involve one single event or life experience. The testimony telling does not always have a well-defined goal, nor certain of how they are expected to "teach." The educative power of narrative learning in these testimonies often goes un-noticed for both the storyteller and the audience. Furthermore, while often the local churches lamented the decrease in people willing to share their faith testimonies. The reasons for the decline are not always identified and resolved.

Where Would the Inquiry Take Place?

The process of data collection could begin with the historical archives that are available. The archives include collection of historical documents in the archives centers and seminary libraries, articles and photographs from various commemorative publications, online web pages and blogs, historical resources of the church's official paper, published autobiographies and personal testimonies. There are also many commemorative or anniversary issues in the churches. These issues preserve our stories as a community of faith. The testimonies in these published church documents have revealed stories of faith and how this faith was learned. The information and stories collected could be useful to either use on their own or as supplements to stories, to validate the time and places, and to point them to events that they may be able to recall.

Storytelling can take place in any setting—in a classroom, church, home, at a restaurant, park, or on the sidewalk. They can occur at any hour and are not restricted by classroom schedule or church's timetable. Yet storytelling can also be used in a structured way in various classroom teaching, church worship and preaching, small group or fellowship gathering. Last but not least, it is useful at funeral services. What matters for the sharing is a setting that encourages the self-revealing disclosure of lived faith experiences. Faith experiences often entail encounter or recognition of one's weakness and thus a need for a superior assistance. This admission is often seen as sign of personal weakness and inferiority that the community in general frowns upon.

While some people are more reserved in speaking out about their personal life event, this reservation can be loosened in a learning sphere where there is mutual respect for the disclosure of personal matters. An authentic narration is dependent on the following factors: integrity of the storyteller, the relationship between the narrator and the audience, and the involvement of the tour-guide-teacher. The practice of sharing their personal testimonies in the church setting has in recent years dwindled. In the last few decades many churches have adopted the small group platform to educate their members. This has facilitated more frequent sharing of their walk with Jesus in their daily lives. Elizabeth Caldwell rightly points out that in a setting of a large crowd, adults often "remain strangers to one another and the teacher"[15] throughout the meetings. The necessity of an open, safe and friendly space is crucial for believers to share their personal life stories. Robert T. O'Gorman highlighted for the need for a safe environment for self-revealing-sharing in the small group, "The educational heart of the small group process is storytelling."[16] He also points out the effect of sharing in a small group setting, "In these grassroots communities, relationships are directed with a shared deep communion, mutual assistance, commonality of ideals, and equality among members."[17] When this safe space is established, we can expect more people encouraged to genuine, intimate and relevant sharing from the participants in the small group.

---

15. Caldwell, "Homemaking," 79.
16. O'Gorman, "Faith Community," 45.
17. Ibid., 47.

In a bible study group, meeting usually starts with Scripture. The making sense moment during the meeting happens "through deliberating on the peers' experience, comparing and contrasting these experiences with the sacred text."[18] The end result is the "emotional bonds and sense of transcendence that develops over an extended period in a primary group."[19] In sum, the sharing of testimonies is creative and generative, creating "a movement of the people from lay passivity to activity, established links between religion and life, and demonstrated the difference between just fulfilling obligations and being faithful, accepted, and responsible members of their communities"[20] Besides the testimony sharing in the small groups, there are other possible venues. It can take place in the Sunday worship, though it often takes a more significant testimony to be called onto a big stage. Outside the church, family, club, society, interest group, school class, or peers may also initiate sharing.

The movement between personal stories and the community the teller resides in is not controllable, nor should there be any attempt to control the freedom of this interaction, and the mutual interactive and collaboration in shaping the epistemological base of the community, and thus the individuals. It is both creativity as well as conformity, but the conformity should come as a result of maximum free negotiation within the community, "for accepting the tradition and for breaking away from it."[21]

How Would the Testimony Be Presented?

Storytelling also incorporates judgment of the storyteller who must decide how the story is formed and told, what to include and what to leave out, what is relevant and what is not. Stories often try to present some specifics, but not necessary the exact replication of a lived event. It is selective to achieve its purpose of telling. In this way, "narratives do not lie idle: they invite, indeed demand, a response from their listeners."[22] The narrative invites retelling, partly through its own merits and partly because it can be used by listeners to communicate and explain their own quandaries and interests to

---

18. Ibid., 48–49.
19. Ibid.
20. Ibid., 53.
21. Mahoney and Yngvesson quoted in Maynes et al., *Telling Stories*, 25.
22. Brophy, *Narrative-Based Practice*, 34.

others.[23] The practice of hearing, reinterpreting, learning and retelling the narrative is familiar, or, at least tacitly, to all learners.

McAdams was right to point out that during the interview, both "the listener and the storyteller should furthermore pay careful attention to the kind of language employed in this opening section, as a clue to personally meaningful images, symbols, and metaphors."[24] In a community that speaks several languages and dialects, the life story interview would be conducted in the language with which the storyteller is most comfortable. After the interview was done, transcribing the dialects into written Mandarin may be more challenging. Therefore, sensitivity to the language and the eventual outcome of the written text would be necessary. It would be ideal if certain terms spoken in dialects could be clarified during the interview and helpful in writing better text as well. It would also be an interesting exercise when the time comes to actually putting spoken words onto paper. A term in a dialect might become a metaphor in itself. Also some terms or phrases that are picked up from the interviewees can be valuable expressions and add strength to the narration.

Who Are Involved in Telling the Testimony?

In telling testimonies of lived faith experiences, there are basic conditions to consider. Who would initiate the testimony telling? Who are the inquirers? Do they have to be scholars? Cultural experts? Local or outside researcher? Who get to tell the testimony? Where would this take place? How would the testimony be presented? What is the aim? When it comes to limitation of resources to conduct narrative research interview, there is the matter of priority to consider. Benham reminds that in narrative inquiry, who get to tell the story and retell, how, for whom, and for what purpose raises the thorny issue of authorial privilege and rights.[25] Telling of faith testimonies takes place in two major settings: in a church-related gathering such as fellowship or small group meetings, and interviews that often leads to a written presentation. The collection of Christian life testimonies can be published and distributed to the members. The fellowship committees or group leaders can organize and plan faith-testimony sharing events. They

---

23. Ibid., 42.
24. McAdams, *Stories*, 257.
25. Benham, "Culturally Relevant Story Making," 513.

may also decide the theme of the faith-testimony sharing, and the people who does the interview.

In the process of finding and sharing the Christian faith testimonies, the teacher is akin to a tour explorer. The concept of the teacher as the guide for the journey is borrowed here from Seymour's insightful image of teacher and learner as co-travelers on a mutual journey.[26] Jerry H. Stone interpreted Seymour's view further and suggests that the travelers are the characters in a narrative. In this journey, the plot unfolds as we share our own story with one another along the pilgrimage road, encourage and remind one another our origins, our position, and our destination. "The teacher cannot provide us with the full fruits of the destination . . . if the fruits of the destination were brought to us then we would not need to travel to them."[27] In this journey, the teacher knows the way because he or she has either learned the way or see the journey ahead. The role of the teacher is to initiate, induct, encourage, teach the story in the sense that it helps others to see and interpret the story, write the story, and promote the story.

The researcher should have a passion in, and respect for, the stories which are their greatest asset in this research. It would require the researcher to be genuinely motivated to hear the stories and to turn these stories into useful narratives for teaching. This attitude would be helpful in guiding the interviewees to share more openly and overcome some of the inhibitions found in them.

The position of the researcher as better educated in the perception of the ordinary people may inhibit their free sharing if they compare and see themselves as less knowledgeable. This might lead some to think that they have nothing worthwhile to contribute and refuse to be interviewed, or not telling some of their life story which they perceive as insignificant. Secondly, the people might tell what they think the researchers want to hear. It is possible that they might leave out some of their "non-Christian" life story. The gentle prodding given at suitable time would alleviate this possible initial difficulty as we recognize the act of telling itself is an act of empowering. Crain and Seymour pointed out that the "very act of hearing gave authority to people's words."[28] The questions asked by the interviewer shape the stories people will tell and therefore become an avenue to their

---

26. Cf. Seymour and Miller, *Contemporary Approaches*, 131–32.
27. Stone, "Narrative Theology," 285.
28. Crain and Seymour, "Ethnographer," 306.

self-understanding.²⁹ Furthermore, the interpretation of the findings affects the people by making sense of the material both for herself or himself, for the faith community, and for the society.³⁰

The pastors would most likely be the initiators of narrative inquiry for several reasons. They are trained and have years of experiences in interpretation of the faith Story, and have built up useful trusting relationship through pastoral ministry that could be put to good use in a narrative inquiry and learning. Their deeper appreciation for the life story of Christian and their relationship with the church members could be valuable to building of trust and integrity that are crucial to a fruitful narration of these personal life experiences.

Due to the exigency to capture her historical narratives, elders are the prime members of the faith community to receive the narrative research interview. Initially, the aim of the research project is to compile life stories as a way to honor the treasure of the uncles and aunties in forming our Christian living. It is also presenting continuity of the church tradition and finding teachable moments in them. Thus the writing could be closer to biographical than didactic. Biographical writing would require a writing skill in story writing. However, the project would become selective as not every life story has enough material to become a biography. The research may also reveal the history of the practices of Christian education in the local church.

At the same time, others are encouraged to share more in the various church settings. For the elders in the church, a snowballing approach would be a good start to collect their faith experiences. As the storytellers are seniors and some of them may have some difficulties in remembering the facts such as time, people and place. The resources from the historical researches could be useful as supplements to their narrations. Furthermore, the photographs and other historical facts could be useful to help them recall and retrieve some of the learning events.³¹

One valuable aspect in narrative inquiry is to deeply respect the elders whose life experiences may differ from the researcher who would most likely be younger. The researcher should attend to the elder members of the

---

29. Ibid.

30. Ibid.

31. Karen Marie Yust proposed the use of visual images such as videos, photographs in improving a reporting. From her idea, I believe the use of these visual and historical aids would enhance the story in the details and vividness. Cf. Yust, "Playing with Mirrors," 90.

household with extra sensitivity to their culture. It would also be fruitful to be more sensitive to the social differences as some are or were poor, lived in villages, experienced changes. Some may have moved through different social status in life. Ultimately, the educational process of an ethnography research could go both ways, each stands to inherit from these uncles and aunties their stories and their wisdom.[32] The interview can also be too revealing:

> Because of their interpersonal dimension, the face-to-face interviews in life history research can also bring about the revelation of long-held secrets. These revelations can lead to the disclosure of significant truths, to be sure, but also present particular methodological and ethical difficulties for both life story narrators and analysts. Narrators or people implicated in their stories may feel that they have revealed too much.[33]

The roles and involvement of the researcher helps individuals to bring out their stories. For narrative inquiry that takes the form of an interview, to gain acceptance as a form of narrative learning, there must be trust in between the researcher and the researched, besides having a safe space, and the integrity of the researcher and teacher. This is especially crucial for those who do not always realize that they have a story to tell and do not feel comfortable to share personal details. The presence of a researcher with sound integrity and being a professional in the matter often creates a sense of confidence. The researcher's ability to maintain caution with what they have learned from collecting or eliciting people's life stories will add to their credibility. They also need to practice transparency in their handling of the information collection: "(1) how they have come to know what they know and (2) where they are situated in the act of creating knowledge."[34]

The credibility of the testimonies presented by the researcher also depends on the transparency of the researcher-interviewee relationship. "By making the narrator-analyst relationship visible throughout the process of collecting and working with personal narratives, analysts can make clearer, stronger, and more credible claims about their interpretation."[35] Where the audience perceived a researcher is motivated by some illicit agenda, he or she and the related work will not be credible in teaching faith.

32. Cf. Crain and Seymour, "Ethnographer," 311–14.
33. Maynes et al., *Telling Stories*, 99.
34. Ibid.
35. Ibid., 125.

Practicing Biblical Narrative Learning

Maynes and others remind us that the role of a researcher-inquirer can be more effective in drawing out the stories when mutual respect is established. Though this is difficult to accomplish in practice, it is both an important ethical and methodological consideration as they navigate the three possibilities of inequalities in status and power between the analyst and the storyteller that could complicate the research situation in the form of "interviewing down," "interviewing up," or crossing racial or cultural boundaries.[36] The researcher-inquirer can also enhance the faith sharing process by guiding the testimony-teller to name the experience. One would not be consciously aware of the meaning of a certain act or event until she or he can "nail" that thing down and name it.

A clear purpose of telling the story, and the eventual interpretation and or affirmative responses, will play a role in making sense of the event(s) in life. The researcher needs to remember that the individuals may have their very own agendas in agreeing to interviews or deciding to write their stories, "The motivation for some narrators is simply the opportunity to get a hearing—often in their later years in life—an opportunity to reflect on their life's accomplishments or to set the record straight after conflicts or misunderstandings."[37] The narration itself has power. It is the power "to talk or write about their lives, or to remain silent; to reveal truths as they see them, or to distort or lie about them. Their interest . . . is to have theirs be the version of history preserved, and told to a well-chosen, relatively influential, or well-connected listener or other selected audience."[38] Also, in the act of telling, the narrators "may incorporate broader public or historical narratives into their life stories; they may utilize them in strategic ways; they may undermine or contradict them."[39] Furthermore, testimony telling has the potential to help the teller integrate his or her life as an individual and a part of the society they belong to, "to understand human lives as governed simultaneously according to the dynamics and temporalities of the individual life course and of collective histories."[40] This reflection or

---

36. Ibid., 121.
37. Ibid., 111.
38. Ibid., 119.
39. Ibid., 60.
40. Ibid., 69. "Narratives told to a specific person in a face-to-face interview situation magnify the impact of intersubjectivity . . . are no less relevant to the analysis of preexisting texts such as diaries and autobiographies. The subjectivity of personal narrative evidence is what makes it distinctly useful for social analysis; interpretation of such evidence necessarily entails intersubjective understanding." Ibid., 124–25.

understanding aligns them to imitate or de-imitate the expectation and practice of the community.

There are other factors that enhance a testimony telling. The skill of the testimony-tellers to use the components of narrative, their linguistic capacity, ability to create dramatic tension, which draw and hold the attention of the listeners as they look for and anticipate resolution of the dilemmas which the characters face. The appropriate pace, which varies as the narrative progresses, allowing breathing spaces to intersperse fast action and tension.[41] The presentation of the testimony-teller is also evident in the performance of oral narratives through "gesture, tone of voice, speech style and manner of telling."[42]

Maynes and others remind us that what makes the works of the narrator distinctive is that in the process of testimony telling they tend to "turn the ethnographic gaze on his or her own life and work. In this respect, auto/ethnographers are at once narrator and analyst."[43] In the moment of transforming their role, they have the great potential of becoming an efficient narrative learner, both as a storyteller and a researcher. In fact, the practice of biblical narrative learning blurs the line between the teacher and learner. Everyone who has lived faith is a potential teacher. However, this does not negate the role that a teacher can play in a biblical narrative learning. The teacher in the traditional sense is still a source of information *plus* a subject of imitation. A narrative teacher is always, first, a narrative learner. A biblical narrative learning is both a process of "getting" the stories and a process of teaching and learning through the Story-stories. From the narrative learning process in John's Gospel, we see the author as a narrative learner and teacher. The learned Story-stories shaped John the author. He had learned from his master-teacher the way of living by faith and then how to teach the Story to the community he loved. He initiated the process of passing on this wise living through showing and telling the stories of faith that is educative for his audience.

In a biblical narrative learning, it is not necessary for both the teacher and the learner to be physically present at the same time, or even for the teacher to be a physical human being. The teacher can at times be present as a physical text existing in various forms of media,[44] or existing in the mem-

41. Cf. Brophy, *Narrative-Based Practice*, 42.
42. Cortazzi and Lin, "Narrative Learning," 651–52.
43. Maynes et al., *Telling Stories*, 94.
44. Letters, for example, are individual documents often written sporadically and

ory of the learner. However, in an interview, the physical presence of the teacher-researcher is expected, but even then, the researcher need not be the teacher—the story is. Though a researcher initiated a narrative inquiry and an interviewee is involved, who is the teacher and who is the learner is not always fixed or defined. A learning moment can occur at the time of narration as the testimony is told and the narrator and or the researcher (who can become a learner in this case) hear the lived faith testimony. The biblical narrative learning process blurs the line between the teacher and learner. The narrator and researcher are both possible learners and teachers in the process of inquiry.

What Is the Aim?

There are two kinds of narrative investigation: descriptive and explanatory. The descriptive task describes the narrative already held by individuals and groups. Its aims is "to render the narrative accounts already in place which are used by individuals or groups as their means for ordering and making temporal events meaningful."[45] "Descriptive narrative research involves detection, selection, and interpretation of the data . . . the test of interview."[46] "The purpose of descriptive research is to present the narrative schemes the storyteller has intended . . . the story allows the person to order and organize his/her experience."[47] The explanatory narrative explains why something happened. "We use the skill of constructing narrative explanations in our lives to understand why we and others act in a particular way. The skill is part of our competence to understand the meaning of sentences."[48]

The use of story is such a powerful tool that accomplishes much where mere propositional statements would at times fail. Swinton and Mowat affirm the power of narrative learning as "a legitimate, rigorous and valid form of knowledge that informs us about the world in ways which are publicly significant. Stories are not simply meaningless personal anecdotes;

---

with strategic aims for specific audiences. Cf. Ibid., 108.
    45. Polkinghorne, *Narrative Knowing*, 161.
    46. Ibid., 169.
    47. Ibid.
    48. Ibid., 171.

they are important sources of knowledge."[49] Story has been a rich resource used in many church ministry settings.

The research could also recover and rebuild the teaching ministry from the past. The targeted people for life story research would be Christians who had been in the church for several decades. Their Christian education experiences are the lived history of the church. While some of the elders would feel challenged to write or explain their past, they are able to tell their life stories. The telling of one's story can be illuminating and aiding to the recovery of the church history. From the researches on life stories, the participants, both researcher and the storyteller, benefited from this process as the story is told, interpreted and retold.[50] This awareness would be helpful for the elderly Christians who may be reserved and lacked confidence in the value of their lives as they draw near to the end of their earthly existence.

Interpret and Imagine-Inspire

A narrative involves and is opened to interpretation. When the interviewees organize lived experiences into meaningful stories, they are in a process that organizes and makes actual past events meaningful. The narrative is more than the events alone; "it consists also of the significance these events have for the narrator in relationship to a particular theme."[51] Rossiter and Clark rightly pointed out that while we do not always have control over many of the events and circumstances of our lives, "we do have some choice as to how we interpret them,"[52] and it happens within what is *given*, "we begin with the actual happenings of our lives."[53]

The ability to interpret and make meaning out of events both pleasant and disappointing "is one of the most valuable aspect of the narrative orientation in adult education because it opens up possibilities."[54] Through

---

49. Swinton and Mowat, *Practical Theology and Qualitative Research*, 38.

50. McAdams told of the many instances where the research subjects were thankful for the experience and even declined the monetary benefit at the end of the participation. Cf. McAdams, *Stories*, 252.

51. Polkinghorne, *Narrative Knowing*, 160.

52. Cf. Rossiter and Clark, *Narrative*, 34. Also cf. Merriam et al., *Learning in Adulthood*, 214.

53. Rossiter and Clark, *Narrative*, 55.

54. Ibid., 34.

this interpretation, narrative informs us of what defines us, which we can construct, analyze, reflect upon, and learn from them.[55] Social psychologists have explored how people respond to stories through the idea of *transportation* into the world of the narrative where the audience is drawn into the unfolding of the drama and took away something from the narrative.[56] When a similar event took place, the audience may react by imitating or by referencing the stories heard and remembered. We "play these stories out in our minds as we seek for a rational explanation, creating quite complex cause-and-effect linkages between events."[57] Because "the world in which the narrative is heard is ever changing, the meaning of each nuance itself alters, develops, takes on new, perhaps greater, perhaps lesser, significance. For all these reasons, narrative is complex not only for the narrator but for the listener."[58] When there are differing interpretations, we are pushed "to re-visit and re-interpret those meanings."[59] Rossiter and Clark further made distinction between objective truth and narrative truth and pointed out that at times, "the facts really do not matter to the meaning of the story. The essential narrative truth of the story is not dependent upon the accuracy of certain facts."[60] However, for biblical narrative learning, the story needs integrity, credibility, thus, the narrator, the teacher, or the presenter are by necessity of sound integrity and or relationship to the audience.

Learning through stories is an undeletable part of our learning process that informs our way of living—both theory and practice. The modernity discrediting of stories as a valid teaching tool has receded due to the disenchantment of modernity. Yet the residue effect of modernity is still found in the emerging countries where the "non-scientific" method in learning is still perceived as second-class. Furthermore, stories as mystical as the biblical narratives that contain miracles and supernatural events are still labeled as unreliable experiences for building theory and practices.

Von Balthasar lamented the "'exactness' of the physical sciences . . . as the model for the life sciences and the humanities . . . the consequence of this restriction are tragic: we get precisely the opposite of what we bargained

---

55. Merriam et al., *Learning in Adulthood*, 215.

56. Cf. Brophy, *Narrative-Based Practice*, 38.

57. Ibid., 38.

58. Ibid., 34.

59. Rossiter and Clark, *Narrative*, 39. More need to be said on this indeterminacy and volatility of the interpretation.

60. Ibid., 55.

for: slavery, not freedom."[61] Our expression of the divine is denigrated to human imagination. The recovery of narrative emancipates the biblical story to spur imagination of a faith-enabled living, especially where faith itself is not defined by any science regulated language or notion. Faith is best learned not by propositional discourses of instruction, but by mimesis of narrative lives. The practice of the faith-related way of life is possible after the impetus to act is activated. While in reality many believers are taking in these stories as their sources of faith learning and object of imitation.

Shults proposes four sets of relationship that offer helpful guides to the usage of faith stories as object of imitation in a biblical narrative learning process:

a. experience and belief

b. truth and knowledge

c. individual and community

d. explanation and understanding[62]

In the relationship between experience and belief, Shults proposes that experience, not merely other beliefs, plays a crucial role in justifying the rationality of a belief. On this ground, we can see the authority of the narrative that is built on lived experiences of the individuals in the community.[63]

Secondly, Shults poses that the objective unity of truth is a necessary condition for knowledge, and the subjective multiplicity of knowledge indicates the fallibility of truth claims.[64] To achieve harmony in this relationship, intelligibility maintains the foundationalist vision of truth as an ideal that drives our inquiry, but we are to "avoid arrogating one's current knowledge as the total and final meta-narrative."[65] On the other hand, fallible nature of human reasoning must be acknowledged, but "does not deny we can have true beliefs, it may consistently offer reasons for accepting fallibilism."[66] Shults does not claim to "have" the truth, but truth is an ideal that "pulls" our search for optimal intelligibility.

In the third set of relationship Shults points out that "rational judgment is an activity of socially situated individuals, and the cultural

---

61. Von Balthasar, *Epilogue*, 23.

62. Cf. Shults, *Postfoundationalist*, 43–77.

63. Ibid., 49.

64. Ibid., 50.

65. Ibid.

66. Ibid., 58.

community indeterminately mediates the criteria of rationality."[67] He urges balance in the reasoning power of the individuals and the communal factors that shape rational judgment.[68] Shults argues that we should affirm the postmodern critique of individualism, "We are shaped by the cultural systems and relations into which we are born. In its relativist forms, non-foundationalism takes this to the extreme and argues that language games are incommensurable, and that each community determines its own rationality."[69] At the same time we need to affirm that what a person judges to be rational is affected by the cultural-historical group of which he or she is a part. We acknowledge the mutuality of the community's role in shaping an individual and the individual who actually has the ability to make a rational judgment. We are open to make a commitment into an ongoing and open dialogue with other traditions, with other disciplines, with one or more communities. The challenge then is how to walk this fine line. This calls for a hermeneutic of harmony, where one should refrain from assuming a position that overrides the others.

The fourth set of relationships aims for universal, trans-contextual understanding, and understanding derives from a particular contextualized explanations. Shults explains the relation of explanation and understanding is both to remove the dichotomy between human and natural science, between thought and matter, or between mind and nature through an interdisciplinary approach. Shults argues that movement between traditional understanding and universally intended explanations enables us to avoid both relativism and absolutism.[70] This is a crucial factor for a practitioner of biblical narrative learning to bear in mind when narrative learning depends much on the interplay of mimesis of one another.

Borrowing Shults' relational frame, biblical narrative learning functions to draw together the small stories of the ordinary and the extraordinary alike, create an understanding that result from the fluid integration of Story-stories,[71] and give rise to imagination and imitation. In the analysis

67. Ibid., 60.
68. Ibid., 59.
69. Ibid., 60.
70. Ibid., 70–71.

71. Buss succinctly summarizes the function of a relational approach where "units, large or small, are neither completely independent from others nor tightly knit internally. Rather, all complexes have within them relations that introduce some divergence, and all are involved in outward relations that both connect and differentiate." Buss, *Concept of Form*, 10.

of the relational nature of narrative learning, there are two "somewhat different but interconnected dualities" at play: "(1) a combination of partial connectivity and partial separateness, and (2) a combination of generality and particularity."[72] Buss adds, "By accepting generality, relational thought allows for the possibility of intellectual knowledge . . . the idea that particulars are partially independent implies that a certain mystery adheres to them. Thus, relational thought accepts in principle a combination of partial knowledge and partial mystery."[73] In biblical narrative learning this understanding of relationality opens the interpretive learning experience to greater possibility, outside the norm of social science that measure, or unable to measure matter such as the inspiration of the Spirit.

Narrative opens up space for interpretation and development that Brophy succinctly summarized:

> Narratives are hugely complex. . . . They enable us to share, discuss and debate all the multifaceted aspects of complex human relationships, systems and organizations. They enable us to represent cause and effect without oversimplification and allow listeners to engage in a situation in a holistic way, recognizing that thoughts, feelings and emotions are at least as important as actions. They enable us to reveal . . . our motivations, feelings, thoughts and beliefs. They also provide a means for excluded and disadvantaged members of society or of organizations to make their voices heard.[74]

On a human and personal level, the creation of narratives in telling lived faith experiences is a way in which "people organize their understanding of what has happened in the recent or distant past." There is a continuance that is never final as narrative is concerned with cause and effect, in the consequences of actions and in explanations for what has been experienced or observed, the individual's ever-evolving interpretation of desired life outcomes and directions.[75]

---

72. Ibid., 66.
73. Ibid.
74. Brophy, *Narrative-Based Practice*, 50.
75. Ibid., 39. Also cf. Rossiter and Clark, *Narrative*, 40.

Practicing Biblical Narrative Learning

Community and Interpretation of Narrative

Interpreting personal narratives that are complex forms of evidence demand our sensitivity to the location of the individual within the community.[76] In interpreting the testimonies narrative, we need to "pay close attention to how genres and their rhetorical mode shape life stories and explicate precisely how analysts are reading their sources in light of the generic characteristics of their sources."[77] The "particular form personal narratives take . . . their temporal dimension . . . and the conditions under which they are produced all shape both what is included in the text and what is not."[78]

A personal life narrative is always closely knitted to the community in which it was birthed and lived.[79] The external context presented by the community and its culture[80] provided the reference points to construct the identity of the characters and recipients. When young, people are socialized into the narrative ways of their culture. Through narrative they are, in turn, socialized into shared knowledge, social experience and cultural values. "Thus 'narrative learning' may be taken as learning narrative and learning through narrative."[81] Yet as Maynes and others rightly reminds, "Individuals are shaped by their contexts but never reducible to them."[82]

In the narrative model, education is about interpreting the world, not just receiving more information about it. It is about integrating new

---

76. Maynes and others asserts, "Lives are lived at the intersection of individual and social dynamics; life stories are correspondingly structured by multiple narrative logics and temporal frames—individual and collective. A life story is typically framed first in reference to the narrator's life course. An individual only directly "experiences" the events of his or her own lifetime, and most common conventions of life storytelling privilege this temporality. At the same time, personal narratives are contextualized by, reflect on, and explore the individual's place in collective events and historical time. They evoke many additional narratives with their own distinct temporalities beyond the individual life." Maynes et al., *Telling Stories*, 43.

77. Ibid., 96.

78. Ibid.

79. "A personal narrative document captures one form and moment in this ongoing narrative self-construction. The selves constructed through and revealed in such narratives are the sites of individual agency and of the particular motivations that ultimately govern both individual actions and self-narratives about them." Ibid., 41–42.

80. Rossiter and Clark gave caution to the socially and culturally defined narrative. Rossiter and Clark, *Narrative*, 56.

81. Cortazzi and Lin, "Narrative Learning," 652–53.

82. Maynes et al., *Telling Stories*, 67.

information and ideas into the one's individual, familial, and cultural narratives. It is a process of reconstructing and producing new discourse that gives meanings to both the old and experiences. "In order to extract meaning from events, people use narrative, which provides a template for ordering experience, identifying the context and thus boundaries of what has occurred and establishing explanations by reference to cause and effect . . . and provide a means for individuals and societies to progress towards closure."[83]

Ruth Behar notes that "life histories are of course always 'translated' or mediated in the first instance by their narrators and are never simple reflections or reports of experiences."[84] Behar alerts the reader to the many steps entailed in translation: The story moves from spoken to written word, from one language to another, and from one cultural context to another.[85] Thus analysts need to be cautious not to draw "dubious conclusions by reading their sources uncritically or may overlook the significance and meaning of contradictions and inconsistencies in the life stories of their subjects" so as not to miss the more complex and nuance readings these narratives can provide.[86] Joan Scott also wrote "testimony from personal experience cannot be read as a transparent form of evidence, but rather is always produced in and through broader discourses that have been the focus of postmodern critique."[87]

The reading of the church is crucial to the interpretation of the story. Like it or not, in reality, the practicing of faith is measured and affected by the community. The community takes a center role in determining the meaning of the story. By community, it can be a small group and the large group. The community of an individual can be as small as just ten people that asserted certain amount of influence in the person's pre-narrative stage. Yet it can expand to a much larger community of thousands or millions when one considers the view and value system of others. Therefore it is crucial that the church is able to embrace a strong reading of the Bible and practice an appropriate hermeneutics principle.[88]

---

83. Brophy, *Narrative-Based Practice*, 42.
84. Maynes et al., *Telling Stories*, 108.
85. Ibid.
86. Ibid., 97.
87. Ibid., 41.
88. K. K. Yeo has been advocating cross-cultural reading that can be applied in the interpreting the Story and the stories. Cf. Yeo, "Cross-cultural Interpretation," 805. Also

Practicing Biblical Narrative Learning

An appreciation of this reality of individuals-community holds implication for the church. Advancement can be appropriated in light of the inevitable flow of understanding and interactive value system, they can become more open to new ideas and practices, and by doing so, become more receptive to the contribution of others in the subject matter. The ability to open up to dialogue, recognizing the limitation of one voice, rejecting the hegemony of one supreme value system, willing to listen, is crucial in the many racial, religious, and cultural discordances in the region.

The second movement of interpreting the testimonies and imagine-inspire is a work of both human and divine. There is difficulty in making precise prediction on the outcome of learning in a biblical narrative learning, as there are many variants involved:

a. The integrity of individuals who share the testimonies

b. The way the testimonies are told—form of presentation—skill and language

c. The reception of the audience through their interpretation,

d. The community of faith and its Story of Faith, and

e. The work of the Holy Spirit in the whole process.

The effort of teacher and learner in this fluid learning movement is to be diligent in presenting the testimony and humbly commit the learning outcome to the Master of the Story and life.

Imitate and Impart

Stories "happened" with complexities beyond quantitative analysis. Each story is formed by events that are not always organized by deliberate planning. Even when it is a deliberate act in certain way, there is no control over all elements. There is always variable in time, space, characters, and combination of multiple elements. The randomness of interactions of the multiple variables makes the stories rich and at the same time unpredictable and not easily replicable. The uniqueness of each story gives it a special quality that tells an experience. Yet, there is similarity that can be affirmative of the other stories. The fluidity and reality of life stories have been operating to enrich the discourses of people. A research in life story could regenerate in them a desire and a way to contribute to refining the biblical education.

see Yeo, *Musing with Confucius and Paul*.

Rossiter and Clark rightly pointed out, "Stories mediate the often perceived, and sometimes real, disconnect between theory and practice."[89]

Hearing a story, the audience can have many types of responses depending on the type of story heard: saddened, enlightened, moved, empathy, sense of loss, delighted, to name a few. The response to a story can also be different depending on the situation of the audience. A story may elicit different imagination in different people at the same instance. The reception of a story is unpredictable. But one thing is more certain: a good story well told always touches the life of an audience—spark their imagination of new alternative course of life that they could choose to imitate.

The community of John has the Laws, a written code of conduct that has become hard and fast rules for the people. With the arrival of Jesus, they have the story of a loving God who came to dwell among his people in flesh as the most affective reiteration and manifestation of his love. In biblical narrative learning, the emphasis is on the message anchored in Jesus, the main character of biblical Christian Story. This anchor gives stability to the fluidity of narratives. As Stone rightly pointed out, the main concern for the critique of narrative education is its apparent relativism.[90] For the Christian task of learning faith, the reading of the Bible takes priority. The Gospels are read in the church "as covenant, not as historical source,"[91] while we are free to use them, historical and literary resources are but supplements and secondary to the text about Jesus.

John takes two resources, the people's tradition and the present life experiences, and seeks to teach his audience how to live in light of these two "stories." He works to ensure that people do not repeat the mistake of forgetting the real sense of God's love and all His deeds of love. The reality is that with elapse of time, people forget and their understanding also faded, and they lost the compassion factor. Over time, the church, reading the Johannine writings, are again facing the dilemma of having a tradition that is ossified in many ways. The church has the continuing stories of love to help them live with adequate faith. However, these stories need to be brought out, made visible to the learning congregation.

Having learned to live with adequate faith in Jesus is what propelled the Johannine characters to give up certain way of living and follow Jesus,

---

89. Rossiter and Clark, *Narrative*, 143.

90. Stone, "Narrative Theology," 266.

91. McKnight in referring to the survival of the early church, points out an insightful reminder for the contemporary church. McKnight and Church, *Hebrews and James*, 4.

Practicing Biblical Narrative Learning

the Son of God who reveals the fullest message of what it means to live life that abides in God the Father. Adequate faith in Jesus is the result of hearing, seeing, and learning the Christ Story. The Story is conveyed through a process that is articulated in the experiences of the characters in the Book of Sign. The Johannine community was taught by the characters and learned to hold onto their faith, to live life dedicated to the mission Jesus entrusted to them.

The disciples are called to imitate these positive characters, become the insiders, share their stories, build up the Family, and reach out to the community. They are subtly warned by the stories of the characters such as Nicodemus who walked out into the dark and did not have adequate faith response. This subtle touch is non-offensive to the non-believers and leaves room for the audience to ponder on the outcome of the Nicodemus' faith response. The disciples, however, are clearly reminded to avoid being outsiders looking at the Christian faith without taking the proper faith response. Nor should they let the future generations become people of inadequate faith and fail to follow Jesus, the Son of God, who has revealed to us how to live in relationship to the Father, in the Family, and in the world.

Imitation does not have to assume simplicity, though it can be simple as it is intuitive to learn through mimesis. It does not need to be reductionistic, though misuse of narrative learning can induce such result. Narrative learning is a complex and ever intriguing continuous process of engagement between self-self, and self-others. In this process learning took place in the following sphere of assumption:

> Articulating connections between new and existing knowledge improves learning. Writing about learning is a way of demonstrating what has been learned. Journal writing accentuates favorable learning conditions—it demands time and space for reflection, encourages independent thought and ownership, enables expressions of feelings, and provides a place to work with ill-structured problems. Reflection encourages deep rather than surface learning.[92]

With the new knowledge and inspiration, the learner is moved to imitate the faith informed by the Story. The reason or motivation to imitate

---

92. Merriam et al., *Learning in Adulthood*, 212. These assumptions are useful in evaluating the practice of the Methodist Women who practice copying the Bible. Each year, the members of Sarawak Methodist Women are given a book or a good section of the Bible to copy by hand. From some of the women who participated they shared a closer reading of the Bible through this act. But they had not articulated the learning principle and how this becomes beneficial to them.

can be many—room for improvement, dissatisfaction with the situation, disequilibrium in knowledge base, seeking transformation, exposure to better example or model and inspired to be better, to name a few. In general, dissatisfaction with the present often motivates imitative learning. For the scope of this research, imitation is chosen for the following reasons:

a. To imitate is natural. It is an instinctive or intuitive human learning process.

b. It is a reflective learning that is common to people in diverse settings.[93]

c. It can be augmented by various teaching skills, such as attention to multiple intelligences in learning that engages the various senses.

d. It is not an act of copying a practice, or uncritically swayed by any persuasion.[94]

e. It is imitative of the example of John's Gospel that is both simple for anyone who wants to read it and yet hugely complex for those who dissect and analyze its content.

f. It is widely practiced in different culture and ethnic groups. It is highly accessible to a wide range of audience who has vast difference in level of education and cultural background.

g. It requires less sophistication in training to use this learning tool.

h. It precludes some of the requirements such as academic training and thus makes everyone a potential teacher and learner.

i. It is highly integrative in bringing the academic and the church nearer in the reading and interpretation of the Bible.

j. It does not have to be a coerced teaching process. While audience in different part of the world may be subjected to coercion in life, what biblical narrative learning can do and at its best is to provide a widest possibility of mimesis. We as a community are to provide the best sources of stories that varies, in theme and aspect of learning, to give a balanced learning.

---

93. For the element of reflective learning in storytelling, cf. McDrury and Alterio, *Learning through Storytelling*, 12–23.

94. I have in mind here the writing of Polanyi that contains implication on narrative learning. "To learn by example is to submit to authority." Polanyi, *Personal Knowledge*, 53, quoted in Ritchie, *Fullness of Knowing*, 206. Furthermore, we do not coerce a submission to an authoritarian rule, but out of love one obeys as an act of a responsive child to a loving God.

k. Imitation provides a ground for generativity.[95]

As a process heavily dependent on the historical events as its content, the foundation of biblical narrative learning calls for an abundant supply of "reliable" stories. Many believers have shared their faith experiences as testimonies of believing in Christ in the various church gatherings. The hearing or sharing of these life experiences is an act of identifying oneself in the long tradition of faith Story. The stories received by audience are interpreted, appreciated and to be imitated. Where there are encouragement and available resources such as writer and publication opportunity, the story is written to create a lasting memory.

The faith testimony may also be taught or recited by teachers or preachers, and further create a legend or myth that is shared in a wider circle of audience. At this stage, a person's life is affirmed and became universalized. This is a process in the development of human being that culminated in what Fowler called universal stage of faith. I believe that the status of universal stage need not be reserved for rarity such as Gandhi and the like. A person whose life in narrated, preserved, shared, inspired the imagination of whoever cross path with it, and is a fruitful example for others to imitate is sufficient to be considered as universalizing in effect. When a story goes "viral" in the cyberspace, it can be an example of a life story reaching a state of wide recognition and is current. A current story more readily connects with the audience and eliminates or reduces complication in interpretation than an old story requires on the part of the audience.

The possibility for imitation is made stronger, as Brophy suggests, when narrative is sensitive to timing, so that the story is told when listeners want to hear what it has to say. It needs to be relevant to listeners' personal frame of reference, so that they understand its significance in relation to their own lives. It should also address topics that feed the listener's curiosity. Thus, it helps the listeners to see the possibilities of imitation. Finally, presentation of narrative may include the use of multimedia, including music to suit the mood or images to reinforce what is said, and information or images that help us to file the story, and its relevance, in our memories.[96]

In the setting of faith testimonies sharing, the audience has a specific learning aim. In a way, they have a narrower scope in their learning aim. They are mostly clear what to expect and know their learning aim in

---

95. McAdams proposes a path of narrative learning that involve the myth making of one self. Cf. McAdams, *Stories*, Chapter 6.

96. Cf. Brophy, *Narrative-Based Practice*, 41.

hearing these testimonies. The aim is to be stronger in faith and to be encouraged and able to make sense of the past, live the present, and anticipate the future. There is less ambiguity in the learning. That makes testimonies sharing all the more imitative as the life experiences are told, wrapped in biblical content.

In this process of biblical narrative learning, there are many educational practices that can be associated with the narrative learning process. The storytelling, interpretation, imitation can be mated to multiple intelligence in learning and other learning practices. Discussion is one of the popular tools that helps with interpretation and negotiation of the faith terrain that leads to imitation. Discussion and plan for action can be used by an individual in his dialogue with oneself, or collectively as a group bible study. Brookfield and Preskill recognize that discussion is not natural to every learner. They emphasize preparation to get discussion started and skills to keep the discussion going.[97] Recent research on biblical narrative learning also suggests the use of questions.[98] Wlodkowski and Ginsberg suggest a motivational framework for cultural responsive teaching where establishing inclusion, developing attitude, enhancing meaning, and engendering experience are carefully structured into the teaching learning process from the beginning of a class. This motivational process is sensitive to students from various cultural backgrounds and works to reduce or remove their fear and resistance to active participation in the class.[99] When they are situated in a non-threatening learning environment they can be guided to confidently and openly voice their opinions.

Narrative learning also involves selection of story. The selection process can happen on two levels. On the level of the teacher, they can help by filtering out those that are of no relevance or less teachable stories. The teacher involved in biblical narrative learning process also uses his or her expertise in their understanding of the faith Story to make selection, recommendation to his audience or committee of writing. On the other level, the community of faith who hear the story would have made some selection either through their critique of its authenticity, integrity of the

---

97. Cf. Brookfield and Preskill, *Discussion as a Way of Teaching*, 34–133. The requirement to "responding to contentious opening statement" is one example of the challenges the average learner. Cf. Brookfield, "How Do We Invite Students into Conversation?" 35–44.

98. Massey, "Narrative Model for Teaching the Bible," 203–4.

99. Wlodkowski and Ginsberg's discussion included those who are not fluent in English language. Cf. Wlodkowski and Ginsberg, *Diversity and Motivation*, 27–60.

narrator, or relevance of the life experience to theirs. In the end, as time goes by, a collection will emerge.

The remembrance of the stories heard is crucial for imitation. Some stories assert their prominence over time and achieve their teaching purpose when corresponding event takes place in a future moment. In John's Gospel, John also *pre-released* the story and admonished his audience that they will eventually understand what he had spoken of in advance (cf. John 14:29). Or, the audience takes time to reconsider the story he or she heard and come to appropriate it at a later time. Where there is instant appropriation, a story remembered is immediately merged into the life story of the audience and became a new story that could and should be told, as it becomes part of the Story.

We are intrinsically historians. We remember and want to pass on what we treasure. Writing out the testimonies is a way to conserve them in a retrievable form. This process helps to organize and make the testimonies accessible to a wider audience both over time and location. The writing of life stories calls us to use the rich language resources. The writer should to one's best possibility, uses the many literary devices available to the language used in representing the story. The usage of literary devices culminates to include the use of physiognomic expression for a fuller expression to foster remembrance. Language in the simple-complex, strange-familiar can be useful for story writing and telling. The writing should avoid mere presentation of hard and fast rules to be handed over to the audience or coming generation. The lively writing should aim to inspire and leave room for imagination. The creation of strange-familiar and engaging the full faculties of human senses are two main goals of the re-presentation of the life story.

The written testimonies can be collected or published in church periodical or anniversary issues. It can also be submitted for publication in Christian magazines or journal. Written testimonies are usually better thought through and the presentation is also more coherent. There is generally less chance for response in this case. However, the value of published testimony lies in its wider circulation as it can gain access to more location and less confined to the listening audience. Written testimonies can also be posted on the webs, either in the blog or social network, thought the later tends to be less on words. A better choice is a dedicated website for the particular theme, person, or event. Of course a testimony in a preserved form is not limited to a written form. It can be a recording that is also publishable on the internet-webs.

Word is the most familiar tool everyone can use to present our testimonies, but mastering it is not always easy. The internet, instant text message, and social network that does not require finesse in language skill has been affecting the precision in our language expression. Language distortion and limitation sets in when there is understanding only among insiders within the group. These languages are not sufficient to, or concentrated enough, to express thought and emotions, faith and other abstract matters. This leaves a vacuum in their language pool and it is often fed and filled by the pop-media where many "wisdom" sayings are shared and absorbed by the audience. The process of writing itself is also a by-product of the spiral growth of biblical narrative learning where testimony-teller may imitate the linguistic devices and learn to create the familiar-strange effect in their testimony telling.

There are elements in events that we cannot communicate through using words alone such as moments of emotion or senses. Furthermore, the average person may be challenged to have the vocabulary, expressions, or simply the literary skill to express or communicate their experiences. To show and tell these experiences may require use of different media. Most people may be able to convey expression such as natural shows of affection, softening of facial expression, and other emotion that they find challenging to write. Therefore, for some, the writing of the life testimonies may need to be assisted or handed over to others who are skilled writer.[100]

CONCLUSION

For the continuation of faith Story, a process of narrative learning is proposed based on the narrative learning as identified above in John's Gospel. A narrative inquiry is envisaged to bring a person's lived faith experience to recognition. Biblical narrative learning is not a novelty or more innovation. Rather it is a task of bringing conscious awareness to those who have not recognized it as a valid way of learning. There are some who have realized the importance of their faith experiences while others may not. It takes an initiative of the researcher to uncover and bring out these lived faith testimonies. The initiation can come from either the person or the educator

---

100. Cf. Becketk and Hager, *Life, Work, and Learning*, 3–9.

Practicing Biblical Narrative Learning

who is designated the task of encouraging and facilitating the uncovering or realization, and affirmation of the lived faith experiences.

A biblical narrative learning involves the sharing of faith testimonies in various settings. The discovery of the Christians' faith stories is a recovery of their voices in the face of multiple voices. It is also a much-needed process to help them develop a sustainable faith tradition to address their unique context and culture. An optimal or completed biblical narrative learning is one where a story that has been heard, interpreted, received and reproduced a new level life experience that can be re-told as another story that is contributive to the Story—our Anchor. With the new story "tied" to the main Anchor, the storyteller who functions like a tour guide is able to point others to the port. As Ferder rightly reminds us, there are "old stories and new stories. They are unfinished stories. They are our stories."[101]

---

101. Ferder, *Enter the Story*, xiii.

Conclusion

The characters in the Gospel of John display two types of faith response to the word and work of Jesus: adequate faith response that led to affirmation of Jesus as Christ from God, or inadequate faith response that denied Jesus and even became enemy of Christ. Each of these events presented a crisis situation. Similarly, the global church faces situations that challenge their reading of the Bible and how they should respond. The critiques against the church often focus on how she failed in upholding moral standards compared to other religions.[1] In the face of this challenge, some churches have become agent of moral education more than proclamation of the gospel as they "relinquished their theological and spiritual vocation as the embodiment of Christ in the world and taken upon themselves a secondary role as persuasive agents of civic righteousness."[2] Christian education in the church has increasingly assumed the role of "teaching polite and inoffensive (i.e., 'civil') behavior than fostering a bold and adventurous spiritual life."[3] Christian education has been supplanted by moral training. In a harsher word, Martin called the church whose ethical norms and strategies are received from cultural traditions rather than primarily from the Gospel, "the church has in effect knelt down to Baal and turned its back on the One True God. . . . When Christian tacitly fears that their faith in God is a mistaken delusion, then religious practice will search for cor-

---

1. "In the public's mind, the most legitimate function of the church today seems to be its *moral* influence." Martin, *Incarnate Ground of Christian Faith*, 5.
2. Ibid., 5.
3. Ibid., 6.

roboration from more culturally legitimate sources."[4] Martin suggests "only as Christian education, . . . orients itself to the true referent of Christian faith, the incarnate Word in Jesus Christ who reveals the Triune God, will Christian education be able to reestablish itself on firm theological ground."[5]

Biblical narrative learning as a form of Christian education is recommended for the church seeking to strengthen her people in biblical faith because narrative learning can occur at any of the three moves, and at any time or type of setting. Without denying the complexity of narrative learning in an academic discussion, the practice of biblical narrative learning is very much a simple process involving accumulation of lived faith experiences from everyday life of ordinary and extraordinary believers. In another word, it constitutes the "wisdom" of the faith community. From this finding and collecting of testimonies, to ownership of information and creation of knowledge, the faith community becomes wiser in their faith practice.

Through biblical narrative learning, we first of all learn from the main character and other characters in John's Gospel to live with adequate faith in God, and we continue this living, showing, and telling a faith that is adequate for the moment, which includes adequate faith to face the unknown future. There is no ultimate example of living by faith except in the Story of Jesus. While we do not possess the full selection of Jesus' faith, we are informed by the story of Jesus' perfect obedience to the Father through love. We are invited to imitate this obedient pattern. The revealing is available to all who are willing to listen to the story—the learners with an open mind to these stories will hear and interpret a way of life, imagine possibilities under the inspiration of the Spirit, and decide to imitate or de-imitate.

Biblical narrative learning is a continual spiral that grows and expands with additional testimonies. The spiral of biblical narrative learning is fluid and does not claim an end-state at any time, yet it can be adequate and arrive at a point of decision and action, in line with the never-ceasing flow of life in time where in reality, none lives in a limbo. Narrative learning is never completed, yet it is efficacious to educate the faith of the individuals and help the person makes the next move in life. The spiral is found in both the stories and the language. As stories are added, the way to represent them is also enhanced as language is used and cultivated, the language is also imitated and grew richer in description as more stories are told and

4. Ibid.
5. Ibid., 4.

CONCLUSION

re-presented in written and/or other forms of media. The presentation keeps improving as we progress, re-think the content, and refine the literary art used to tell the testimonies. The individuals and the community (both their testimonies and the testimony-telling) are constantly infused in this spiral—life will continue with a difference that is informed by the Story.

CONTRIBUTION TO CHRISTIAN EDUCATION

We need to be more attentive to the characteristics of learners and avoid a rigid approach in the behavioral and cognitive frames that boxed-in the learners and generally labeled them through a broad generic description of each age group. With greater availability of information, the trend for children to begin more educational activities at a younger age, and the possibility of longer period of education for individuals that is extending into young adulthood is changing the landscape of the learner community. The fluidity within each age group has grown beyond simplicity of traditional age-based categorization that we can no longer assume a universal way of learning for all the learners.

The diversity of learners and the attention to the voices to different groups, such as the socially or religiously oppressed, less advantaged, and gender bias are part of current education consideration that need to be addressed. The movement of inquiry and invent in biblical narrative learning emphatically seeks the voices of the people, encourages and gives each individuals, regardless of how the norm of the community perceives them as insignificant or pays overly attention. Biblical narrative learning also contributes to availability of story as illustration to a teaching and does much more.[6] The telling of a lived faith experience itself is a learning experience. The teller does not cease to learn when she or he tells the testimony for the first or the fifth time. The reflection, remembrance, and the interaction with the audience will continue to fire imagination each time the testimony is shared and reflected upon.

To break out of the confinement of traditional education theory and practice, we need an education practice that can revitalize the lethargic faith formation, and one that can help the believers to relate our Christian faith to the challenges of the complexities and ambiguities of the fluidic

---

6. Hsiao's writing lacks the story about the people, the curriculum, and the author himself. His work has been largely on the teaching skill and the administration of educational ministry in the church.

postmodern thinking. Thomas Groome, in the wake of postmodern and its challenges to teaching the Bible as authoritative Word of God, affirms the Christian tradition and emphasis on its authority in the process of Christian education drew my attention. Groome's five movements trace the passing-on of faith with both continuity and discontinuity.

Groome's five movements is a process that leans toward rational thinking involving discussion, and arriving at a decision and a course of action.[7] Biblical narrative learning differs in that it includes similar acts such as discussions and reasoning, it further pays keen attention to affective learning. Best possibility of learning is when personal reflection occurs during the narration time, and it can happen within both the testimony-teller and the hearer or reader.[8] Groome repositions storytelling as a key teaching method in Christian education and attracts attention. His notion of the present "story" entails some form of narrative inquiry. Groome's *shared praxis* could have expanded into narrative inquiry, but this aspect is not in his work.

In the wave of narrative learning practiced outside the United States, Ivor Goodson caught my attention as his work with a group of researchers in the United Kingdom holds a valuable example for researching the individuals as narrative learner. Goodson and his team wrote three books from this research project. *Narrative Learning* is the report of the project, from which *Narrative Pedagogy* and *Improved Learning through the Life Course* followed.[9] Goodson's research holds several significant implications for biblical narrative learning. First of all, in the mold of biblical narrative learning that is presented in this research, Goodson's *Narrative Learning* is a *showing* of how an independent narrative research work is done and what can be revealed in this process. Secondly, *Narrative Pedagogy* is a *telling* of his work that reveals the importance of narrative learning as a process within an individual as a person recounts lived life experiences and interpret these experiences in this process of telling. The third book is the practical application of the finding and practices in adult life-long learning.

Goodson and his team and other narrative researchers in Australia and New Zealand are part of a recovery of an old tradition in learning that is intuitive. These researchers often put into practice the idea of narrative

---

7. Cf. Groome, *Christian Religious Education*, 208–23.

8. Cf. Ha, "Familiar-Strange," 167.

9. Biesta et al., *Improved Learning through the Life Course*. This is the third volume from their research project in which Goodson is one of the five authors.

Conclusion

learning that build on the conceptual frame from North American theorists like Jerome Bruner and Polkinghorne. The result of these researches in the field is informative for the North American narrative researchers as all these contributions will be part of the growing spiral of narrative learning.

One of the conclusions drawn from his research raised an issue as one considers how the narrative research can be part of biblical narrative learning. Goodson concludes that narrative learning is not sufficient to offer a way to better life which starkly contrasts with the Johannine promise of a life abundance in Jesus. I see in this conclusion a lack of presumption in a grand narrative. I believe Goodson's research is restricted by the presumption that framed his research methodology. The research took place outside of a religious setting and the wish to refrain from any form of ideal prevented the interviewers referencing to the Story (or any grand narrative) that Groome advocated in *shared praxis*. Biblical narrative learning asserts the necessity of a grand narrative as anchor to learning a meaningful and authentic living. From John's Gospel, we see that to live with adequate faith entails a practice of living in the love of God, and propagating this love in one's daily life in relation with self and others. This love is exemplified by the life of Jesus, and John's purpose of writing the Gospel is to help others to know and imitate this way of living an abundant life.

Proponents of narrative learning (Clandinin, Rossiter, Brophy, Dickelmann and others included), focus mainly on adult learners. However, with the development and their greater capacity of younger people to reflect, I believe it can be expanded into younger age groups such as emerging adult, and even possible with adolescent. Most of the current narrative researches focus on the adult in non-Christian setting and professional vocation and practices. My research offers two possibilities for Christian education. Firstly, it prepares the church to conduct narrative inquiry and gain greater understanding into the contemporary faith formation under the challenges of the postmodern and the overflow of information. It offers a Bible-based, Christ-focused way of relational learning and living faith that is guided by the love principle. Secondly, the biblical narrative learning departs from sole reliance of faith formation on social science theory that is not designed to teach the rich mystery of divine and the abstract subject such as faith and love in Christian education.

The biblical narrative learning offers examples that encourage imitation (not exact copy) of living faith that glorify the household of God. It also adds volume to the Voice. It counters the shiftiness and directionless of current narrative learning researches by refocusing on the tradition of biblical text. At the same time the skill of narrative inquiry or life story research will enrich both the researched and the researcher.

A dedicated effort in teaching the Bible through narrative learning leans on the works of many predecessors, and also seeks to continue, expand, and improve on the spiral progress in narrative learning. Dorothy Lee introduced the possibility of reading the John's narrative from a fresh perspective—that is, to read with our five senses. She pointed out, "faith cannot appear and develop without such imagery, so foundational is it to the world of the fourth evangelist."[10] She pointed out the reader benefits from reading with five senses in its ability to create "a transformation in the reader's imagination . . . the new imaging of a God."[11] Her conclusion is theologically significant and laid the foundation for a greater possibility of coming to know God, and a fuller experience in building relationship with God as this reading rises above conventional learning, through mere lectures, that is often the case in the process of didactic teaching.

Lee has identified the theological significance of reading John's Gospel with five senses that can be broadly applied to readers of differing ability such as reasoning and education. It is encouraging and promising for both reading and teaching the Bible in all cultures. However, Lee does not expand on how this is significant in Christian education. Reading the Gospel with the five senses enables us to re-imagine an ossified text through lively re-presentation of a past event. In the case of reading John's Gospel, such reading strategy coincides with John's writing strategy—using the plot, the characters, and literary devices to communicate a realistic testimony of Jesus.

Reading John's Gospel in five senses also reminds us the need to be intentional testimony writers or tellers. The presentation should be attentive to the use of literary devices that maximize imagination of the audience or reader. The ability of reader to re-live the past in the present is crucial for both affective learning and remembrance. The former is evidenced in the theological theme of love in John's Gospel, and the latter is emphatic in John's writing that he taught so that followers of Christ will remember, and imagine the way of life in loving relationship with God and one another under the inspiration of the Spirit.

---

10. Lee, "John and the Five Senses," 115.
11. Ibid., 125–26.

Conclusion

RECOMMENDATION FOR THE LOCAL CHURCH

Introducing the concept of biblical narrative learning into the church will be challenging. The faith community will need to understand and be convinced that it is meaningful to her faith development, and become willing to be contributing partner in this process. The teachers will need to be familiar with the components and the movements, learn the languages well, and gain mastery over storytelling. The present practice of sharing personal testimonies in the church can be researched, and improved in terms of the showing and telling in order to be more effective in informing the way of life in the faith community and beyond. The Johannine example shows his sensitivity to the plot and characterization, his linguistic touches, and his interpretation of the past tradition or stories are some of the keys to life story research and teaching.

For the beginners in telling personal lived faith testimonies, the telling could initially see some poor composition that lacks a clear subject or is out of focus. This can distort or make it hard for the audience to catch the theme of the testimony. An unclear presentation may limit the learner's ability to interpret the testimony and turn it into a learning moment. With training, the testimony teller will learn to use a basic plot and be guided on using various themes to focus the sharing. While almost any event in life is a possible theme, the themes include: healing, helps in moment of suffering, making decision in various life choices, callings, providence of life's essentials, overcoming emotional stress, and so forth. The stories are not limited to the story of individuals but also the story of curriculum, organization, community, and a host of possibilities is out there. Yet even a basic story can be complex, reflecting the complexity of human existence.

The oral form of testimonies often needs more refinement. It may not be well thought out, and the presentation also tends to be not so well structured. This is what a powerful biblical narrative learning tries to avert and avoid. Thus we need to teach the church how to use the components of narrative learning to ensure the quality of the narrative and effectiveness of its presentation to teach adequate faith. They can be 1) better organized, 2) written down, 3) reviewed, 4) refined, and 5) disseminated through encouragement and guidance.

Narrative learning has already informed much of the practice in the field of education in terms of methods, and adult educators use stories in their teaching routinely, to illuminate content, to facilitate learning, and to link learning to the life experiences of the learners. Learning methods

Biblical Narrative Learning

such as case studies, learning journals, diaries, simulations, autobiographical writing, and many other methods that have narrative at their root are all familiar pedagogical tools in education.

Furthermore, a biblical narrative learning can integrate with many current education theories such as transformative learning (Mezirow), use of discussion in learning (as part of interpretive process in narrative learning, Stephen D. Brookfield), multiple intelligence learning theory (as part of learning through multiple modes of presentation, Gardner, Bracke and Tye), and motivate adult learning (especially for adult learners who would be more liberated to learn while recognize their unique place in the learning process, Raymond J. Wlodkowski).[12] The effort will benefit the whole community as we reflect and learn from these researches and re-present the Gospel through our lives—past and present—informing the future.

In light of the present practices in the church, biblical narrative learning can be applied in the present practice of copying the Bible, giving it greater meaning than mere moving of the pen. The person can embark on a process of narrative learning as the Story unfold slowly before her or him, giving time to recall, interpret, and imagine while the Story is realized as an image or message. The Spirit can further inspire the person for imitation. In a similar way, memorizing the Bible verses can be better appreciated especially among the younger generations. The practice can be interesting if each verse memorized is related to some story in real life. The format of the Bible memorization handbook can also be designed to facilitate remembrance of the verses.

The regular scheduled testimony sharing during the church groups gathering can also take some variations to encourage individuals to share their lived faith experiences. Some fellowship groups select and interview an individual member each month and make the person the "Star of the Month." The interview starts with asking the interviewee general questions about her or his family, education, vocation, hobbies and any other aspects of life the group may find interesting. The interview would move on to include telling personal faith experiences when the interviewees may reveal some significant faith encounters or learning. This process is helpful to build bonds among the members and at the same time uncover the faith journey of the individuals.

---

12. These are some of the possible ways narrative learning can work alongside other modes of learning.

Conclusion

The use of literary devices in telling testimonies of lived faith experiences can be applied in two ways. First of all is an imitation of the various literary devices in John's Gospel to create the familiar-strange, to explain, to recreate or present an event in a lively—realistic—image that registers with the audience. Secondly, as a process of imitation and recreation, the language(s) can be reconfigured to create a fresh presentation of a testimony or a teaching point in the narrative. A testimony can be summarized into a key teaching with a particular focus on living Christian faith. The good use of literary devices and the play with the language itself is also imitative and build the eloquence and beauty of the narrative.[13]

The practice of a believer sharing faith testimonies in the church takes lots of courage and, most often, determination. It involves the disclosure of personal details and admittance of one's weakness that the community in general perceive as un-glorious. In order to invite more church members into this sharing and building up of faith narratives, forming a sizable data that can feed the community's imagination, the researcher-teacher needs to encourage building of a non-judgmental community. It takes a safe environment—the people, the culture—to encourage sharing. I suggest a dedicated ministry to encourage and collect testimonies by a group of researchers, with an eye for the work to involve writers and publishers.[14] The church can assist by introducing to the researchers those who have faith testimonies. At the same time, we need to train more researchers who know the Story well, are able to provide a sound interpretation, and with the literary skill to represent the testimonies well.

In this fast changing and fluidic generation, the task of narrative research is ever changing the horizons of both the researched subject and the researcher. Life story research will be a continuous and growing learning experience. There are issues that we can never prepare well enough, nor should we try to, before we enter the site, but there is one who can be prepared as best as possible: the researcher. With the increment of experiences and continuous reflection, improvement will come. The researches will sharpen the art of conducting interviews, skills in collecting data, analyses of data, and writing the report. The initial researcher(s) will also be training more researchers to continue the life story research among different groups

13. The narrator will always exercise caution and restrain that the use of literary devices does not aim at, or create, fictitious or untruthful presentation.

14. I have in mind here a collection of Christian faith testimonies in good details, as inspired by Mathison, *Treasures of the Transformed Life*. Also cf. Walsh, *Dictionary of Christian Biography* which carries rather brief stories of individuals.

and different problems. Change often begins with, and needs to start from, the education leadership.[15] The seminary is an ideal starting place of a new curriculum that could transform the learning community. A drastic change or introduction to an idea foreign to the audience is a risk. Introducing and learning a new concept will continue to be a challenge, but it is a hurdle that we must cross with faith in the resilience of the Christian community to excel.

Biblical narrative learning, as a major route by which people learn about faith, is not intended as the only way of learning faith. There is definitely room for other modes of learning such as lectures and reading. The process of narrative learning is incorporated in, and is able to work through, all modes of teaching and learning skill. It can reach across multiple disciplines. At the same time, there is always room for biblical narrative learning to gain from sincere conversation with other disciplines. The arrival of technology that brings information into many rooms (both physical and spiritual) hastens the necessity of the church to be active and engaging others.[16] A dominant approach to interpretation and teaching the biblical text is counter-productive and only works to isolate oneself from the others. The benefit of a biblically strong anchor will be crucial as the churches examine their stories, reassess their faith position, and move forward in the midst of their challenges to not only survive, but to revive the church.

The task of Christian education is to affirm and enhance learning among the believers while making available resources and guidance. We often learn through the community their stories of success, sometimes even building their life perspectives from the hearsay, the legends of past and present-day. But the community is growing apart. The voices of the stories are growing thin. They need to keep the stories alive and pass on their stories. A way forward could include setting the desirable criteria and improving the telling of biblical faith stories to become fruitful learning experiences. The inherent danger of miss-education in this situation is real. We do not seek to be revolutionary, but we seek refreshing way of knowing that continue to evolve and change the learning environment and the learners.

---

15. For further references on narrative learning and educational leadership, the three-volume Narrative Leadership Collection edited by Larry A. Goleman is a helpful starting point.

16. The possibility of digital text and its effect on the readers and the learning experience is worth further exploring.

Bibliography

Anderson, Paul N. *The Christology of the Fourth Gospel: Its Unity and Disunity in the Light of John 6*. Tübingen: Mohr Siebeck, 1996.

———. *The Fourth Gospel and the Quest for Jesus: Modern Foundations Reconsidered*. New York: T. & T. Clark, 2006.

———. *The Riddles of the Fourth Gospel: An Introduction to John*. Minneapolis: Fortress, 2011.

Anderson, Paul N., et al., ed. *John, Jesus, and History, vol. 1: Critical Appraisals of Critical Reviews*. Atlanta, GA: SBL, 2007.

———. *John, Jesus, and History, vol. 2: Aspects of Historicity in the Fourth Gospel*. Atlanta, GA: SBL, 2007.

Anderson, Ray S. *On Being Human: Essays in Theological Anthropology*. Grand Rapids: Eerdmans, 1982.

Arnett, Jeffrey Jensen. *Emerging Adulthoods: The Winding Road from the Late Teens through the Twenties*. New York: Oxford University Press, 2004.

Aune, David E. *The Westminster Dictionary of New Testament and Early Christian Literature and Rhetoric*. Louisville, KY: Westminster John Knox, 2003.

Bal, Mieke, and David Jobling, eds. *On Storytelling: Essays in Narratology*. Sonoma, CA: Polebridge, 1991.

Bauckham, Richard. "The Audience of the Fourth Gospel." In *Jesus in Johannine Tradition*, edited by Robert T. Fortna and Tom Thatcher, 101–12. Louisville, KY: Westminster John Knox, 2001.

———. *Jesus and the Eyewitnesses: The Gospels as Eyewitness Testimony*. Grand Rapids: Baker Academic, 2006.

———. *The Testimony of the Beloved Disciple: Narrative, History, and Theology in the Gospel of John*. Grand Rapids: Eerdmans, 2007.

Bauckham, Richard, ed. *The Book of Acts in Its Palestinian Setting*. Grand Rapids: Eerdmans, 1995.

Bauckham, Richard, and Carl Mosser, eds. *The Gospel of John and Christian Theology*. Grand Rapids: Eerdmans, 2008.

Bausch, William J. *Storytelling: Imagination and Faith*. Mystic, CT: Twenty-Third Publications, 1984.

Bibliography

Beale, G. K., and D. A. Carson, eds. *Commentary on the New Testament use of the Old Testament*. Grand Rapids: Baker Academic, 2007.

Beasley-Murray, George R. *John*. Word Biblical Commentary 36. Waco: Word, 1987.

Beattie, Mary. *The Quest for Meaning: Narratives of Teaching, Learning and the Arts*. Boston: Sense, 2009.

Benham, Maenette K. P. "Moʻōlelo: On Culturally Relevant Story Making from an Indigenous Perspective." In *Handbook of Narrative Inquiry: Mapping a Methodology*, edited by D. Jean Clandinin, 512–34. Thousand Oaks, CA: Sage, 2007.

Bennema, Cornelis. "A Theory of Character in the Fourth Gospel with Reference to Ancient and Modern Literature." *Biblical Interpretation* 17 (2009) 375–421.

———. *Encountering Jesus: Character Studies in the Gospel of John*. Milton Keynes: Paternoster, 2009.

———. *The Power of Saving Wisdom: An Investigation of Spirit and Wisdom in Relationship to the Soteriology of the Fourth Gospel*. Tübingen: Mohr Siebeck, 2002.

Berger, Klaus. *Identity and Experience in the New Testament*. Translated by Charles Muenchow. Minneapolis: Fortress, 2003.

Biesta, Gert J. J., et al. *Improved Learning through the Life Course*. New York: Routledge, 2011.

Birren, James E., et al., eds. *Aging and Biography: Explorations in Adult Development*. New York: Springer, 1996.

Blair, Christine Eaton. *The Art of Teaching the Bible: A Practical Guide for Adults*. Louisville, KY: Geneva, 2001.

Bondi, Richard. "The Elements of Character." *The Journal of Religious Ethics* 12.2 (1984) 201–18.

Bonney, William. *Caused to Believe: The Doubting Thomas Story as the Climax of John's Christological Narrative*. Leiden: Brill, 2002.

Boys, Mary C. *Educating in Faith: Maps and Visions*. San Francisco: Harper and Row, 1989.

Bracke, John M., and Karen B Tye. *Teaching the Bible in the Church*. St. Louis: Chalice, 2003.

Brenner, Athalya, and Frank H. Polak, eds. *Performing Memory in Biblical Narrative and Beyond*. Sheffield: Sheffield Phoenix, 2009.

Brodie, Thomas L. *The Gospel According to John: A Literary and Theological Commentary*. New York: Oxford University Press, 1993.

———. *The Quest for the Origin of John's Gospel: A Source-Oriented Approach*. New York: Oxford University Press, 1993.

Brookfield, Stephen D. "How Do We Invite Students into Conversation?" In *Teaching Reflectively in Theological Contexts: Promises and Contradictions*, edited by Mary E. Hess and Stephen D. Brookfield, 35–44. Malabar: Krieger, 2008.

Brookfield, Stephen D., and Stephen Preskill. *Discussion as a Way of Teaching: Tools and Techniques for University Teachers*. Buckingham: SRHE, 1999.

Brophy, Peter. *Narrative-Based Practice*. Surrey: Ashgate, 2009.

Brown, Raymond E. *The Gospel According to John, vol. 1 & 2*. New York: Doubleday, 1966.

———. *An Introduction to the Gospel of John*. Edited by Francis J. Moloney. New York: Doubleday, 2003.

———. *An Introduction to the New Testament*. New York: Doubleday, 1997.

Bruce, Barbara A. *Triangular Teaching: A New Way of Teaching the Bible to Adults*. Nashville: Abingdon, 2007.

Bibliography

Brueggemann, Walter. *The Creative Word: Canon as A Model for Biblical Education*. Philadelphia: Fortress, 1982.
Bruner, Frederick Dale. *The Gospel of John: A Commentary*. Grand Rapids: Eerdmans, 2012.
Bruner, Jerome. *Actual Minds, Possible Worlds*. Cambridge: Harvard University Press, 1986.
———. *Acts of Meaning*. Cambridge: Harvard University Press, 1990.
Burke, T Patrick. "Theologian as Storyteller and Philosopher." *Horizons* 4.2 (1977) 207–15.
Buss, Martin J. *The Concept of Form in the Twentieth Century*. Sheffield: Sheffield Phoenix, 2008.
Caldwell, Elizabeth. "Religious Instruction: Homemaking." In *Mapping Christian Education: Approaches to Congregational Learning*, edited by Jack L. Seymour, 74–89. Nashville: Abingdon, 1997.
Capps, Donald. *The Decades of Life: A Guide to Human Development*. Louisville, KY: Westminster John Knox, 2008.
Carson, D. A. "Syntactical and Text-Critical Observations on John 20:30–31: One More Round on the Purpose of the Fourth Gospel." *JBL* 124.4 (2005) 693–714.
———. "The Challenge of the Balkanization of Johannine Studies." In *John, Jesus, and History, Volume 1: Critical Appraisals of Critical Reviews*, edited by Paul N. Anderson et al., 133–59. Atlanta, GA: SBL, 2007.
Carter, Warren. *John and Empire: Initial Explorations*. New York: T. & T. Clark, 2008.
———. *John: Storyteller, Interpreter, Evangelist*. Peabody, MA: Hendrickson, 2006.
———. *The Roman Empire and the New Testament: An Essential Guide*. Nashville: Abingdon, 2006.
Chamberlayne, Pure, et al. *The Turn to Biographical Methods in Social Science: Comparative Issues ad Examples*. London: Routledge, 2000.
Clandinin, D. Jean ed. *Handbook of Narrative Inquiry: Mapping a Methodology*. Thousand Oaks, CA: Sage, 2007.
Clandinin, D. Jean, and F. Michael Connelly, eds. *Narrative Inquiry: Experience and Story in Qualitative Research*. San Francisco: Jossey-Bass, 2000.
Clark, M. Carolyn, and Marsha Rossiter. "Narrative Learning in Adulthood." In *Third Update on Adult Learning Theory*, edited by Sharan B. Merriam, 61–70. San Francisco: Jossey-Bass, 2008.
Conway, Collen M. *Men and Women in the Fourth Gospel: Gender and Johannine Characterization*. Atlanta, GA: SBL, 1999.
Cortazzi, Martin, and Lixian Lin. "Narrative Learning, EAL and Cognitive Development." *Early Child Development and Care* 177.6/7 (2007) 645–60.
Crain, Margaret Ann, and Jack L. Seymour. "The Ethnographer as Minister: Ethnographic Research in Ministry." *Religious Education* 91.3 (1996) 299–315.
Cranton, Patricia. *Understanding and Promoting Transformative Learning: A Guide for Educators of Adults*. San Francisco: Jossey-Bass, 1994.
Cranton, Patricia, ed. *Authenticity in Teaching: New Directions for Adult and Continuing Education*, No.111. San Francisco: Jossey-Bass, 2006.
Crenshaw, James L. *Education in Ancient Israel: Across the Deadening Silence*. New York: Doubleday, 1998.
Culpepper, R. Alan. *Anatomy of the Fourth Gospel: A Study in Literary Design*. Philadelphia: Fortress, 1983.
———. *The Gospel and Letters of John*. Nashville: Abingdon, 1998.

Bibliography

Cunningham, David S., ed. *To Teach, to Delight, and to Move: Theological Education in a Post-Christian World*. Eugene, OR: Cascade, 2004.

Daniels, Harry, et al., eds. *The Cambridge Companion to Vygotsky*. New York: Cambridge, 2007.

Danker, Frederick William, ed. *Greek-English Lexicon of the New Testament and Other Early Christian Literature*, 3rd ed. Chicago: University of Chicago, 2000.

Diekelmann, Nancy, and John Diekelmann. *Schooling Learning Teaching: Toward Narrative Pedagogy*. Bloomington: iUniverse, 2009.

Domeris, W. R. "The Johannine Drama." *Journal of Theology for Southern Africa* 42 (1983) 29–35.

Duke, Paul D. *Irony in the Fourth Gospel*. Atlanta, GA: John Knox, 1985.

Du Rand, Paul A. "The Creation Motif in the Fourth Gospel: Perspectives on its Narratological Function within a Judaistic Background." In *Theology and Christology in the Fourth Gospel*, edited by Gilbert van Belle et al., 21–46. Leuven: Leuven University, 2005.

Dunn, James D. G. "John's Gospel and the Oral Gospel Tradition." In *The Fourth Gospel in First-Century Media Culture*, edited by Anthony Le Donne and Tom Thatcher, 157–85. New York: T. & T. Clark, 2011.

Ehrman, Bart D. *The New Testament: A Historical Introduction to the Early Christian Writings*, 2nd ed. New York: Oxford University Press, 2000.

Erikson, Erik H. *The Life Cycle Completed: A Review*. New York: W. W. Norton, 1982.

Esler, Philip F., ed. *The Early Christian World*, vol. 1. London: Routledge, 2000.

Esler, Philip F., and Ronald Piper. *Lazarus, Mary, and Martha: Social-Scientific Approaches to the Gospel of John*. Minneapolis: Fortress, 2006.

Esterline, David V., and Ogbu U. Kalu, eds. *Shaping Beloved Community: Multicultural Theological Education*. Louisville, KY: Westminster John Knox, 2006.

Evans, Craig A., and H. Daniel Zacharias, eds. *Early Christian Literature and Intertextuality, vol. 2: Exegetical Studies*. New York: T. & T. Clark, 2009.

Felch, Susan M. "Dialogism." In *Dictionary for Theological Interpretation of the Bible*, edited by Kevin J. Vanhoozer, 173–5. Grand Rapids: Baker Academic, 2005.

Ferder, Fran. *Enter the Story: Biblical Metaphors for Our Lives*. Maryknoll, NY: Orbis, 2010.

Ferguson, Everett. *Backgrounds of Early Christianity*, 3rd ed. Grand Rapids: Eerdmans, 2003.

Fiensy, David A. "The Composition of the Jerusalem Church." In *The Book of Acts in Its Palestinian Setting*, edited by Richard Bauckham, 213–36. Grand Rapids: Eerdmans, 1995.

Fishbane, Michael. *Sacred Attunement: A Jewish Theology*. Chicago: University of Chicago, 2008.

Fokkelman, J.P. *Reading Biblical Narrative: An Introductory Guide*. Louisville, KY: Deo, 1999.

Fortna, Robert Tomson. *The Fourth Gospel and its Predecessor: From Narrative Source to Present Gospel*. Philadelphia: Fortress, 1988.

———. *The Gospel of Signs*. Cambridge: Cambridge University Press, 1970.

Fortna, Robert Tomson, and Tom Thatcher, eds. *Jesus in Johannine Tradition*. Louisville, KY: Westminster John Knox, 2001.

Fowler, James W. *Stages of Faith: The Psychology of Human Development and the Quest for Meaning*. San Francisco: Harper and Row, 1981.

Bibliography

Fowler, James W., et al. *Stages of Faith and Religious Development: Implications for Church, Education, and Society*. New York: Crossroad, 1991.

———. *Trajectories in Faith: Life Stories of Malcolm X, Anne Hutchinson, Blaise Pascal, Ludwig Wittgenstein, & Dietrich Bonhoeffer*. Nashville: Abingdon, 1980.

Frank, Thomas Edward. *The Soul of the Congregation: An Invitation to Congregational Reflection*. Nashville: Abingdon, 2000.

Friesen, Steven J. "Justice or God's Will? Early Christian Explanations of Poverty." In *Wealth and Poverty in Early Church and Society*, edited by Susan R. Holman, 17–36. Grand Rapids: Baker Academic, 2008.

Gamble, Harry Y. *Books and Readers in the Early Church: A History of Early Christian Texts*. New Haven, CT: Yale University, 1995.

Gardner, Howard. *Multiple Intelligences: The Theory in Practice*. New York: Basic Books, 1993.

Gill, David W. J., and Conrad Gempf, eds. *The Book of Acts in Its First Century Setting, vol. 2: The Book of Acts in Its Graeco-Roman Setting*. Grand Rapids: Eerdmans, 1994.

Gilmour, Peter. "Life Narratives: Expressions of Diverse Spiritualities." *Religious Education* 87.4 (1992) 545–57.

Girard, René. *The Girard Reader*. Edited by James G. Williams. New York: Crossroad, 1996.

———. *Mimesis and Theory: Essays on Literature and Criticism, 1953–2005*. Edited by Robert Doran. Stanford: Stanford University Press, 2008.

———. *Things Hidden since the Foundation of the World*. Translated by Stephen Bann (Books II & III) and Michael Metteer (Book I). Stanford: Stanford University Press, 1987.

Golemon, Larry A., ed. *Finding Our Story: Narrative Leadership and Congregational Change*. Herndon, VA: Alban Institute, 2010.

———. *Living Our Story: Narrative Leadership and Congregational Culture*. Herndon, VA: Alban Institute, 2010.

———. *Teaching Our Story: Narrative Leadership and Pastoral Formation*. Herndon, VA: Alban Institute, 2010.

Gooder, Paula. *Searching for Meaning: An Introduction to Interpreting the New Testament*. Louisville, KY: Westminster John Knox, 2009.

Goodman, Martin. *Judaism in the Roman World*. Leiden: Brill, 2007.

Goodson, Ivor F., et al. *Narrative Learning*. London: Routledge, 2010.

Goodson, Ivor, and Scherto R. Gill. *Narrative Pedagogy: Life Story and Learning*. New York: Peter Lang, 2011.

Goodley, Dan, et al. *Researching Life Stories: Method, Theory and Analyses in a Biographical Age*. London: Routledge Falmer, 2004.

Graham, Elaine, et al. *Theological Reflection: Method*. London: SCM, 2005.

Green, Joel B. *Reading Scripture as Wesleyans*. Nashville: Abingdon, 2010.

Grenz, Stanley J. "The Social God and the Relational Self: Toward a Theology of the Imago Dei in the Postmodern Context." In *Personal Identity in Theological Perspective*, edited by Richard Lints, Michael S. Horton, and Mark R. Talbot, 70–94. Grand Rapids: Eerdmans, 2006.

Groome, Thomas H. *Christian Religious Education: Sharing Our Story and Vision*. San Francisco: Harper & Row, 1980.

———. *Educating for Life: A Spiritual Vision for Every Teacher and Parent*. New York: Crossroad, 1998.

Bibliography

———. *Sharing Faith: A Comprehensive Approach to Religious Education and Pastoral Ministry, The Way of Shared Praxis*. New York: Harper Collins, 1991.

Gudmundsdottir, Sigrun. "The Narrative Nature of Pedagogical Content Knowledge." In *Narrative in Teaching, Learning, and Research*, edited by Hunter McEwan, and Kieran Egan, 24–38. New York: Teachers College Press, 1995.

Ha, Tung-Chiew. "Familiar-Strange: Teaching the Scripture as John Would Teach." *Religious Education* 109.2 (2014) 162–72.

Harris, Maria. *Women and Teaching*. New York: Paulist, 1988.

Harstine, Stan. *Moses as a Character in the Fourth Gospel: A Study of Ancient Reading Techniques*. Sheffield: Sheffield Academic, 2002.

Harvey, John D. *Listening To The Text: Oral Patterning in Paul's Letters*. Grand Rapids: Baker, 1998.

Hess, Mary E., and Stephen D. Brookfield, eds. *Teaching Reflectively in Theological Contexts: Promises and Contradictions*. Malabar: Krieger, 2008.

Hester, James D., and J. David Hester, eds. *Rhetorics in the New Millennium: Promise and Fulfillment*. New York: T. & T. Clark, 2010.

Holland, Scott. *How Do Stories Save Us?: An Essay on the Question with the Theological Hermeneutics of David Tracy in View*. Louvain: Peeters, 2006.

Holman, Susan R. ed. *Wealth and Poverty in Early Church and Society*. Grand Rapids: Baker Academic, 2008.

Hooley, Neil. *Narrative Life: Democratic Curriculum and Indigenous Learning*. New York: Springer, 2009.

Horrell, David G. "Early Jewish Christianity." In *The Early Christian World, Vol. 1*, ed. Philip F. Esler, 136–67. London: Routledge, 2000.

Horsley, Richard A. *Hearing the Whole Story: The Politics of Plot in Mark's Gospel*. Louisville, KY: Westminster John Knox, 2001.

———. *Jesus in Context: Power, People and Performance*. Minneapolis: Fortress, 2008.

———. *Scribes, Visionaries, and the Politics of Second Temple Judea*. Louisville, KY: Westminster John Knox, 2007.

Howard, James M. "The Significance of Minor Characters in the Gospel of John." *Bibliotheca Sacra* 163 (2006) 63–78.

Howard-Brook, Wes. *Becoming the Children of God: John's Gospel and Radical Discipleship*. Maryknoll, NY: Orbis, 1994.

Hsiao, Andrew. *A Handbook on Christian Religious Education*. Hong Kong: Daosheng, 2007.

———. *Introduction to Christian Religious Education*. Hong Kong: Daosheng, 1986.

Hultgren, Stephen. *Narrative Elements in the Double Tradition: A Study of Their Place within the Framework of the Gospel Narrative*. Berlin: Walter de Gruyter, 2002.

Hylen, Susan E. *Imperfect Believers: Ambiguous Characters in the Gospel of John*. Louisville, KY: Westminster John Knox, 2009.

Hyman, Garvin. *The Predicament of Postmodern Theology*. Louisville, KY: Westminster John Knox, 2001.

Inbody, Tyron. *The Faith of Christian Church: An Introduction to Theology*. Grand Rapids: Eerdmans, 2005.

Jack, Alison M. *Scottish Fiction as Gospel Exegesis: Four Case Studies*. Sheffield: Sheffield Phoenix, 2010.

Katongole, Emmanuel M. *A Future for Africa: Critical Essays in Christian Social Imagination*. Scranton, PA: University of Scranton, 2005.

Bibliography

Keener, Craig S. *The Gospel of John: A Commentary*, vol. 1 & 2. Peabody, MA: Hendrickson, 2003.

Kennedy, George A. *Classical Rhetoric and Its Christian and Secular Tradition from Ancient to Modern Times*, 2nd revised and enlarged. Chapel Hill, NC: University of North Carolina Press, 1999.

———. *Invention and Method: Two Rhetorical Treatises from the Hermogenic Corpus*. Translated with Introductions and Notes. Atlanta, GA: SBL, 2005.

———. *Progymnasmata: Greek Textbooks of Prose Composition and Rhetoric*. Translated with Introductions and Notes. Atlanta, GA: SBL, 2003.

Kim, Dongsoo, "The Paraclete: The Spirit of the Church." *Asian Journal of Pentecostal Studies* 5.2 (2002) 255–70.

Kim, Eunjoo Mary. *Preaching the Presence of God: A Homiletic from an Asian American Perspective*. Valley Forge, PA: Judson, 1999.

Kincheloe, Joe L. *Knowledge and Critical Pedagogy: An Introduction*. New York: Springer, 2008.

Kinlaw, Pamela E. *The Christ is Jesus: Metamorphosis, Possession, and Johannine Christology*. Brill: SBL, 2005.

Kingsbury, Jack Dean ed. *Gospel Interpretation: Narrative-Critical & Social-Scientific Approaches*. Harrisburg, PA: Trinity, 1997.

Kitchen, Julian, Darlene Ciuffetelli Parker, and Debbie Pushor ed. *Narrative Inquires into Curriculum Making in Teacher Education*. Bingley: Emerald, 2011.

Klink III, Edward W. ed. *The Audience of the Gospels: The Origin and Function of the Gospels in Early Christianity*. London: T. & T. Clark, 2010.

Klutz, Todd. "Paul and the Development of Gentile Christianity." In *The Early Christian World, Vol. 1*, edited by Philip F. Esler, 168–97. London: Routledge, 2000.

Koester, Craig R. "Jesus as the Way to the Father in Johannine Theology (John 14:6)." In *Theology and Christology in the Fourth Gospel: Essays by the Members of the Snts Johannine Writings Seminars*, edited by G. van Belle et al., 117–34. Leuven: Leuven University, 2005.

———. *The Word of Life: A Theology of John's Gospel*. Grand Rapids: Eerdmans, 2008.

Koester, Helmut. *Ancient Christian Gospels: Their History and Development*. Philadelphia: Trinity, 1990.

———. *History, Culture, and Religion of the Hellenistic Age, Introduction to the New Testament*, vol. 1 & 2. Philadelphia: Fortress, 1982.

Köstenberger, Andreas J. "Hearing the Old Testament in the New: A Response." In *Hearing the Old Testament in the New Testament*, edited by Stanley E. Porter, 255–94. Grand Rapids: Eerdmans, 2006.

———. "John." In *Commentary on the New Testament use of the Old Testament*, edited by G. K. Beale, and D. A. Carson, 415–512. Grand Rapids: Baker Academic, 2007.

———. *A Theology of John's Gospel and Letters: The Words, the Christ, the Son of God*. Grand Rapids: Zondervan, 2009.

Köstenberger, Andreas J., and Scott R. Swain. *Father, Son and Spirit: The Trinity and John's Gospel*. Downers Grove, IL: InterVarsity, 2008.

Kuhn, Karl Allen. *The Heart of Biblical Narrative: Rediscovering Biblical Appeal to the Emotions*. Minneapolis: Fortress, 2009.

Kysar, Robert. *John the Maverick Gospel*, 3rd ed. Louisville, KY: Westminster John Knox, 2007.

BIBLIOGRAPHY

———. *Voyages with John: Charting the Fourth Gospel*. Waco, TX: Baylor University Press, 2005.
Labahn, Michael. "Scripture Talks because Jesus Talks: The Narrative Rhetoric of Persuading and Creativity in John's Use of Scripture." In *The Fourth Gospel in First-Century Media Culture*, edited by Anthony Le Donne and Tom Thatcher, 133–54. New York: T. & T. Clark, 2011.
Larsen, Kasper Bro. *Recognizing the Stranger: Recognition Scenes in the Gospel of John*. Leiden & Boston: Brill, 2008.
Lauritzen, Carol, and Michael Jaeger. *Integrating Learning through Story: The Narrative Curriculum*. Albany, NY: Delmar, 1997.
Lawless, Elaine. *Holy Women, Wholly Women: Sharing Ministries of Wholeness through Life Stories and Reciprocal Ethnography*. Philadelphia: University of Pennsylvania, 1993.
Lee, Dorothy. "The Gospel of John and the Five Senses." *JBL* 129.1 (2010) 115–27.
Levine, Lee I., ed. *Jerusalem: Its Sanctity and Centrality to Judaism, Christianity, and Islam*. New York: Continuum, 1999.
Levinskaya, Irina. *The Book of Acts in Its Diaspora Setting*. Grand Rapids: Eerdmans, 1996.
Lincoln, Andrew. *The Gospel According to Saint John*. Black's New Testament Commentaries. London: Continuum, 2005.
———. "The Lazarus Story: A Literary Perspective." In *The Gospel of John and Christian Theology*, edited by Richard Bauckham, and Carl Mosser, 211–32. Grand Rapids: Eerdmans, 2008.
Lints, Richard. "Imaging and Idolatry: The Sociality of Personhood in the Canon." In *Personal Identity in Theological Perspective*, edited by Richard Lints, Michael S. Horton, and Mark R. Talbot, 204–25. Grand Rapids: Eerdmans, 2006.
Loader, William. "Jesus and the Law in John." In *Theology and Christology in the Fourth Gospel: Essays by the Members of the Snts Johannine Writings Seminars*, edited by G. van Belle et al., 135–54. Leuven: Leuven University, 2005.
Loder, James. *The Logic of the Spirit: Human Development in Theological Perspective*. San Francisco: Jossey-Bass, 1998.
Loughlin, Gerard. *Telling God's Story: Bible, Church and Narrative Theology*. Cambridge: Cambridge University Press, 1996.
Louw, Johannes P., and Eugene A. Nida, ed. *Greek-English Lexicon of the New Testament: Based on Semantic Domains*. BibleWorks, LLC, Version 5.0.020w, 2001.
Lozada Jr., Francisco, and Tom Thatcher. *New Currents through John: A Global Perspective*. Atlanta, GA: SBL, 2006.
Malina, Bruce J. *The New Testament World: Insights from Cultural Anthropology*, 3rd ed. Louisville, KY: Westminster John Knox, 2001.
Malina, Bruce J., and Richard L. Rohrbaugh. *Social-Science Commentary on the Gospel of John*. Minneapolis: Fortress, 1998.
Marshall, I. Howard. *A Concise New Testament Theology*. Downers Grove, IL: InterVarsity Academic, 2008.
Martin, Dale B. *Pedagogy of the Bible: An Analysis and Proposal*. Louisville, KY: Westminster John Knox, 2008.
Martin, Luther H. "Graeco-Roman Philosophy and Religion." In *The Early Christian World, Vol. 1*, edited by Philip F. Esler, 53–79. London: Routledge, 2000.
Martin, Michael W. *Judas and the Rhetoric of Comparison in the Fourth Gospel*. Sheffield: Sheffield Phoenix, 2010.

Bibliography

Martin, Robert K. *The Incarnate Ground of Christian Faith: Toward a Christian Theological Epistemology for the Educational Ministry of the Church*. Lanham, MD: University Press of America, 1998.

Martin, Vincent. *A House Divided: The Parting of the Ways between Synagogue and Church*. Mahwah, NJ: Paulist, 1995.

Martyn, J. Louis. *History and Theology in the Fourth Gospel*, 3rd ed. Louisville, KY: Westminster John Knox, 2003.

Massey, Karen. "The Narrative Model for Teaching the Bible." *Review and Expositor* 107 (2010) 197–206.

Mathison, John, ed. *Treasures of the Transformed Life: Satisfying Your Soul's Thirst for More*. Nashville: Abingdon, 2006.

Matthews, Victor H. *More Than Meets The Ear*. Grand Rapids: Eerdmans, 2008.

Maynes, Mary Jo, et al. *Telling Stories: The Use of Personal Narratives in Social Sciences and History*. Ithaca, NY: Cornell University Press, 2008.

McAdams, Dan P. *The Stories We Live By: Personal Myths and the Making of the Self*. New York: Guildford, 1993.

McDrury, Janice, and Maxine Alterio. *Learning through Storytelling in Higher Education: Using Reflection and Experience to Improve Learning*. Kindle edition. Taylor & Francis e-Library, 2004.

McEwan, Hunter, and Kieran Egan, ed. *Narrative in Teaching, Learning, and Research*. New York: Teachers College, 1995.

McHugh, John F. *A Critical and Exegetical Commentary on John 1–4*. New York: T. & T. Clark, 2009.

McKnight, Edgar V., and Christopher Church. *Hebrews and James*. Smyth & Helwys Bible Commentary. Marcon, GA: Smyth & Helwys, 2004.

Meeks, Wayne A. *The First Urban Christians: the Social World of the Apostle Paul*. New Haven, CT: Yale University Press, 1983.

———. *The Moral World of the First Christians*. Philadelphia: Westminster, 1986.

Menken, Maarten J. J. "Observations on the Significance of the Old Testament in the Fourth Gospel." In *Theology and Christology in the Fourth Gospel: Essays by the Members of the SNTS Johannine Writings Seminars*, edited by G. Van Belle, et al., 155–75. Leuven: Leuven University Press, 2005.

Merriam, Sharan B., ed. *Third Update on Adult Learning Theory*. San Francisco: Jossey-Bass, 2008.

Merriam, Sharan B., et al. *Non-Western Perspectives on Learning and Knowing*. Malabar, FL: Krieger, 2007.

———. *Learning in Adulthood: A Comprehensive Guide*, 3rd ed. San Francisco: Wiley & Sons, 2007.

Metzger, Paul Louis. *The Gospel of John: When Love Comes to Town*. Downers Grove, IL: InterVarsity, 2010.

Mezirow, Jack. *Transformative Dimensions of Adult Learning*. San Francisco: Jossey-Bass, 1991.

Michaels, Ramsey. *The Gospel of John*, NICNT. Grand Rapids: Eerdmans, 2010.

Michelson, Elana. "Autobiography and Selfhood in the Practice of Adult Learning." *Adult Education Quarterly* 61.1 (2011) 3–21.

Miller, Paul. "They Saw His Glory and Spoke of Him: The Gospel of John and the Old Testament." In *Hearing the Old Testament in the New Testament*, edited by Stanley E. Porter, 127–51. Grand Rapids: Eerdmans, 2006.

Bibliography

Miller, Randolph Crump. *Theologies of Religious Education*. Birmingham, AL: Religious Education, 1995.

Mlakuzhil, S. J., George. *The Christocentric Literary Structure of the Fourth Gospel*. Roma: Editrice Pontificio Istituto Biblico, 1987.

Muirhead, Ian A. *Education in the New Testament*. New York: Associated Press, 1965.

Moloney, Francis J. *The Living Voice of the Gospels*. Peabody, MA: Hendrickson, 2007.

———. *The Gospel of John*. Sacra Pagina 4. Collegeville, MN: Liturgical, 1998.

Moxnes, Halvor. *The Economy of the Kingdom: Social Conflict and Economic Relations in Luke's Gospel*. Philadelphia: Fortress, 1988.

Moyise, Steve. *The Old Testament in the New: An Introduction*. London: Continuum, 2001.

Newsome, James D. *Greeks, Romans, Jews: Currents of Culture and Belief in New Testament World*. Philadelphia: Trinity, 1992.

Neyrey, Jerome H. *The Gospel of John*. New Cambridge Bible Commentary. New York: Cambridge University Press, 2007.

———. *The Gospel of John in Cultural and Rhetorical Perspective*. Grand Rapids: Eerdmans, 2009.

Neyrey, Jerome H, and Eric C. Stewart, eds. *The Social World of the New Testament: Insights and Models*. Peabody, MA: Hendrickson, 2008.

Ngien, Dennis. *Gifted Response: The Triune God as the Causative Agency of Our Responsive Worship*. Milton Keynes: Paternoster, 2008.

O'Brien, Kelli. "Written That You May Believe: John 20 and Narrative Rhetoric." *Catholic Biblical Quarterly* 67.2 (2008) 284–302.

O'Day, Gail R, and Susan E. Hylen. *John*. Louisville, KY: Westminster John Knox, 2006.

O'Gorman, Robert T. "The Faith Community." In *Mapping Christian Education: Approaches to Congregational Learning*, edited by Jack L. Seymour, 41–57. Nashville: Abingdon, 1997.

Olsson, Birger. "'All My Teaching was Done in Synagogues . . .' John 18:20." In *Theology and Christology in the Fourth Gospel: Essays by the Members of the SNTS Johannine Writings Seminar*, edited by G. Van Belle, et al., 203–24. Leuven: Leuven University Press, 2005.

Osmer, Richard Robert. *The Teaching Ministry of Congregations*. Louisville, KY: Westminster John Knox, 2005

Patte, Daniel. *Discipleship According to the Sermon on the Mount: Four Legitimate Readings, Four Plausible Views of Discipleship, and Their Relative Values*. Valley Forge, PA: Trinity, 1996.

Pazmiño, Robert W. *Foundational Issues in Christian Education: An Introduction in Evangelical Perspective*, 2nd ed. Grand Rapids: Baker, 1997.

Phillips, Peter M. *The Prologue of the Fourth Gospel: A Sequential Reading*. New York: T. & T. Clark, 2006.

Pinnegar, Stefinee, and J. Gary Daynes. "Locating Narrative Inquiry Historically: Thematics in the Turn to Narrative." In *Handbook of Narrative Inquiry: Mapping a Methodology*, edited by D. Jean Clandinin, 3-34. Thousand Oaks, CA: Sage, 2007.

Polkinghorne, D. E. *Narrative Knowing and the Human Sciences*. New York: State University of the New York Press, 1988.

———. "Narrative Knowing and Study of Lives." In *Aging and Biography: Explorations in Adult Development*, edited by James E. Birren et al., 77–99. New York: Springer, 1996.

Porter, Stanley E., ed. *Hearing the Old Testament in the New Testament*. Grand Rapids: Eerdmans, 2006.

Bibliography

Powell, Mark Allen. *Introducing the New Testament: A Historical, Literary, and Theological Survey.* Grand Rapids: Baker Academic, 2009.

Preistly, Jack G. "Concepts with Blurred Edges: Story and Religious Imagination." *Religious Education* 78.3 (1983) 377–89.

Pryor, John W. *John: Evangelist of the Covenant People: The Narrative and Themes of the Fourth Gospel.* Downers Grove, IL: InterVarsity, 1992.

Rajak, Tessa. "The Location of Cultures in Second Temple Palestine: The Evidence of Josephus." In *The Book of Acts in Its Palestinian Setting*, edited by Richard Bauckham, 1–14. Grand Rapids: Eerdmans, 1995.

Raschke, Carl. *The Next Reformation: Why Evangelicals Must Embrace Postmodernity.* Grand Rapids: Baker Academic, 2004.

Resseguie, James L. *Narrative Criticism of the New Testament: An Introduction.* Grand Rapids: Baker Academic, 2005.

———. *The Strange Gospel: Narrative Design and Point of View in John.* Leiden: Brill, 2001.

Ricoeur, Paul. *Time and Narrative*, vol. 1. Translated by Kathleen McLaughlin and David Pellauer. Chicago: University of Chicago Press, 1984.

Ritchie, Daniel E. *The Fullness of Knowing: Modernity and Postmodernity from Defoe to Gadamer.* Waco, TX: Baylor University Press, 2010.

Robbins, Vernon K. *The Invention of Christian Discourse*, vol. 1. Dorset: Deo, 2009.

Roetzel, Calvin J. *The World that Shaped the New Testament*, rev. ed. Louisville, KY: Westminster John Knox, 2002.

Rosenfeld, Ben Zion. *Torah Centers and Rabbinic Activity in Palestine 70–400 CE.* Leiden: Brill, 2010.

Rossiter, Marsha, and M. Carolyn Clark. *Narrative and the Practice of Adult Education.* Malabar, FL: Krieger, 2007.

Sadananda, Daniel Rathnakara. *The Johannine Exegesis of God: An Exploration into the Johannine Understanding of God.* Berlin: Walter de Gruyter, 2004.

Schmithals, Walter. *The Theology of the First Christians.* Louisville, KY: Westminster John Knox, 1997.

Schnackenburg, Rudolf. *The Gospel according to St John, Volume One, Introduction and Commentary on Chapters 1–4.* Translated by Kevin Smyth. New York: Herder and Herder, 1968.

———. *Jesus in the Gospels: A Biblical Christology.* Louisville, KY: Westminster John Knox, 1995.

Schreiner, Thomas R. *New Testament Theology: Magnifying God in Christ.* Grand Rapids: Baker Academic, 2008.

Schwehn, Mark R., and Dorothy C. Bass, eds. *Leading Lives That Matter: What We Should Do and Who We Should Be.* Grand Rapids: Eerdmans, 2006.

Scott, Ian W. *Paul's Way of Knowing: Story, Experience, and the Spirit.* Grand Rapids: Baker Academic, 2006.

Sergovia, Fernanado F., ed. *What is John? Volume 1: Readers and Readings of the Fourth Gospel.* Atlanta, GA: Scholars, 1996.

Segovia, Fernando F., and Mary Ann Tolbert, eds. *Teaching the Bible: The Discourses and Politics of Biblical Pedagogy.* Maryknoll, NY: Orbis, 1998.

Seymour, Jack L., ed. *Mapping Christian Education: Approaches to Congregational Learning.* Nashville: Abingdon, 1997.

Bibliography

Seymour, Jack L., et al. *The Church in the Education of the Public.* Nashville: Abingdon, 1984.

———. *Educating Christians: The Intersection of Meaning, Learning, and Vocation.* Nashville: Abingdon, 1993.

Seymour, Jack L., and Donald E. Miller. *Contemporary Approaches to Christian Education.* Nashville: Abingdon, 1982.

Shults, F. Leron. *Christology and Science.* Grand Rapids: Eerdmans, 2008.

———. *The Postfoundationalist Task of Theology.* Grand Rapids: Eerdmans, 1999.

Skarsaune, Oskar. *In the Shadow of the Temple: Jewish Influences on Early Christianity.* Downers Grove, IL: InterVasity, 2002.

Skinner, Christopher W. *John and Thomas—Gospels in Conflict?: Johannine Characterization and the Thomas Question.* Eugene, OR: Pickwick, 2009.

Smith, D. Moody. *John.* Abingdon New Testament Commentaries. Nashville: Abingdon, 1999.

———. *The Theology of the Gospel of John.* Cambridge: Cambridge University Press, 1995.

Smith, Justin Marc. "About Friends, by Friends, for Others: Author-Subject Relationships in Contemporary Greco-Roman Biographies." In *The Audience of the Gospels: The Origin and Function of the Gospels in Early Christianity*, edited by Edward W. Klink III, 49–67. London: T. & T. Clark, 2010.

Song, C. S. *The Believing Heart: An Invitation to Story Theology.* Minneapolis: Fortress, 1999.

Staley, Jeffrey L. "What Can Postmodern Approach to the Fourth Gospel Add to Contemporary Debates About Its Historical Situation?" In *Jesus in Johannine Tradition*, edited by Robert T. Fortna and Tom Thatcher, 47–58. Louisville, KY: Westminster John Knox, 2001.

Stamps, Dennis L. "The Use of the Old Testament in the New Testament as a Rhetorical Device: A Methodological Proposal." In *Hearing the Old Testament in the New Testament*, edited by Stanley E. Porter, 9–37. Grand Rapids: Eerdmans, 2006.

Stemberger, Günter. *Jewish Contemporaries of Jesus: Pharisees, Sadducees, Essenes.* Translated by Alan W. Mahnke. Minneapolis: Augsburg Fortress, 1995.

Stibbe, Mark W. G. *The Gospel of John as Literature: An Anthology of Twentieth-Century Perspectives.* Leiden: Brill, 1993.

———. *John as Storyteller: Narrative Criticism and the Fourth Gospel.* Cambridge: Cambridge University Press, 1992.

Stone, Jerry H. "Narrative Theology and Religious Education." In *Theologies of Religious Education*, edited by Randolph Crump Miller, 255–85. Birmingham, AL: Religious Education, 1995.

Swinton, John, and Harriet Mowat. *Practical Theology and Qualitative Research.* London: SCMP, 2006.

Talbert, Charles H. *Reading John: A Literary and Theological Commentary on the Fourth Gospel and the Johannine Epistles*, rev. ed. Macon, GA: Smyth & Helwys, 2005.

Tan, Jason. "Pulling Together amid Globalization: National Education in Singapore Schools." In *Changing Education Leadership, Innovation and Development in a Globalizing Asia Pacific*, edited by Peter D. Hershock et al., 183–98. Hong Kong: University of Hong Kong, 2007.

Thatcher, Tom "The Legend of the Beloved Disciple." In *Jesus in Johannine Tradition*, edited by Robert T. Fortna, and Tom Thatcher, 91–99. Louisville, KY: Westminster John Knox, 2001.

Bibliography

———. *Why John Wrote a Gospel: Jesus-Memory-History*. Louisville, KY: Westminster John Knox, 2006.

Thatcher, Tom, ed. *What We Have Heard From The Beginning: The Past, Present, and Future of Johannine Studies*. Waco, TX: Baylor University, 2007.

Thatcher, Tom, and Stephen D. Moore, ed. *Anatomies of Narrative Criticism*. Atlanta, GA: SBL, 2008.

Thiselton, Anthony C. *Hermeneutics: An Introduction*. Grand Rapids: Eerdmans, 2009.

———. *New Horizons in Hermeneutics*. Grand Rapids: Zondervan, 1992.

———. *Thiselton on Hermeneutics: Collected Works with New Essays*. Grand Rapids: Eerdmans, 2006.

Tovey, Derek. *Narrative Art and Act in the Fourth Gospel*. Sheffield: Sheffield, 1997.

Tsang, Sam, and Nancy Ou. *Eternal Word Spoken: A Literary Study on Characterization in John's Gospel*. Hong Kong: Logos, 2006.

Usher, Robin, and Richard Edwards. *Lifelong Learning—Signs, Discourses, Practices*. Dordrecht: Springer, 2007.

Van Belle, G., et al., eds. *Repetitions and Variations in the Fourth Gospels: Style, Text, Interpretation*. Leuven: Peeters, 2009.

———. *Theology and Christology In the Fourth Gospel: Essays by the Members of the SNTS Johannine Writings Seminar*. Leuven: Peeters, 2005.

Van der Watt, Jan G. *Family of the King: Dynamics of Metaphor in the Gospel According to John*. Leiden: Brill, 2000.

Van Engen, John, ed. *Educating People of Faith: Exploring the History of Jewish and Christian Communities*. Grand Rapids: Eerdmans, 2004.

Van Huyssteen, J. Wentzel. *Essays in Postfoundationalist Theology*. Grand Rapids: Eerdmans, 1997.

Van Oers, Bert, et al., ed. *The Transformation of Learning: Advances in Cultural-Historical Activity Theory*. New York: Cambridge University Press, 2008.

Van Schalkwyk, Gertina J. "Collage Life Story Elicitation Technique: A Representational Technique for Scaffolding Autobiographical Memories." *The Qualitative Report* 15.3 (2010) 675–95.

Van Voorst, Robert E. *Reading the New Testament Today*. Belmont, CA: Wadsworth, 2005.

Vanhoozer, Kevin J. *The Drama of Doctrine: A Canonical Linguistic Approach to Christian Theology*. Louisville, KY: Westminster John Knox, 2005.

———. *Remythologizing Theology: Divine Action, Passion, and Authorship*. Cambridge: Cambridge University Press. 2010.

Vanhoozer, Kevin J., ed. *Dictionary for Theological Interpretation of the Bible*. Grand Rapids: Baker Academic, 2005.

Von Balthasar, Hans Ur. *Epilogue*. Translated by Edward T. Oakes, SJ. San Francisco: Ignatius, 2004.

Von Wahlde, Urban C. *The Gospel and Letters of John*, vol. 1 & 2, Eerdmans Critical Commentary. Grand Rapids: Eerdmans, 2010.

Voorwinde, Stephen. *Jesus' Emotions in the Fourth Gospel: Human or Divine?* London: T. & T. Clark, 2005.

Walsh, Jerome T. *Old Testament Narrative: A Guide to Interpretation*. Louisville, KY: Westminster John Knox, 2009.

Walsh, Michael, ed. *Dictionary of Christian Biography*. Collegeville, MN: Liturgical, 2001.

Weimer, Maryellen. *Learner-Centered Teaching: Five Key Changes to Practice*. San Francisco: Jossey-Bass, 2002.

Bibliography

Wenell, Karen J. *Jesus and the Land: Sacred and Social Space in Second Temple Judaism.* London: T. & T. Clark, 2007.
Westerhoff, III, John H. *Will Our Children Have Faith.* Harrisburg, PA: Morehouse, 2000.
Whitters, Mark F. "Discipleship in John: Four Profiles." *Word & World* 18 (1998) 422–27.
William, Cartin H. "Abraham as a Figure of Memory in John 8:31–59." In *The Fourth Gospel in First-Century Media Culture*, edited by Anthony Le Donne and Tom Thatcher, 205–22. New York: T. & T. Clark, 2011.
Wimberly, Anne E. Streaty. *Soul Stories: African American Christian Education*, rev. ed. Nashville: Abingdon, 2005.
Witherington III, Ben. *Jesus the Sage: the Pilgrimage of Wisdom.* Minneapolis: Fortress, 1994.
———. *John's Wisdom: A Commentary on the Fourth Gospel.* Louisville, KY: Westminster John Knox, 1995.
———. *New Testament History: A Narrative Account.* Grand Rapids: Baker Academic, 2001.
———. *The New Testament Story.* Grand Rapids: Eerdmans, 2004.
Wlodkowski, Raymond J., and Margery B. Ginsberg. *Diversity and Motivation: Culturally Responsive Teaching.* San Francisco: Jossey-Bass, 1995.
Yeo, K. K. *Chairman Mao Meets the Apostle Paul.* Grand Rapids: Brazos, 2002.
———. *Musing with Confucius and Paul: Toward a Chinese Christian Theology.* Eugene, OR: Cascade, 2008.
Yeo, K. K., ed. *Navigating Romans through Cultures.* London: T. & T. Clark, 2004.
Yieh, John. *One Teacher: Jesus' Teaching Role in Matthew's Gospel Report.* Berlin: Walter de Gruyter, 2004.
Yust, Karen Marie. "Playing with Mirrors: Narrative Inquiry and Congregational Consultation." *Religious Education* 104.1 (2009) 84–93.

Index

adequate faith, xiii, xiv, xvi, 57–58, 65, 74, 79, 81–82, 106, 109, 112, 115–16, 120, 122, 124–27, 129, 130, 133–39, 144–45, 147–49, 152–55, 157, 161, 163, 164, 166, 184–85, 193, 194, 197, 199
affective, 8, 9, 73, 79, 83, 84, 106, 107, 124, 141–42, 144, 156, 184, 196, 198
anchor, xii–xvi, 15, 17, 19, 30–31, 33–35, 147, 150, 153, 157–58, 161, 164, 184, 191, 197, 202
aporias, 59
Aristotle, 9–10, 15, 25–26, 63, 104
audience, *passim*
authentic,
    living, xii–xiii, 31–36, 74, 105, 197
    self, 33
autonomy, 30, 44

biography, 3–4, 9, 23–24, 62–65, 72, 74–75, 82, 97, 106, 164, 171
bios, 41, 61–62

challenges,
    Johannnie community, 40–41, 48, 56–57, 61, 75–76, 107, 110, 145

Church, 150, 156, 158, 161, 202
character, characterization *passim*
chiastic, 80, 82, 125–26, 135
christological, 68
curriculum, 24, 137, 148, 160, 195, 199, 202

dialogue, 13, 27, 28, 36, 37, 73, 80, 93, 101, 119, 120, 123, 179, 183, 188
diaspora, 42–45, 48, 50, 51, 53, 58, 60, 75, 76
didactic, 25, 64, 67, 70, 73, 80–81, 104, 106, 137, 171, 198
double entendres, 92, 99, 102, 104
drama, dramatic, 5, 11, 43, 96–97, 100, 111, 114, 117, 124, 132, 146, 156, 174, 177

economic, 31, 44, 56,
education,
    Christian, *passim*
    Graeco-Roman, 48–49
emplotment, 7, 15, 80, 127, 138, 148
enfleshment, 6–7, 157
eyewitness, 139

217

Index

family, xiv, 1, 10, 18, 20, 47, 48, 56–59, 71–75, 82, 116, 125, 136, 137, 139, 143, 148, 150, 157, 162, 164–66, 168, 185, 200
five senses, 26, 105, 148, 198
Fowler, James, 19–20, 187
freedom, 4, 27, 32, 33, 71, 124, 168, 178

Gadamer, 25
Girard, Rene, 15–18
Groome, Thomas, 26–29, 36, 38, 153, 159, 196–97
gymnasium, 49

Hellenistic, Hellenization, 41–44, 48–50, 52, 53, 61, 63–68, 75
hermeneutics, xv, 13, 27, 34, 69, 156, 179, 182
Holy Spirit, 34–35, 87, 144, 154, 183
honor-shame, 48, 55
human development, 16, 19–20, 97

imagination-inspiration, 78, 134, 158
imagine-inspire, xiv, 153, 154, 176–83
imitate and impart, xiv, 153–54, 183–90
incarnation, 32, 35, 148
inquire and invent, xiv, 153, 161–76
insider, 30, 47, 80–82, 101, 112, 116, 119, 125, 127, 137, 185, 190
inspiration, 17, 180, 185, 194, 198
imitate, *passim*
irony, 88, 92, 94, 99–102

Judaism, 41–43, 47, 53, 56, 61, 62, 75

language, xii, xiii, 6–7, 33, 37, 42–43, 48, 52–53, 58, 61, 68, 75, 90, 92, 99, 105–8, 138, 146, 152–53, 155, 163, 169, 178–79, 182–83, 188–90, 194, 199, 201
linguistic features, xii, 79, 83, 93
literary device, xiii, xv, 61–62, 78, 91–94, 99–102, 104–9, 125, 135–36, 144, 148, 153, 155–57, 160, 161, 189, 198, 201

meaning making, 7, 10, 18, 22, 23, 29, 158

media, xii, xiii, 7, 29, 46, 65, 105, 106, 153, 155, 156, 162, 174, 187
memory, 11, 21, 22, 33, 37, 49, 59, 61, 76, 104, 105, 107, 115, 157–60, 187
mimesis, xiii, 15–19, 89, 157, 162, 178, 179, 185, 186
misunderstanding, 85, 88–89, 92, 94, 99, 100–102, 104, 148
motivation, 10, 97, 111, 173, 180, 181, 185, 188

narration thickness, 123
narrative *asides*, 102, 118
narrative learning,
  biblical, *passim*
  component, xiii, 2, 78, 83, 105, 107, 108, 152–53, 156–58, 163–64, 174, 199
  content, 20–22, 28, 29, 79–80, 140, 195, 199
  function, 13–19, 38, 179
  inquiry, xiii, 2, 3, 9, 38, 150, 153, 155, 159, 162–63, 169, 171–72, 175, 190, 196–98
  pedagogy, 3–4, 9
  practice, 3–4, 9, 22–23, 26, 28–29, 37–38, 108, 150, 174, 194, 196
  presentation, xii, xiii–xiv, 21, 36, 153, 156, 164, 187, 199, 201
  sources, 8, 10
  structure, 15, 79, 89, 122, 164

outsider, 30, 47, 53, 81–82, 101, 103, 113, 116, 120, 130, 185

patron-client, 55
personhood, 2, 17, 30, 32–36, 97
persuasion, 67, 68, 79, 186
Pharisees, 45–47, 55, 60, 74, 120–22, 125, 132, 137
phraseological, 92–93, 99, 101, 144
physiognomic, xii, 94, 105, 106, 148, 153, 160, 189
plot, xiii, 7, 9–13, 15, 78–79, 83, 85, 87, 104, 107, 110, 111, 123, 142, 153, 156, 157, 160, 163, 164, 170, 198, 199

INDEX

point of view, xii, 12, 14, 83, 85, 92, 95–99, 104, 119, 129, 140, 156, 158
praxis, 26–27, 153, 159, 196–97
psychological, 92–93, 97–99, 144, 148

recognition, 1, 3, 5, 9, 35, 37, 62, 106, 112, 117, 126, 139, 142, 143, 149, 165, 167, 187, 190
reflective, 9, 10, 19, 79, 155, 186
relational, 32, 34–35, 73, 142, 155, 163, 179–80, 197
remember, xiii–xiv, 11, 14, 17, 28, 38, 61, 62, 65, 73, 104–5, 109, 114–15, 133, 135–36, 138, 144, 148–49, 161–63, 171, 173, 177, 189, 198
re-presentation, xv, 5–6, 65, 155, 157, 189, 198
researcher, 5, 14, 17, 38, 99, 150, 153, 160–61, 169–75, 176, 190, 196–98, 201
resurrection, 35, 38, 60, 80–81, 89, 95, 96, 98, 99, 114, 124, 127, 132, 136–37, 145
Ricoeur, 9–10, 15, 23, 38
Roman Empire, 44, 48, 52–54

Second Temple, 41–43, 46–47, 50–51, 54–55, 60

showing and telling, xiii, 32, 36, 72, 76, 78–81, 105–7, 110–11, 118, 126, 147–49, 154–55, 174, 199
sign-event, 80–81, 89, 123, 125, 127–32, 137–38
spatial, 92–95, 127, 129, 132, 144
story-linking, 27–28
storytelling, xii–xiii, 2–19, 20–29, 38, 84, 94, 104, 105, 109, 127, 140, 147, 150, 152, 160, 162, 164, 167, 168, 181, 186, 188, 196, 199
style, 12, 59, 68, 90–91, 156, 158, 174
suspense, 13, 23, 110, 112, 125, 127–40, 144
symbolism, 88, 99, 103–4
synagogue, 44–48, 50–51, 53–54, 56, 60–61, 69, 75, 118–20
syncretism, 41, 42, 45–46, 65, 75
Synoptic, 41, 57, 59–61, 92, 111–12, 116–19, 127, 132, 147, 150, 165

temporal, 12, 15, 92–93, 95, 96, 110, 127–29, 132, 137, 144, 175, 181
testimony, *passim*
teaching session, 114, 117–19

vision, 27, 36, 54, 71–72, 93, 134, 159, 178
Vygotsky, 5–6

www.ingramcontent.com/pod-product-compliance
Lightning Source LLC
Chambersburg PA
CBHW051640230426
43669CB00013B/2386